PIANO · VOCAL · GUITAR

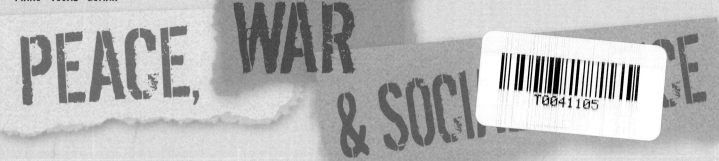

PEACE, WAR & SOCIAL [illegible]

T0041105

ISBN 0-634-08662-6

HAL•LEONARD® CORPORATION

7777 W. BLUEMOUND RD. P.O. BOX 13819 MILWAUKEE, WI 53213

For all works contained herein:
Unauthorized copying, arranging, adapting, recording or public performance is an infringement of copyright.
Infringers are liable under the law.

Visit Hal Leonard Online at
www.halleonard.com

ABRAHAM, MARTIN AND JOHN

Words and Music by
RICHARD HOLLER

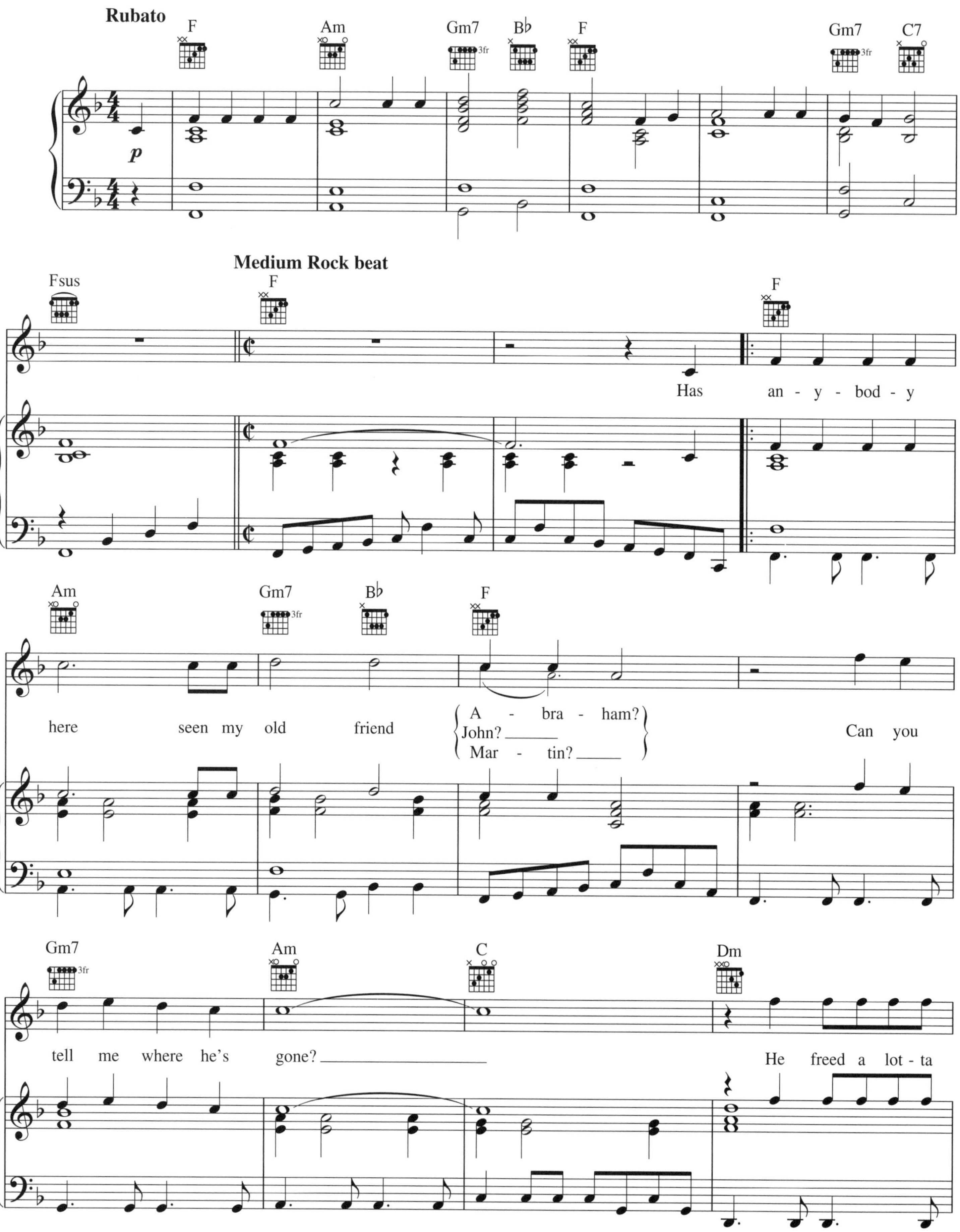

Copyright © 1968, 1970 (Renewed) by Regent Music Corp. (BMI) and Beardsley Tunes
International Copyright Secured All Rights Reserved
Used by Permission

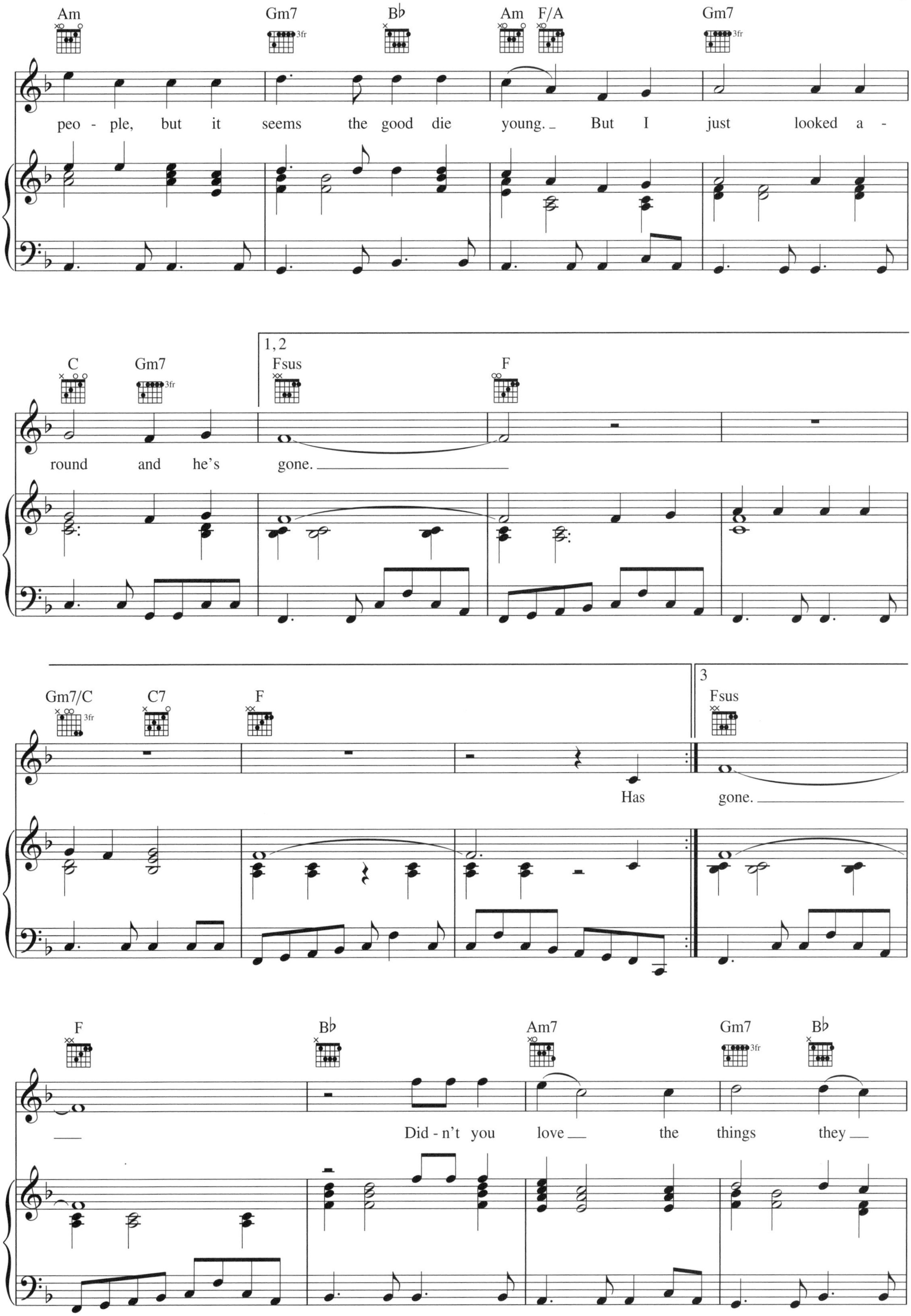
Am Gm7 B♭ Am F/A Gm7
3fr
peo - ple, but it seems the good die young. But I just looked a -
C Gm7
1, 2
Fsus F
round and he's gone.
Gm7/C C7 F
3
Fsus
Has gone.
F B♭ Am7 Gm7 B♭
Did - n't you love the things they

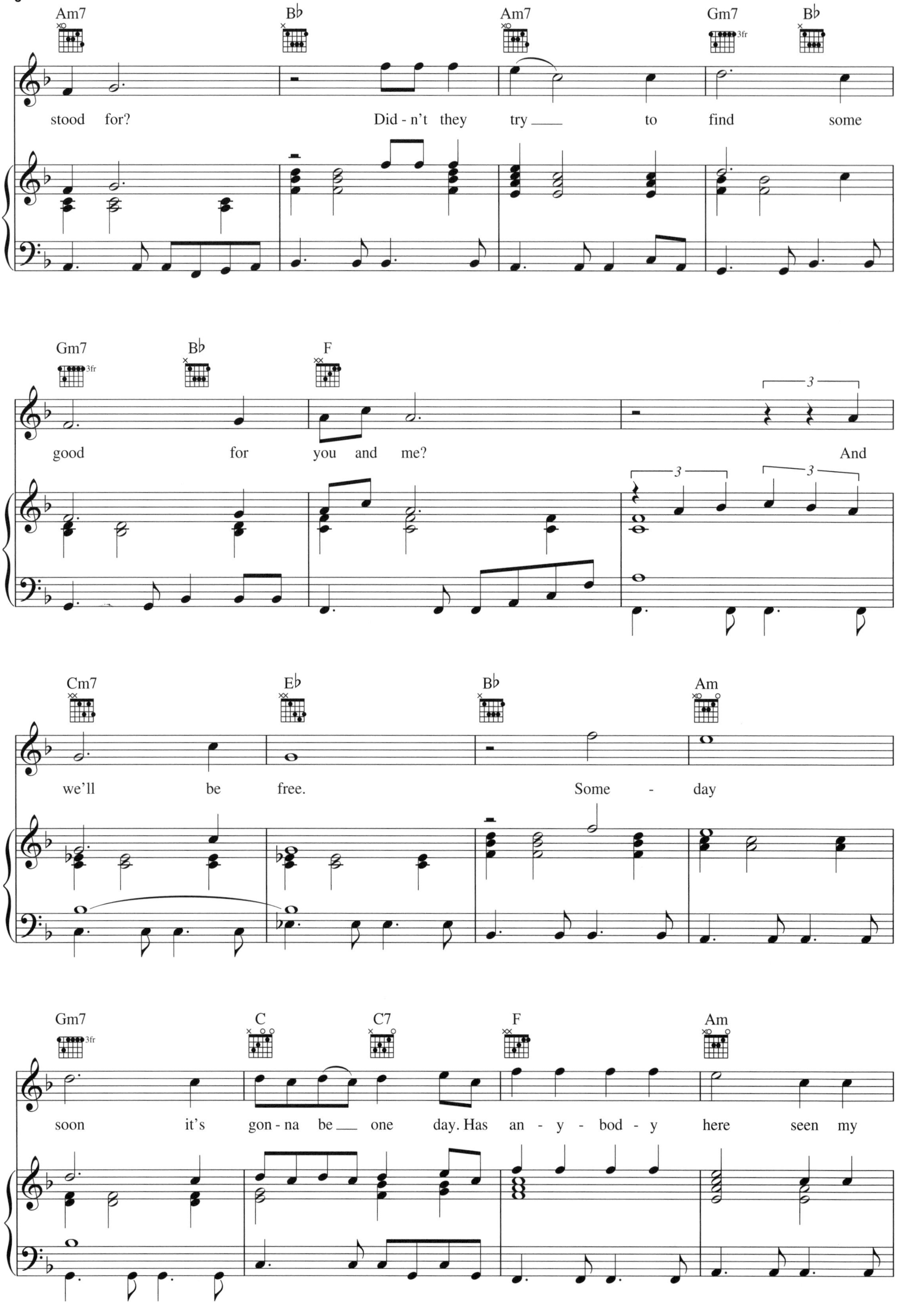
Am7 B♭ Am7 Gm7 B♭
3fr
stood for? Did - n't they try to find some
Gm7 B♭ F
3fr
3
good for you and me? And
3 3
Cm7 E♭ B♭ Am
we'll be free. Some - day
Gm7 C C7 F Am
3fr
soon it's gon - na be one day. Has an - y - bod - y here seen my

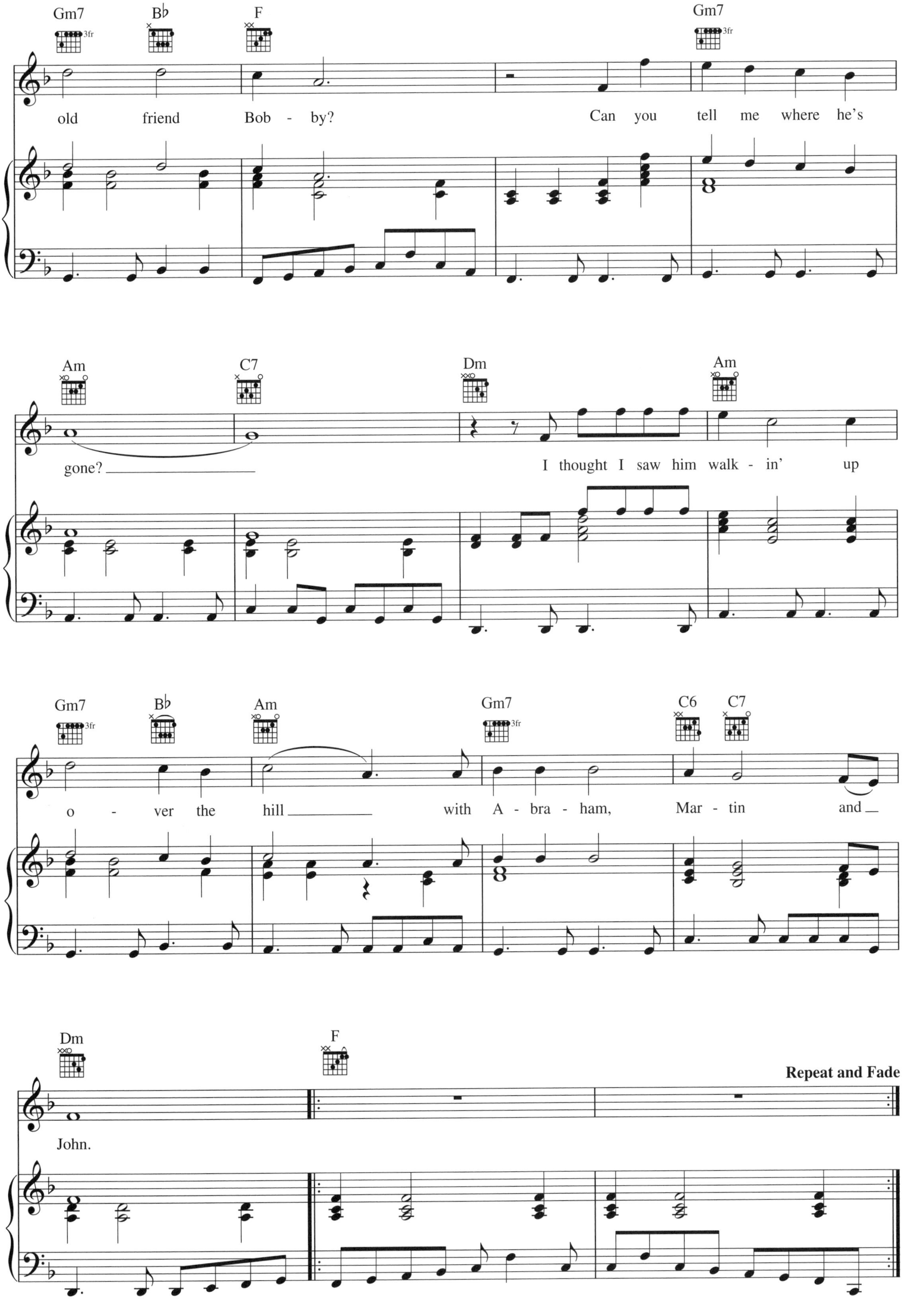
Gm7
B♭
F
Gm7
3fr
old friend Bob - by? Can you tell me where he's
Am
C7
Dm
Am
gone?
I thought I saw him walk - in' up
Gm7
B♭
Am
Gm7
C6
C7
o - ver the hill with A - bra - ham, Mar - tin and
Dm
F
Repeat and Fade
John.

BLACK AND WHITE

Words by DAVID ARKIN
Music by EARL ROBINSON

Moderate Rock

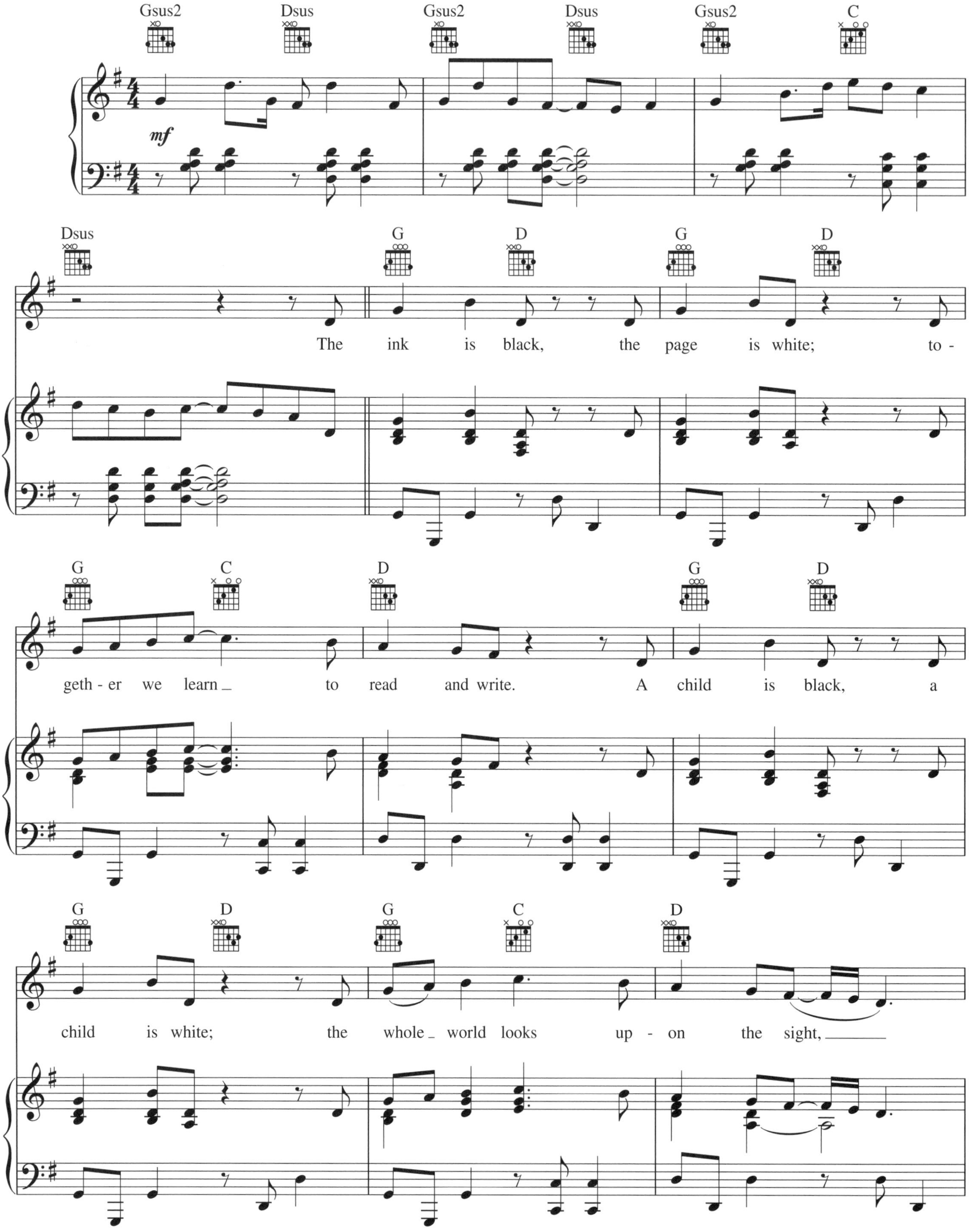

Copyright © 1956 (Renewed) by Templeton Publishing, a division of Shawnee Press, Inc. (ASCAP)
International Copyright Secured All Rights Reserved
Reprinted by Permission

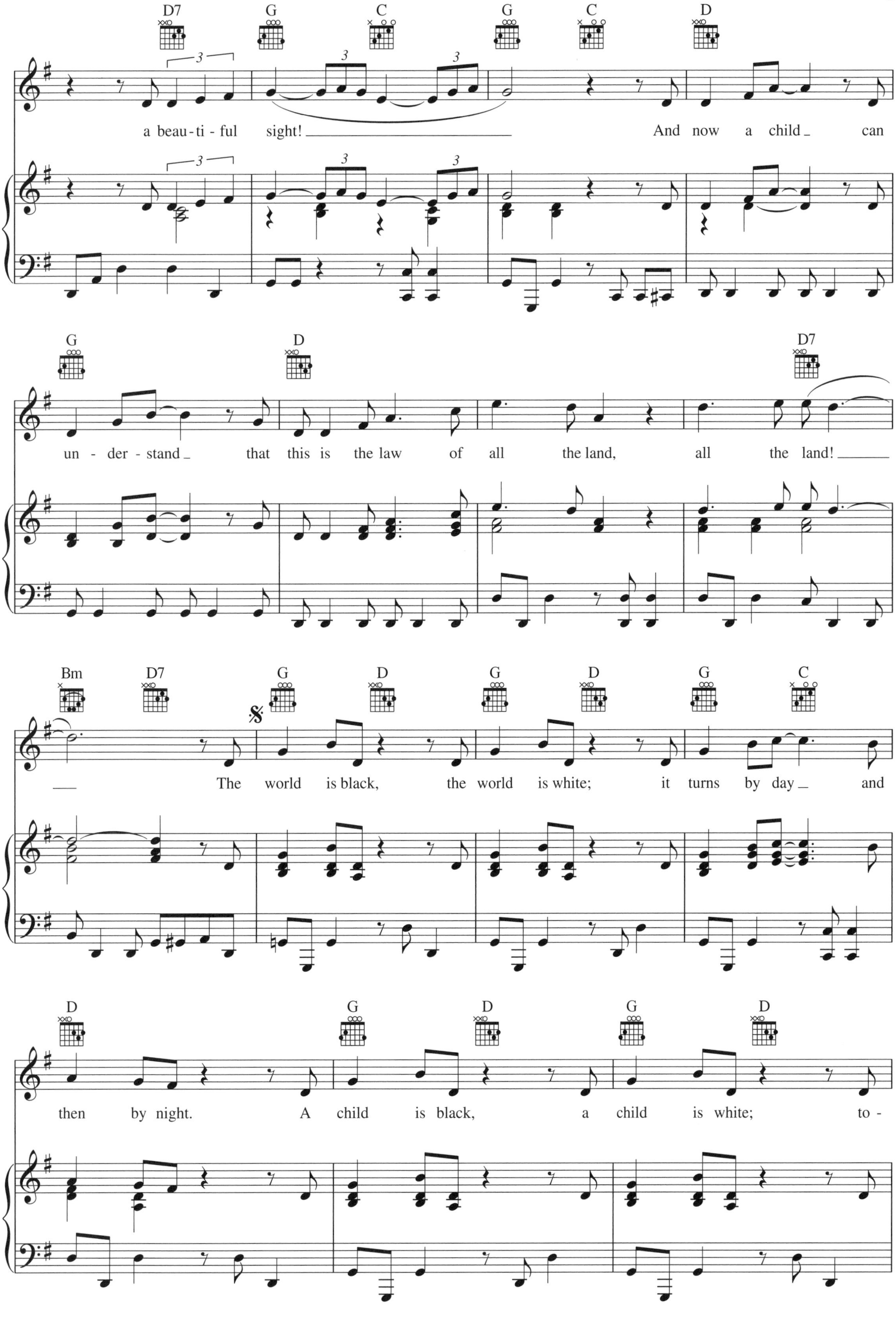
D7 G C G C D
a beau-ti-ful sight! And now a child can
G D D7
un-der-stand that this is the law of all the land, all the land!
Bm D7 G D G D G C
The world is black, the world is white; it turns by day and
D G D G D
then by night. A child is black, a child is white; to-

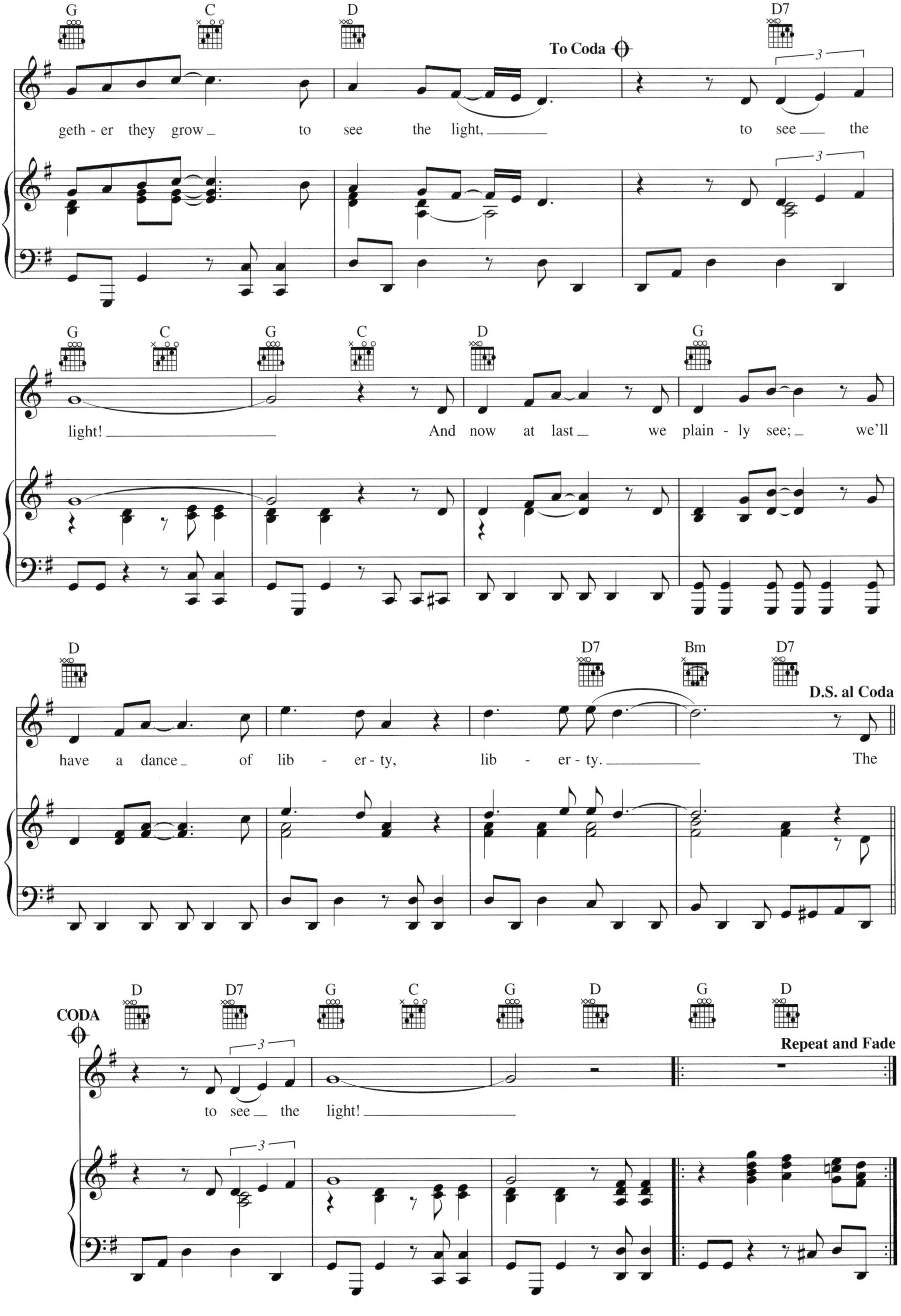
G C D D7
To Coda
geth - er they grow to see the light, to see the
G C G C D G
light! And now at last we plain - ly see; we'll
D D7 Bm D7
D.S. al Coda
have a dance of lib - er - ty, lib - er - ty. The
CODA
D D7 G C G D G D
Repeat and Fade
to see the light!

BUFFALO SOLDIER

Words and Music by NOEL WILLIAMS
and BOB MARLEY

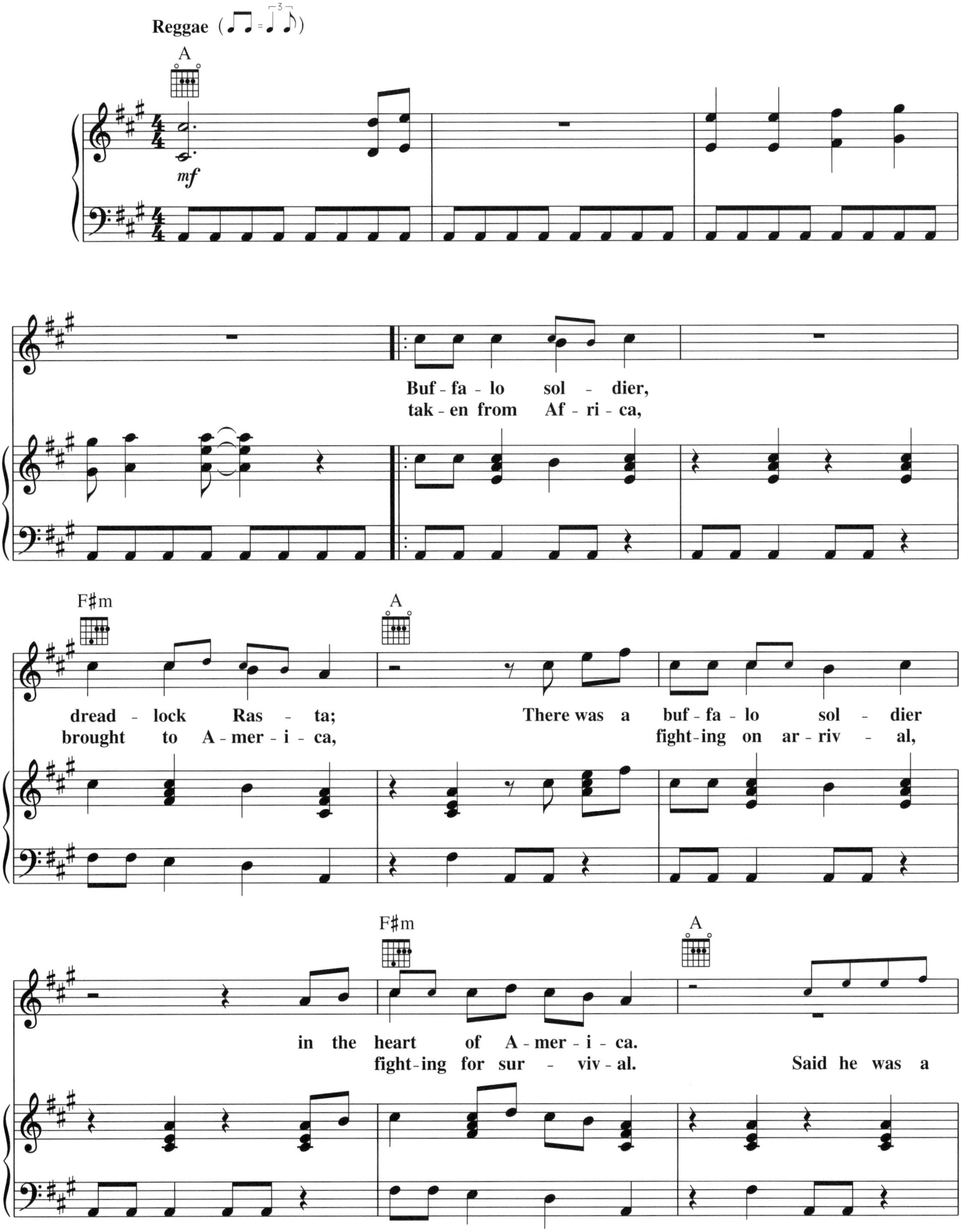

© 1983 EMI LONGITUDE MUSIC and MUSIC SALES CORPORATION
All Rights Reserved International Copyright Secured Used by Permission

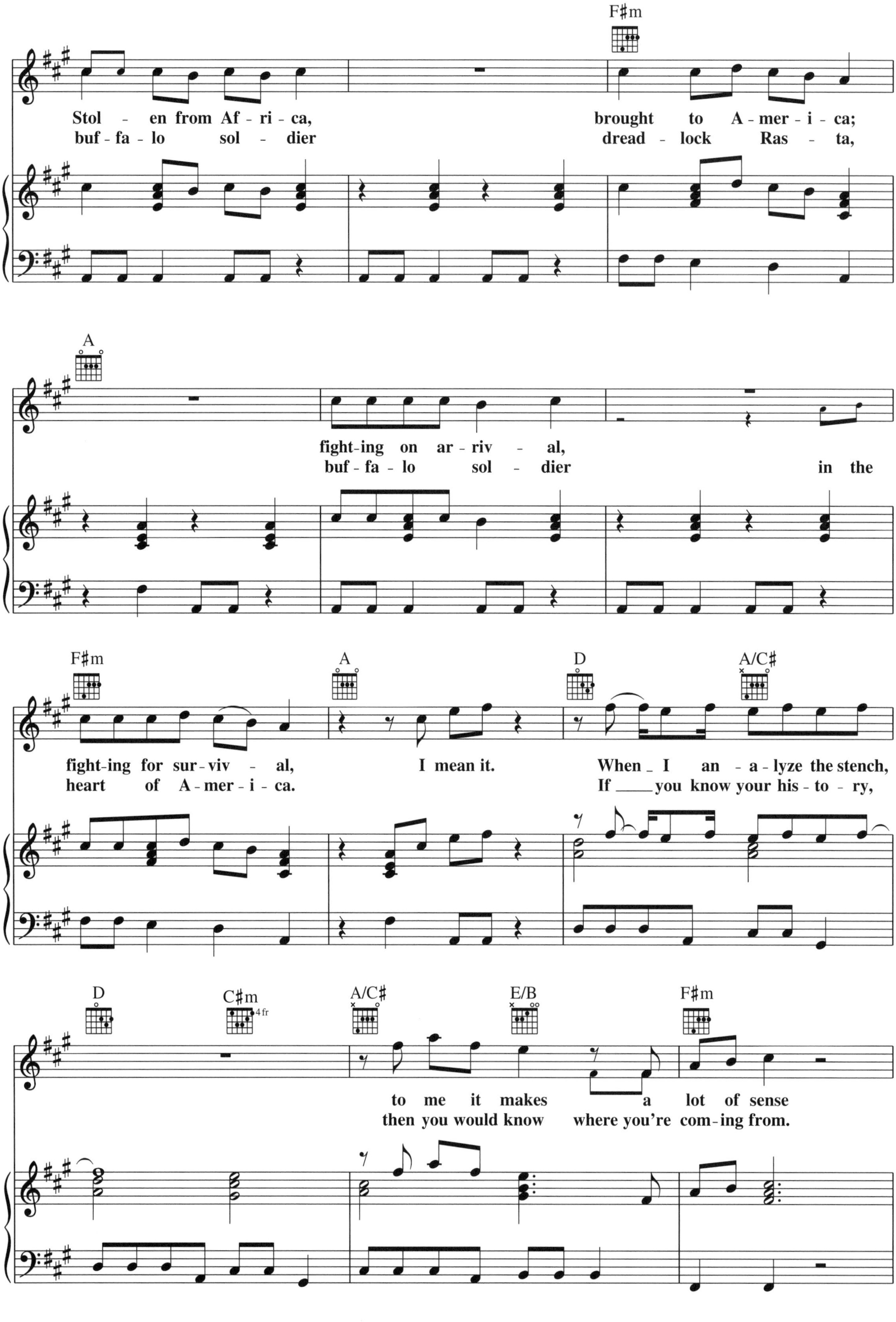
F♯m
Stol - en from Af - ri - ca, brought to A - mer - i - ca;
buf - fa - lo sol - dier dread - lock Ras - ta,
A
fight - ing on ar - riv - al,
buf - fa - lo sol - dier in the
F♯m
A
D
A/C♯
fight - ing for sur - viv - al, I mean it. When I an - a - lyze the stench,
heart of A - mer - i - ca. If you know your his - to - ry,
D
C♯m
4fr
A/C♯
E/B
F♯m
to me it makes a lot of sense
then you would know where you're com - ing from.

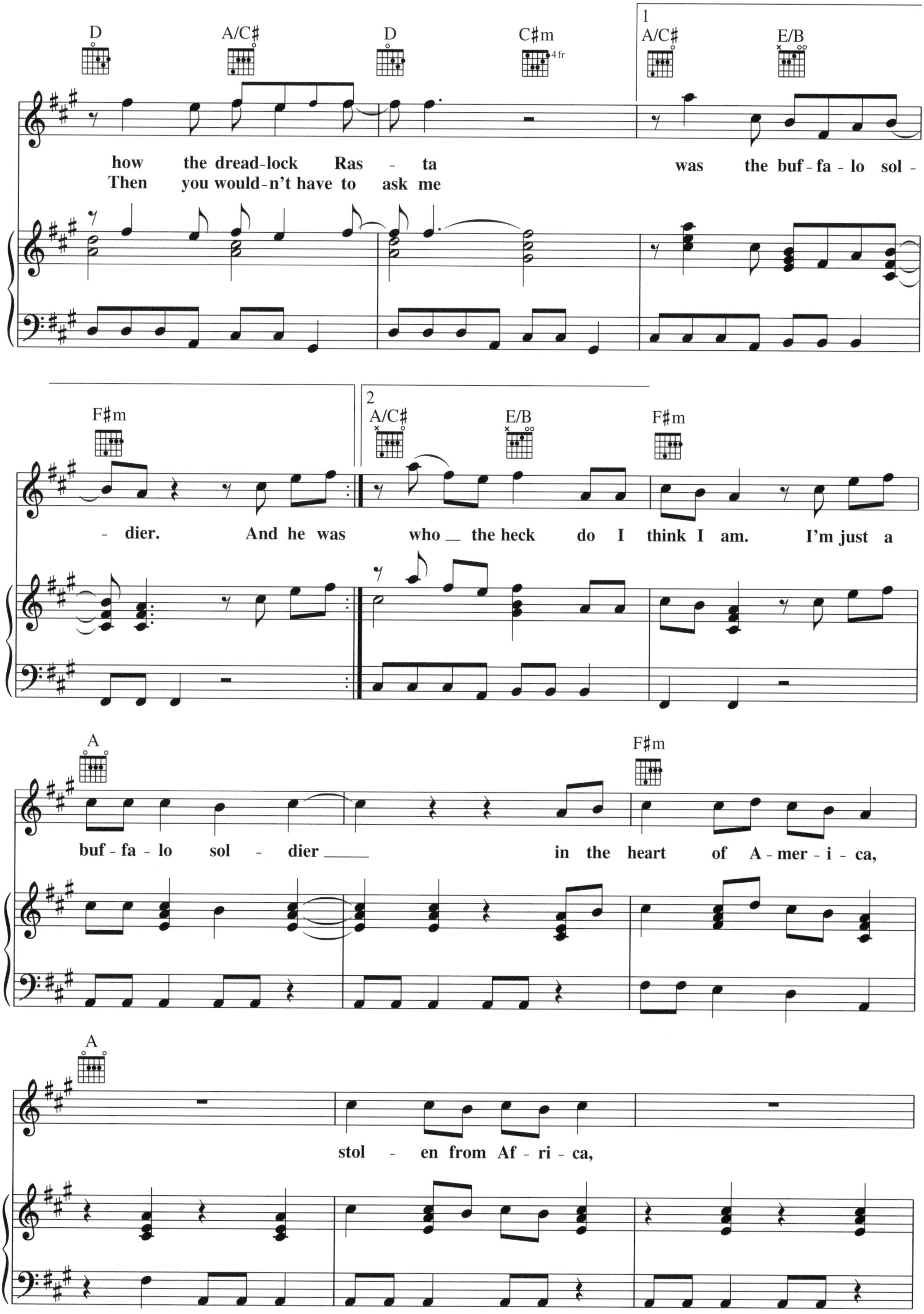
D A/C♯ D C♯m 4fr
1
A/C♯ E/B
how the dread-lock Ras - ta was the buf - fa - lo sol -
Then you would-n't have to ask me
F♯m
2
A/C♯ E/B F♯m
- dier. And he was who _ the heck do I think I am. I'm just a
A F♯m
buf - fa - lo sol - dier _ in the heart of A - mer - i - ca,
A
stol - en from Af - ri - ca,

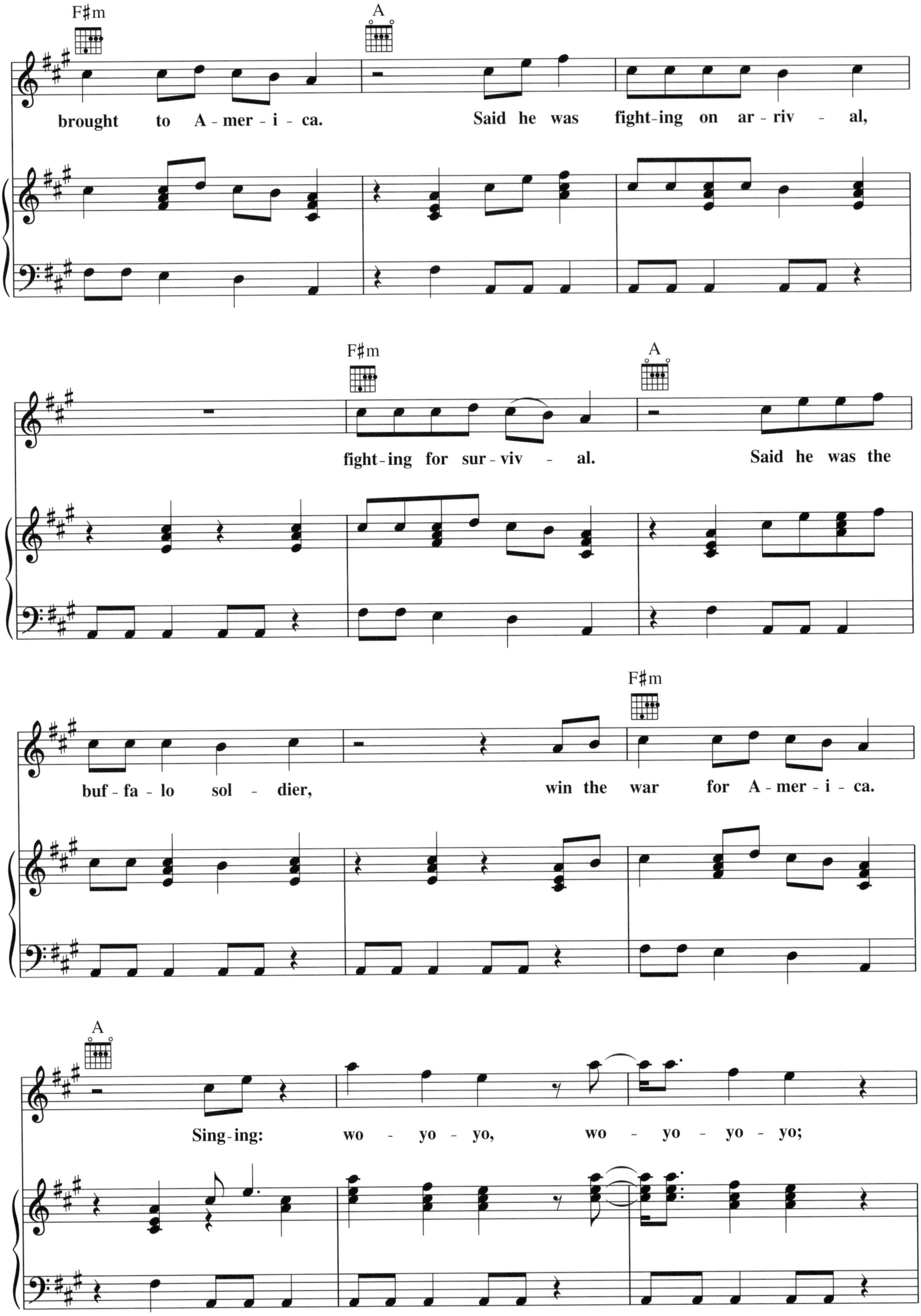
F♯m
A
brought to A - mer - i - ca. Said he was fight - ing on ar - riv - al,
F♯m
A
fight - ing for sur - viv - al. Said he was the
F♯m
buf - fa - lo sol - dier, win the war for A - mer - i - ca.
A
Sing - ing: wo - yo - yo, wo - yo - yo - yo;

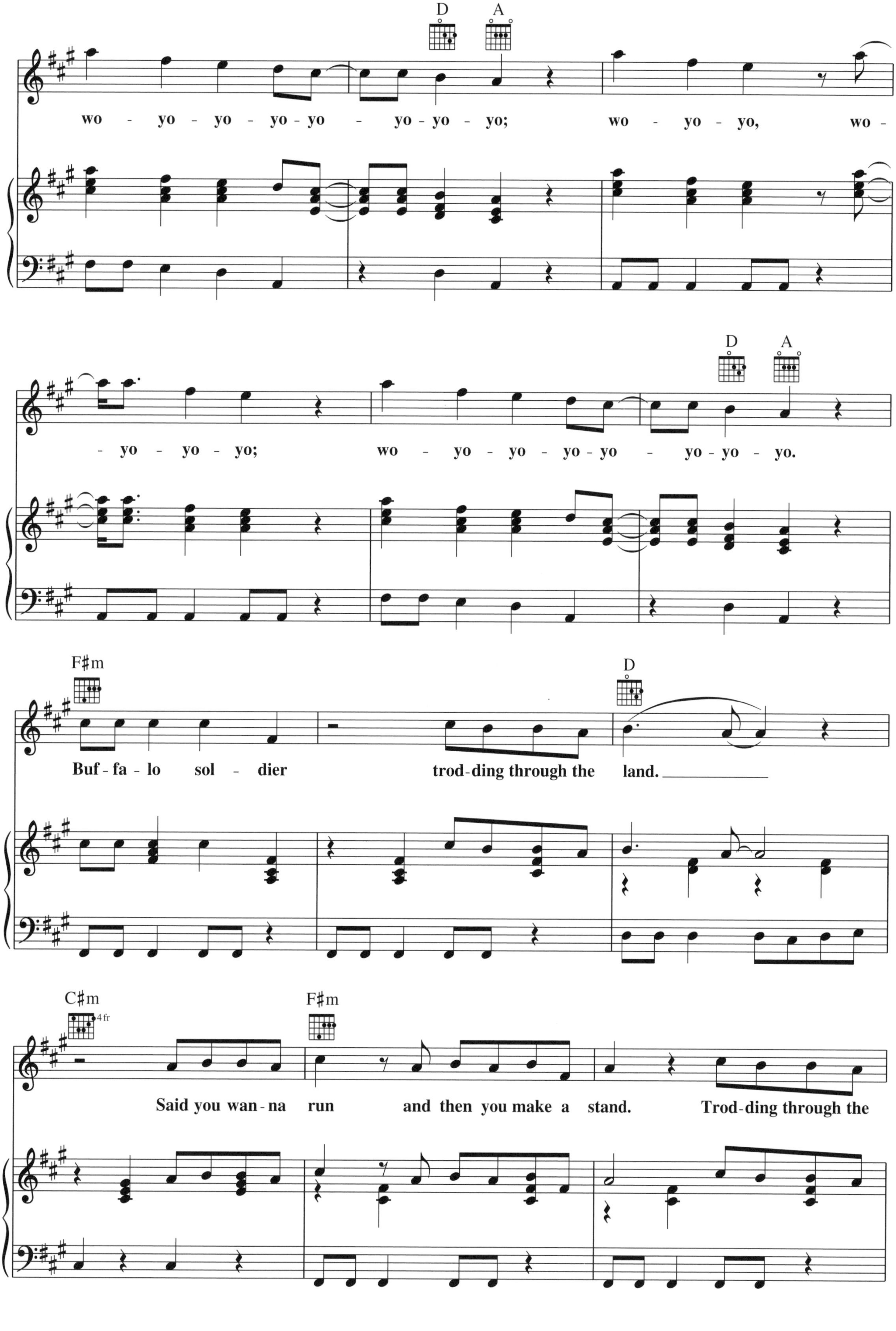
D
A
wo - yo - yo - yo - yo - yo - yo - yo; wo - yo - yo, wo -
D
A
- yo - yo - yo; wo - yo - yo - yo - yo - yo - yo - yo.
F#m
D
Buf - fa - lo sol - dier trod - ding through the land.
C#m
4fr
F#m
Said you wan - na run and then you make a stand. Trod - ding through the

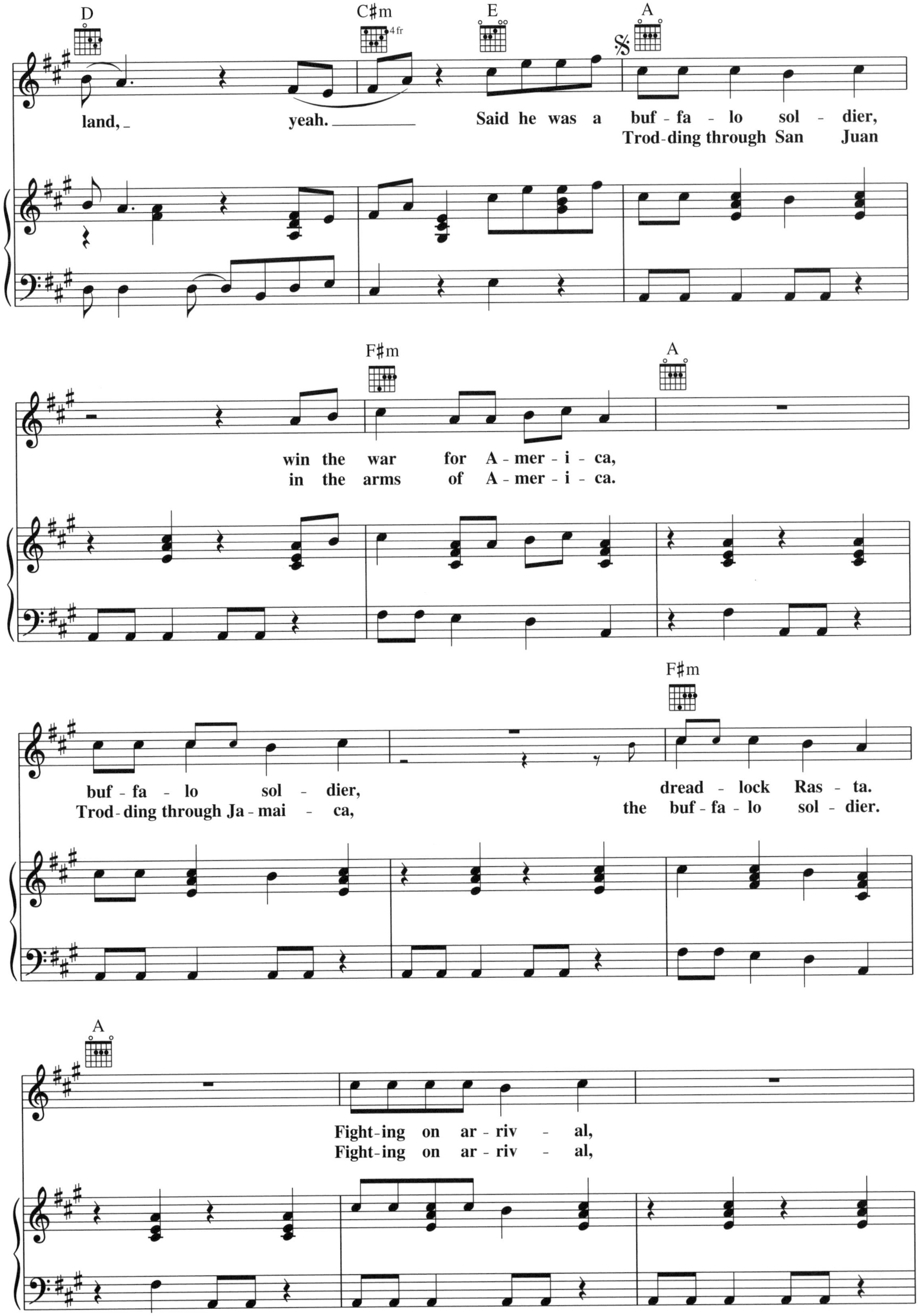
D
C♯m
E
A
land, _
yeah. _______
Said he was a
buf - fa - lo sol - dier,
Trod-ding through San Juan
F♯m
A
win the war for A - mer - i - ca,
in the arms of A - mer - i - ca.
F♯m
buf - fa - lo sol - dier,
Trod-ding through Ja - mai - ca,
dread - lock Ras - ta.
the buf - fa - lo sol - dier.
A
Fight-ing on ar - riv - al,
Fight-ing on ar - riv - al,

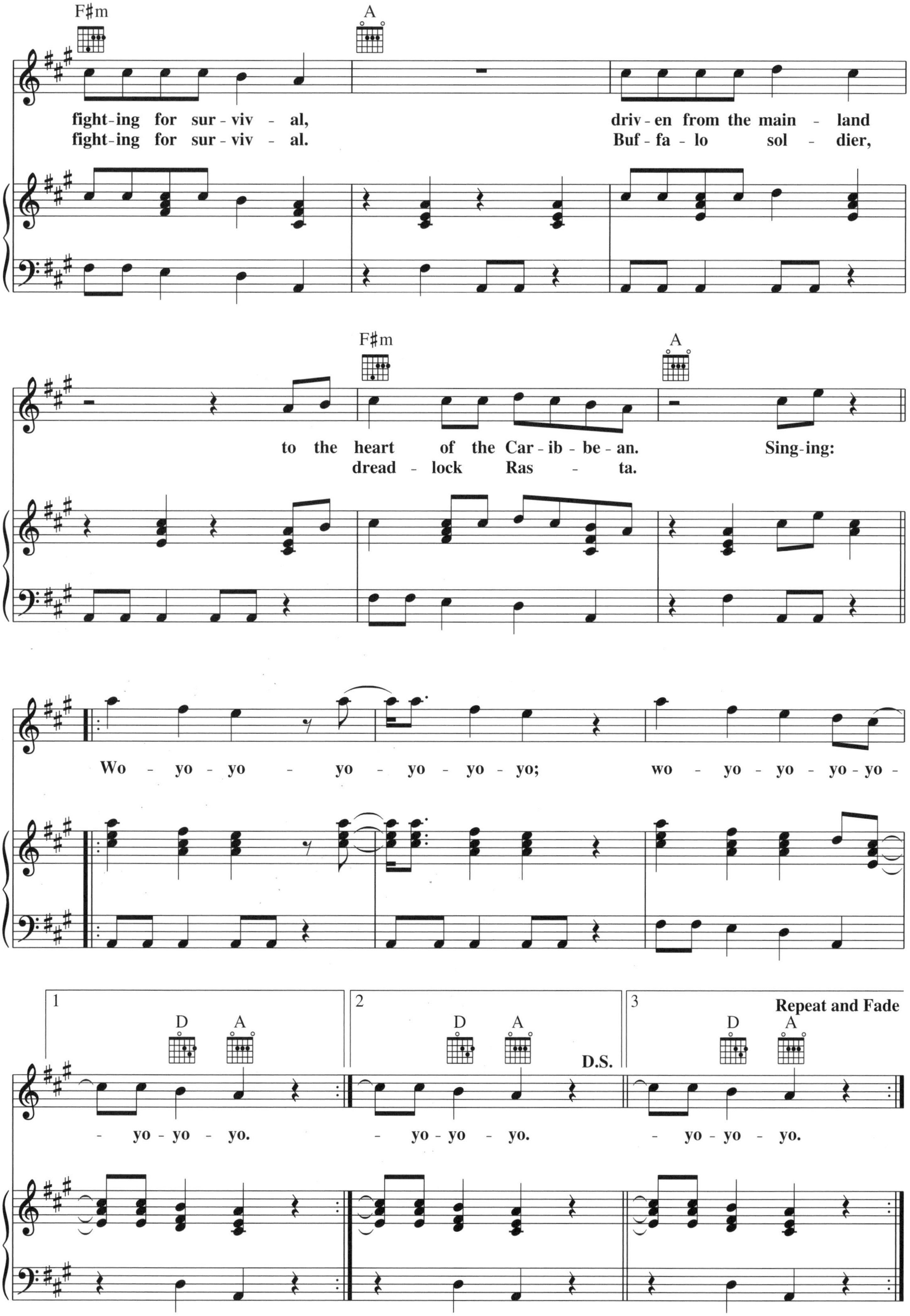
F♯m
A
fight-ing for sur-viv - al,
driv-en from the main - land
fight-ing for sur-viv - al.
Buf-fa-lo sol - dier,
F♯m
A
to the heart of the Car-ib-be-an.
Sing-ing:
dread - lock Ras - ta.
Wo - yo - yo - yo - yo - yo - yo;
wo - yo - yo - yo - yo -
1
D
A
- yo - yo - yo.
2
D
A
D.S.
- yo - yo - yo.
3
Repeat and Fade
D
A
- yo - yo - yo.

EVE OF DESTRUCTION

Words and Music by P.F. SLOAN
and STEVE BARRI

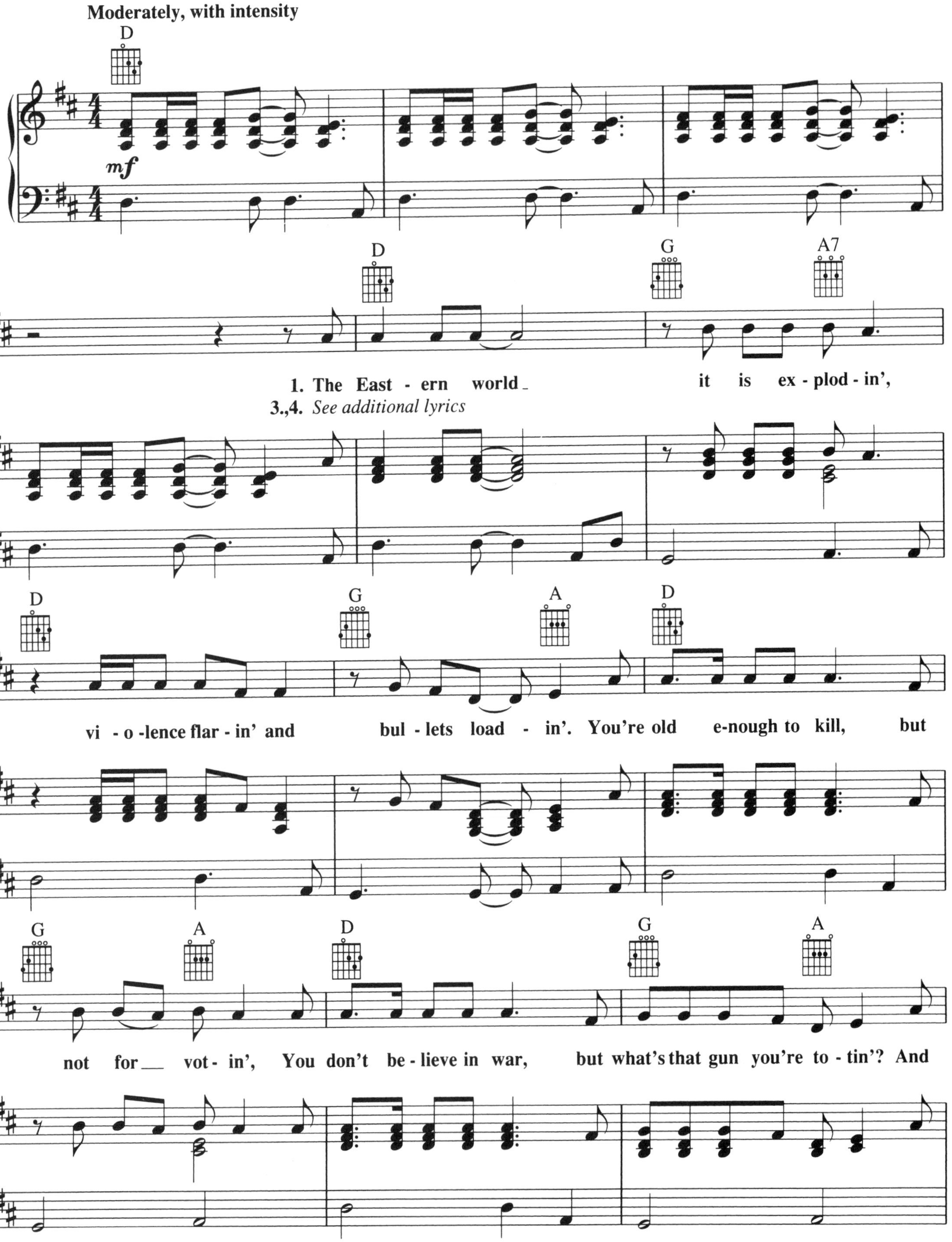

Copyright © 1965 UNIVERSAL MUSIC CORP.
Copyright Renewed
All Rights Reserved Used by Permission

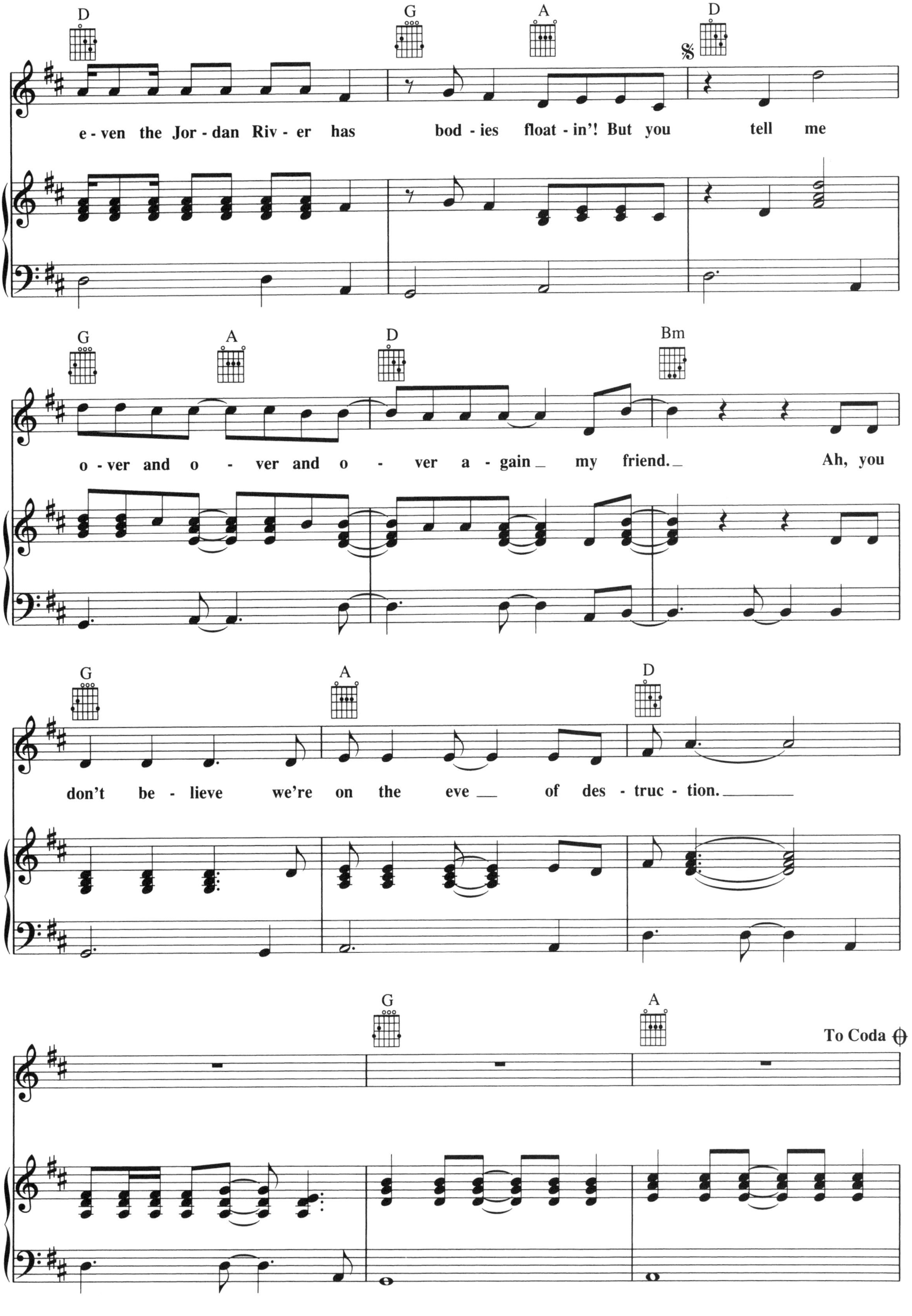
D
G
A
D
e - ven the Jor - dan Riv - er has bod - ies float - in'! But you tell me
G
A
D
Bm
o - ver and o - ver and o - ver a - gain my friend. Ah, you
G
A
D
don't be - lieve we're on the eve of des - truc - tion.
G
A
To Coda

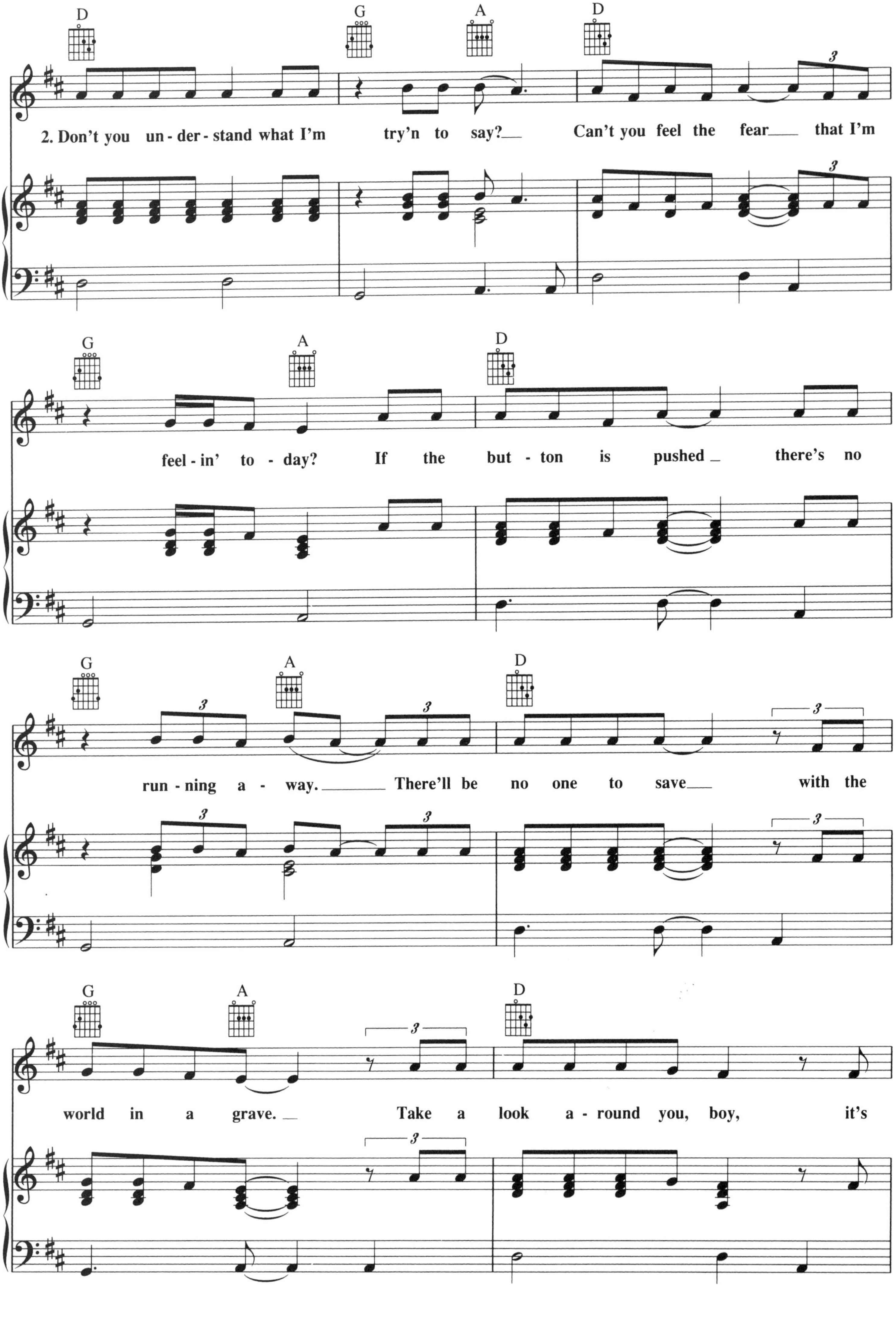
D G A D
3
2. Don't you un - der - stand what I'm try'n to say? Can't you feel the fear that I'm
3
G A D
feel - in' to - day? If the but - ton is pushed there's no
G A D
3 3 3
run - ning a - way. There'll be no one to save with the
3 3 3
G A D
3
world in a grave. Take a look a - round you, boy, it's
3

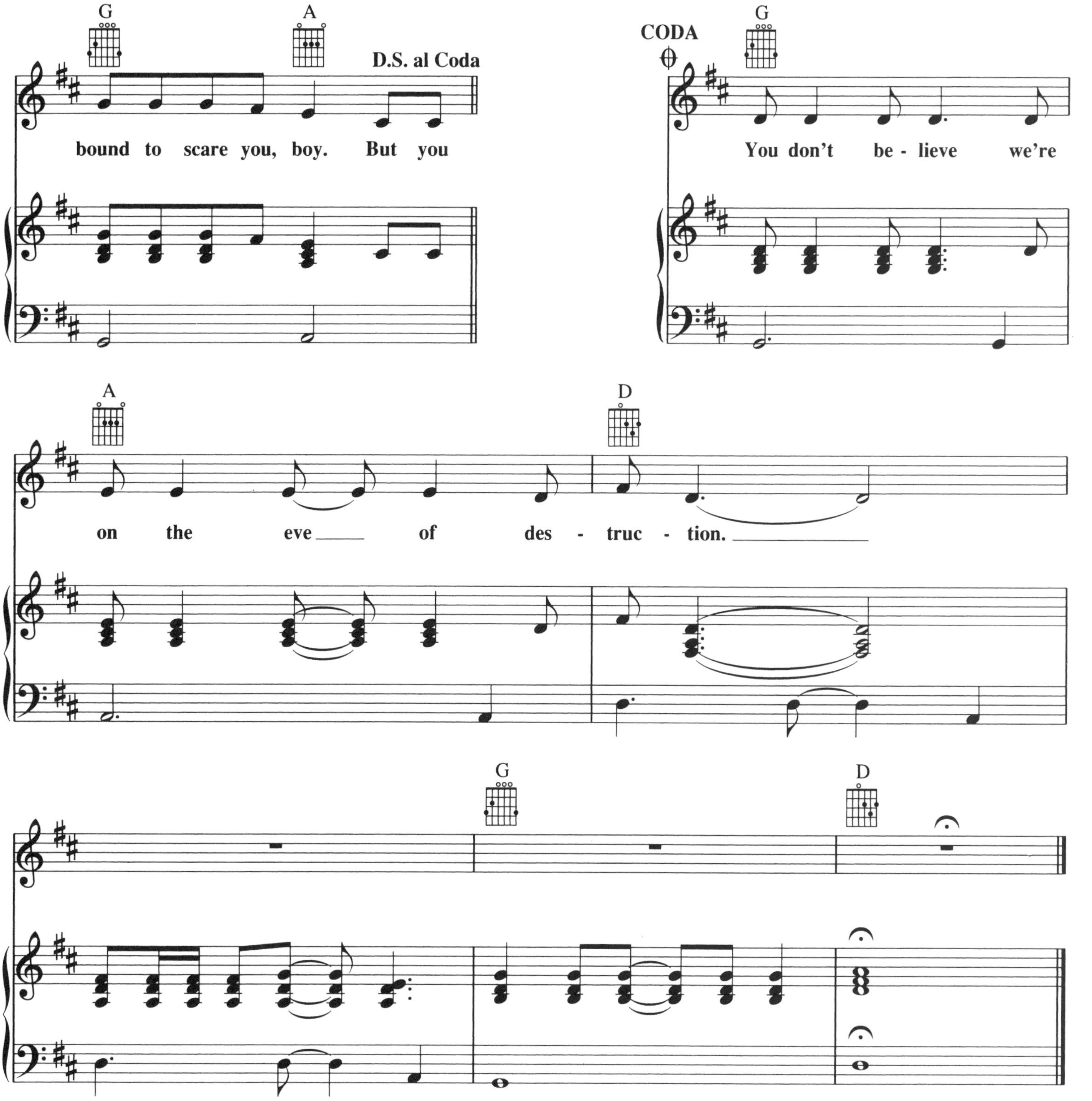

Additional Lyrics

3. My blood's so mad feels like coagulatin'
I'm sittin' here just contemplatin'
You can't twist the truth it knows no regulatin'
And a handful of Senators don't pass legislation
Marches alone can't bring integration
When human respect is disintegratin'
This whole crazy world is just too frustatin'.
(To Chorus:)

4. Think of all the hate there is in Red China
Then take a look around to Selma, Alabama!
You may leave here for four days in space
But when you return, it's the same old place,
The pounding drums, the pride and disgrace
You can bury your dead, but don't leave a trace
Hate your next door neighbor, but don't forget to say grace.
(To Chorus:)

FREEDOM

Words and Music by
PAUL McCARTNEY

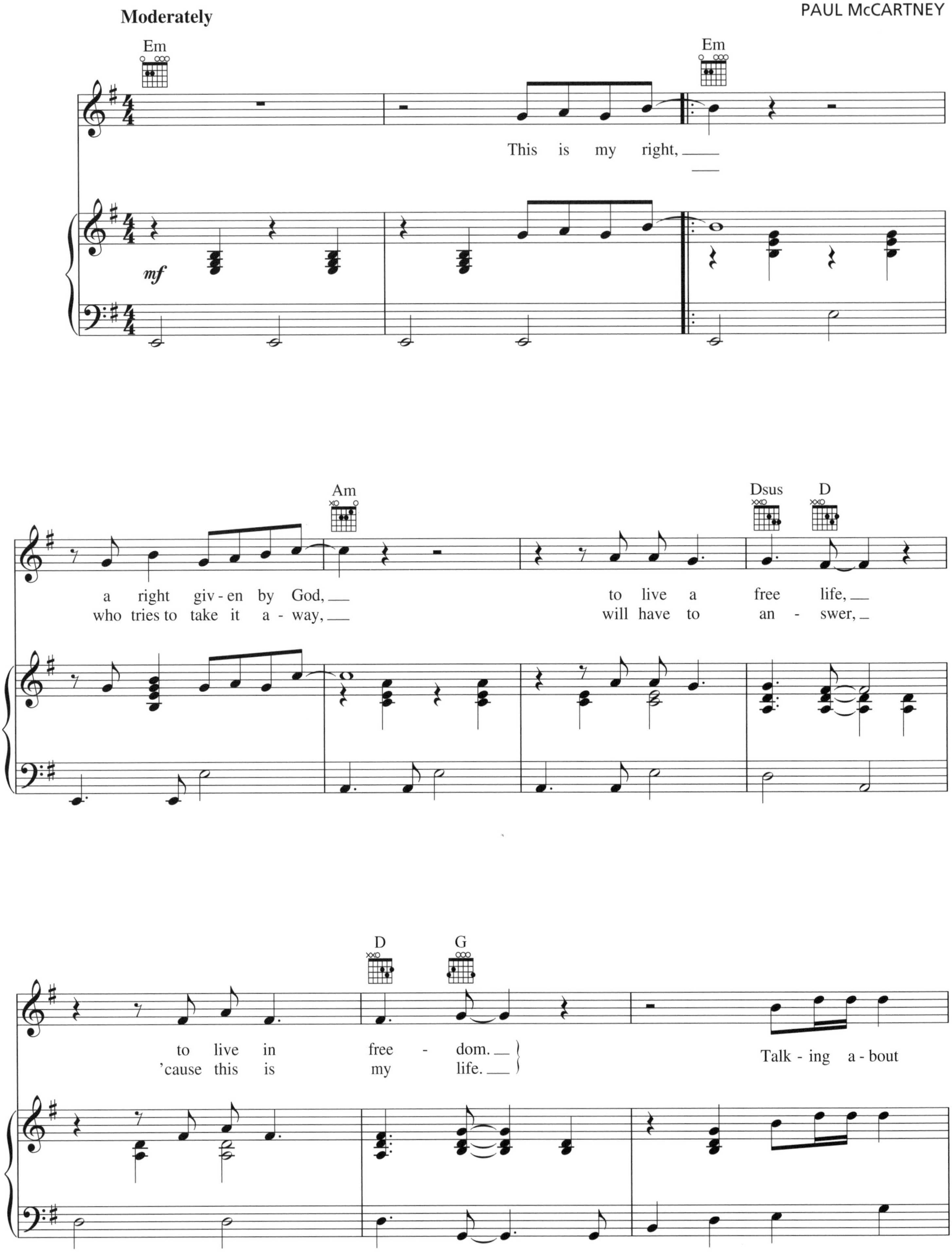

© 2001 MPL COMMUNICATIONS LTD.
Administered by MPL COMMUNICATIONS, INC.
All Rights Reserved

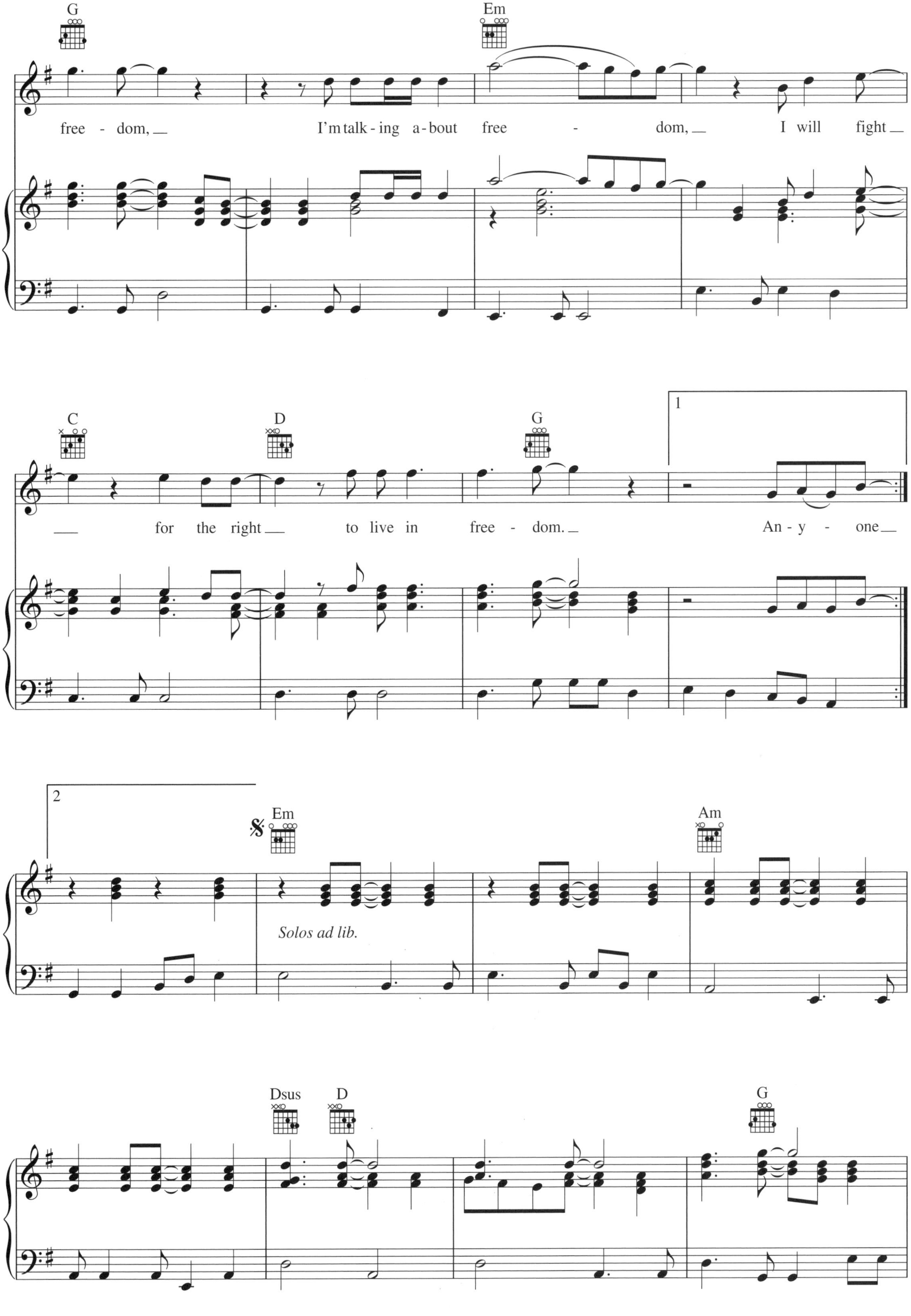
G
Em
free - dom, __ I'm talk - ing a - bout free - dom, __ I will fight __
C
D
G
1
__ for the right __ to live in free - dom. __ An - y - one __
2
Em
Am
Solos ad lib.
Dsus
D
G

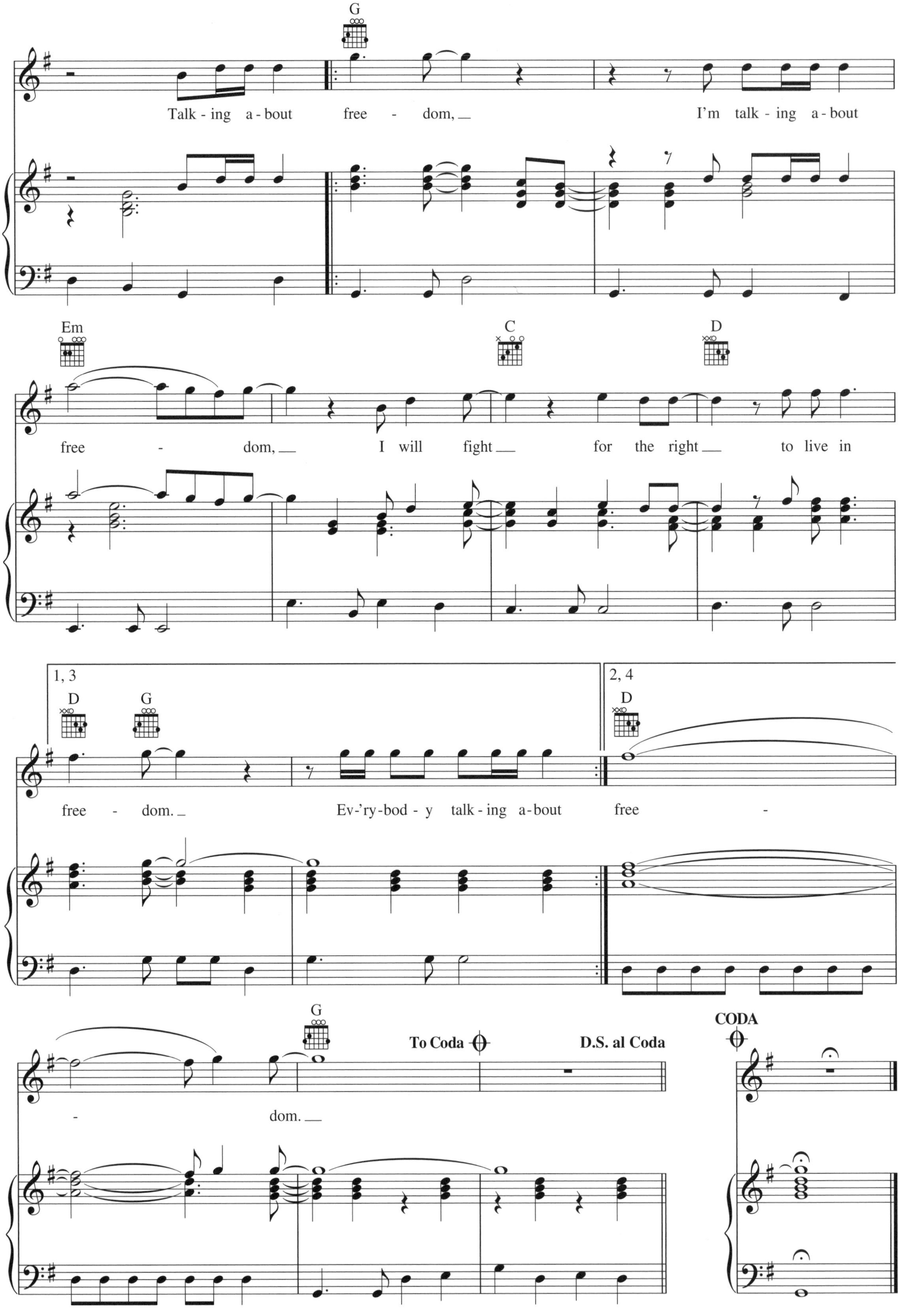
G
Talk - ing a - bout free - dom, I'm talk - ing a - bout
Em
C
D
free - dom, I will fight for the right to live in
1, 3
D
G
free - dom. Ev-'ry-bod - y talk - ing a - bout
2, 4
D
free -
G
- dom.
To Coda
D.S. al Coda
CODA

GIVE PEACE A CHANCE

Words and Music by
JOHN LENNON

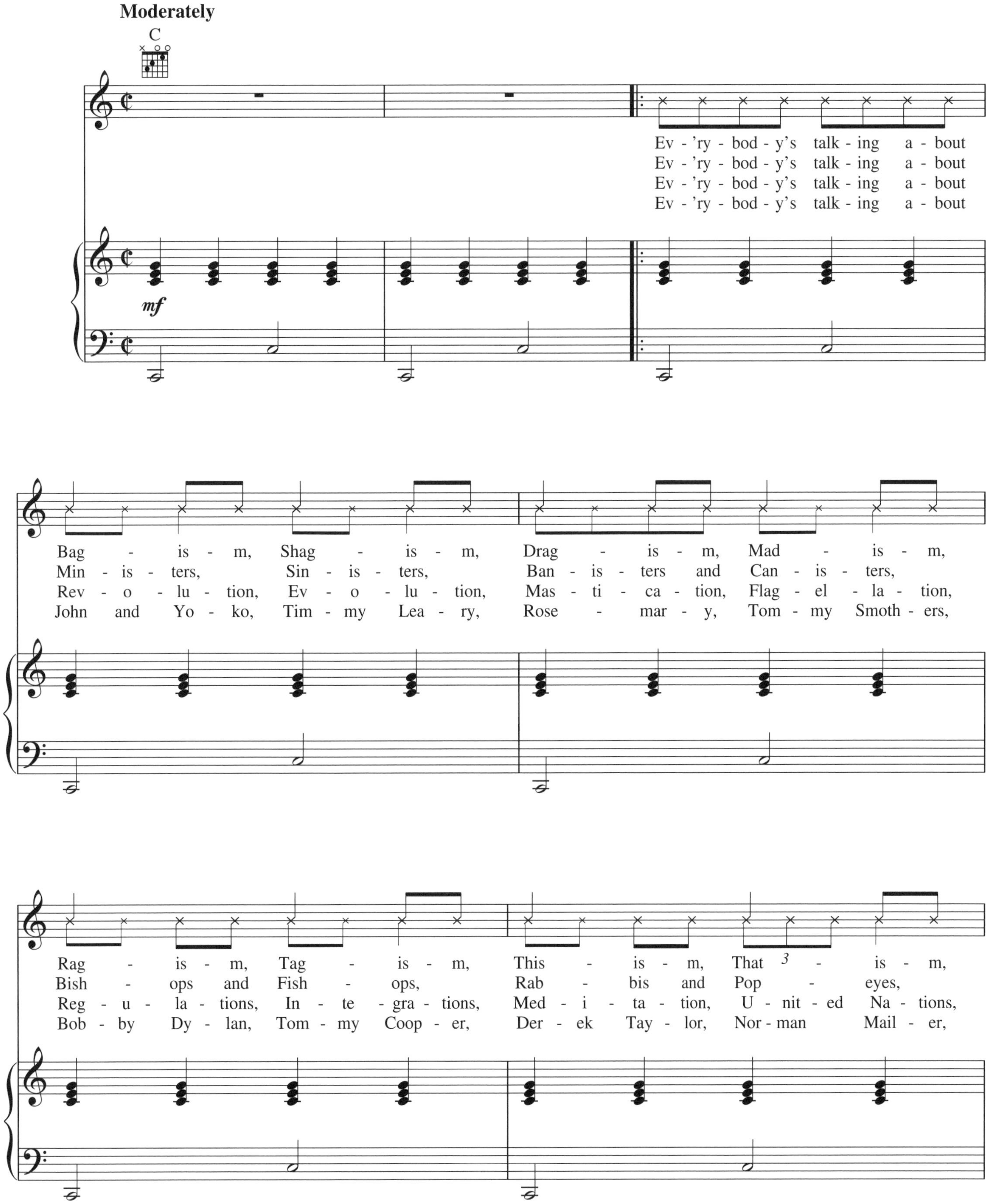

Copyright © 1969 Sony/ATV Songs LLC
Copyright Renewed
All Rights Administered by Sony/ATV Music Publishing, 8 Music Square West, Nashville, Tn 37203
International Copyright Secured All Rights Reserved

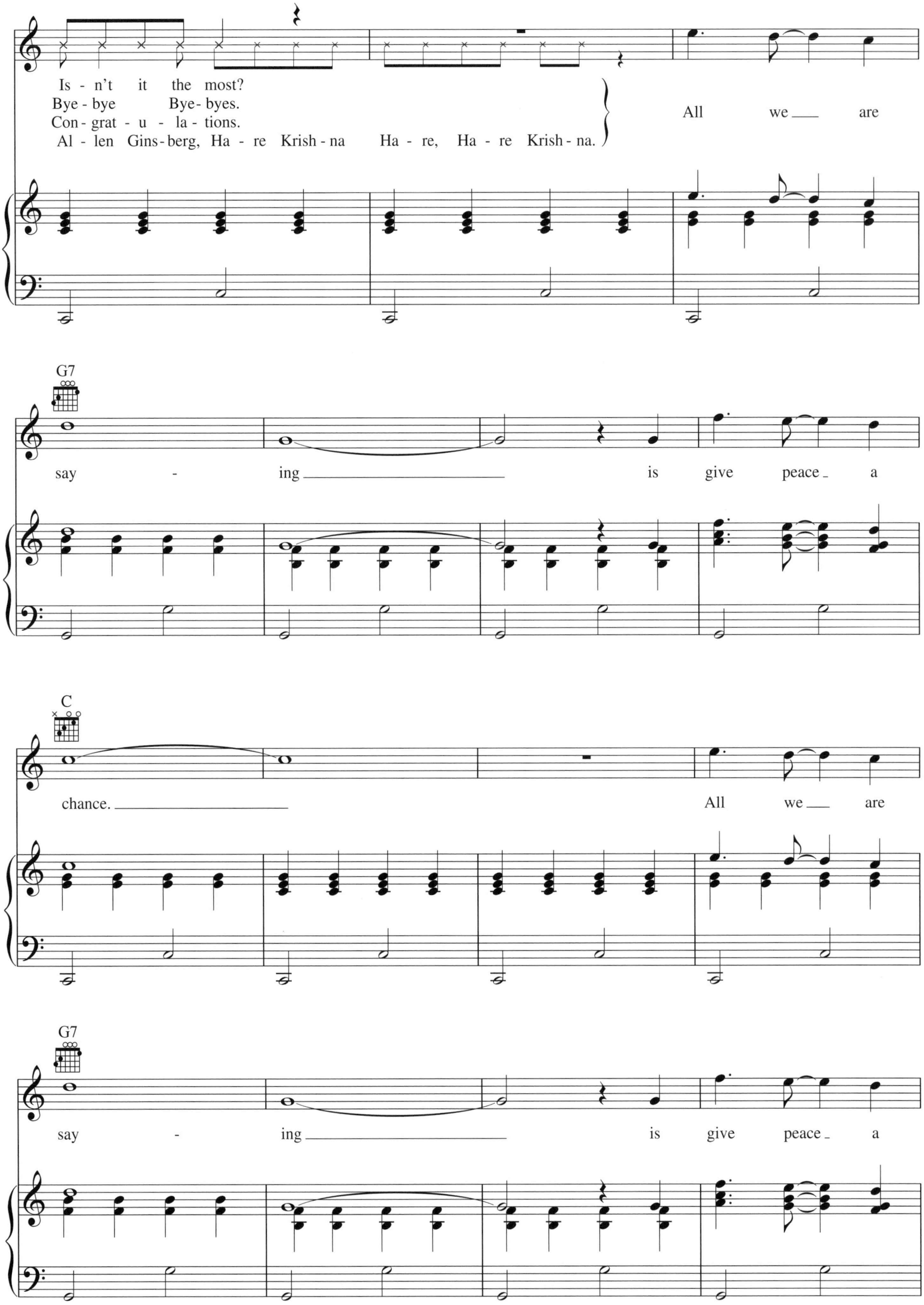
Is - n't it the most?
Bye - bye Bye - byes.
Con - grat - u - la - tions.
Al - len Gins - berg, Ha - re Krish - na Ha - re, Ha - re Krish - na.
All we are
G7
say - ing is give peace a
C
chance.
All we are
G7
say - ing is give peace a

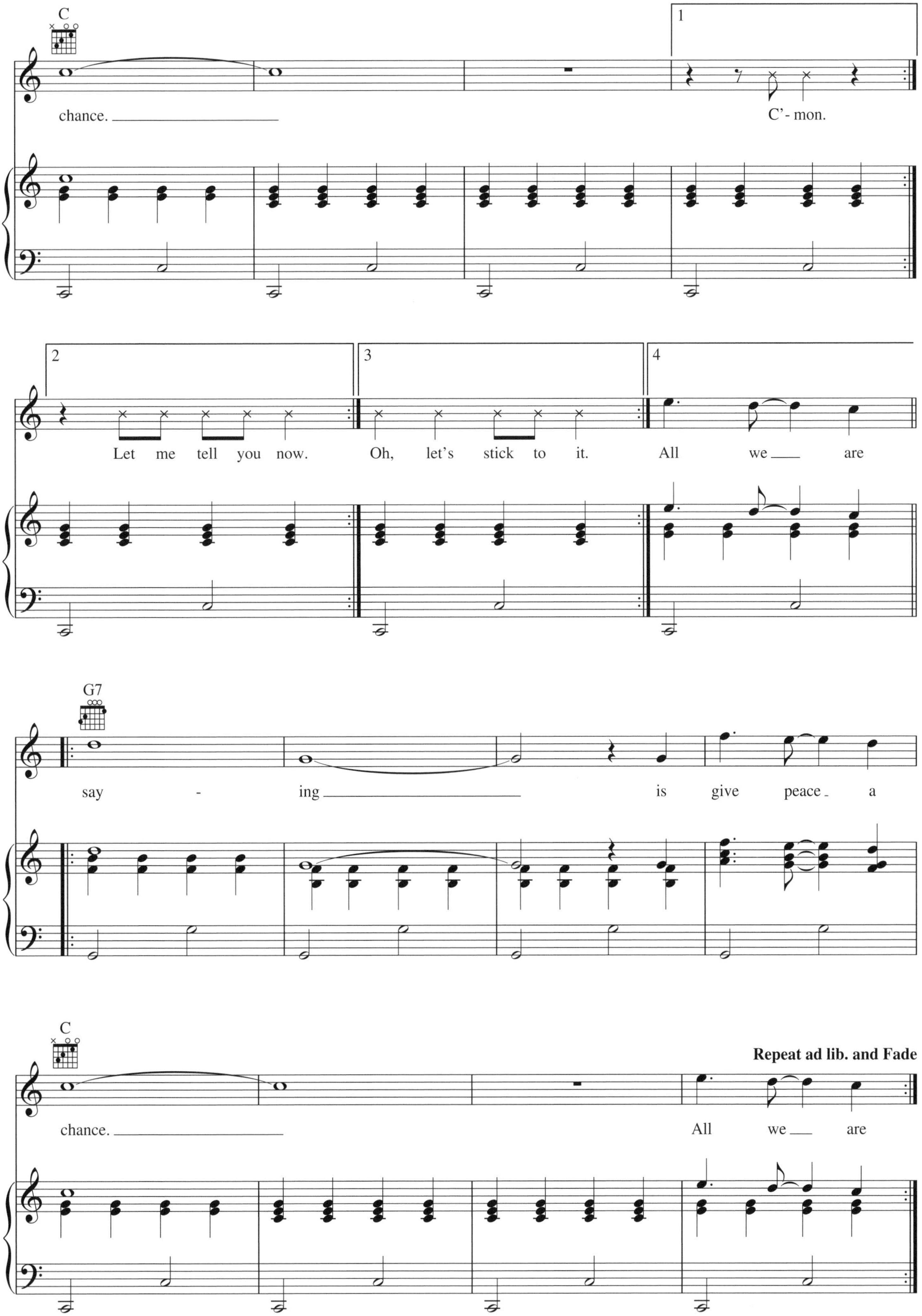
C
1
chance. C'- mon.
2
3
4
Let me tell you now. Oh, let's stick to it. All we are
G7
say - ing is give peace a
C
Repeat ad lib. and Fade
chance. All we are

HE AIN'T HEAVY... HE'S MY BROTHER

Words and Music by BOB RUSSELL
and BOBBY SCOTT

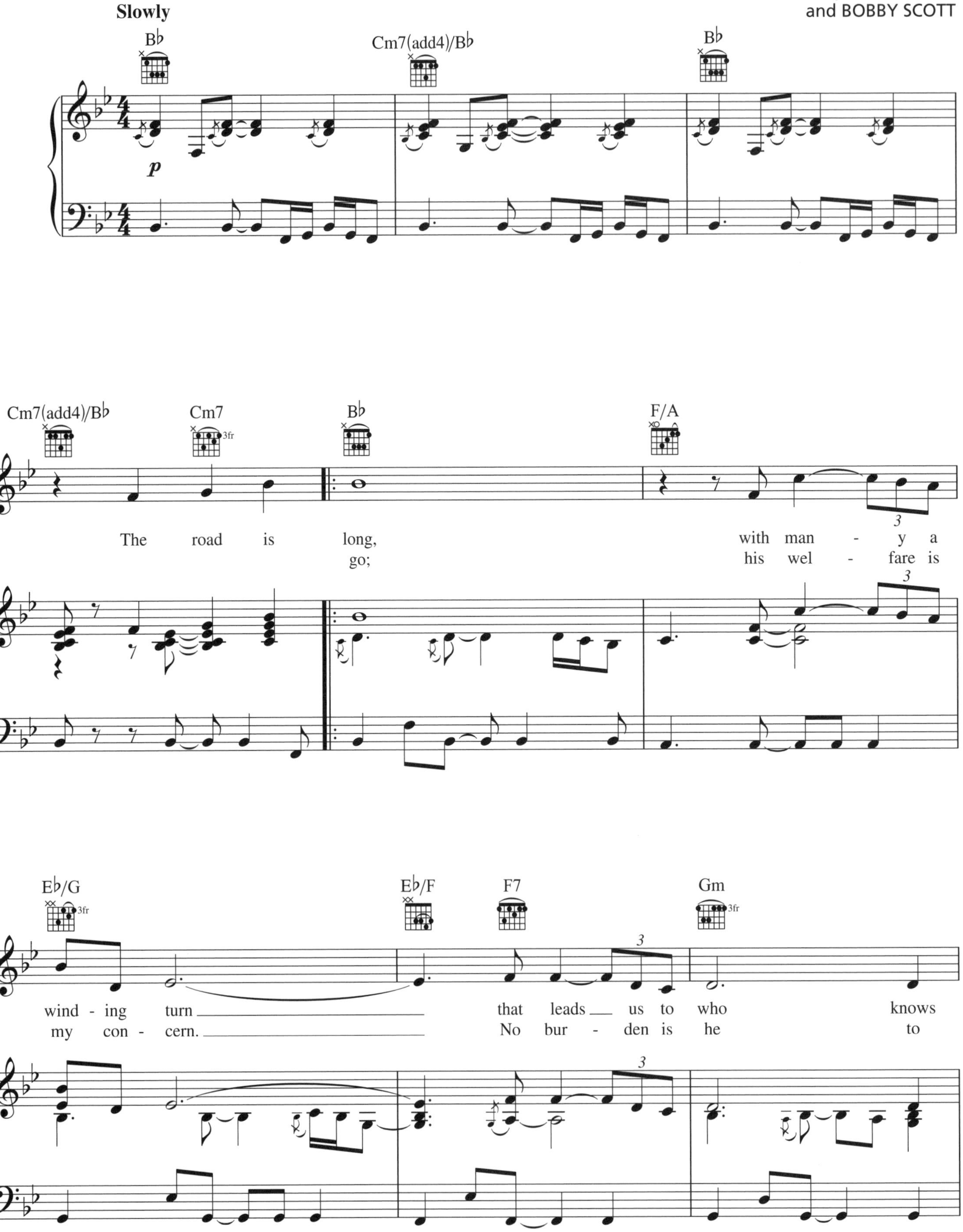
Slowly
B♭
Cm7(add4)/B♭
B♭
p
Cm7(add4)/B♭
Cm7
B♭
F/A
The road is long, with man - y a
go; his wel - fare is
E♭/G
E♭/F
F7
Gm
wind - ing turn that leads us to who knows
my con - cern. No bur - den is he to

© Copyright 1969 HARRISON MUSIC CORP. and JENNY MUSIC
Copyright Renewed
International Copyright Secured All Rights Reserved

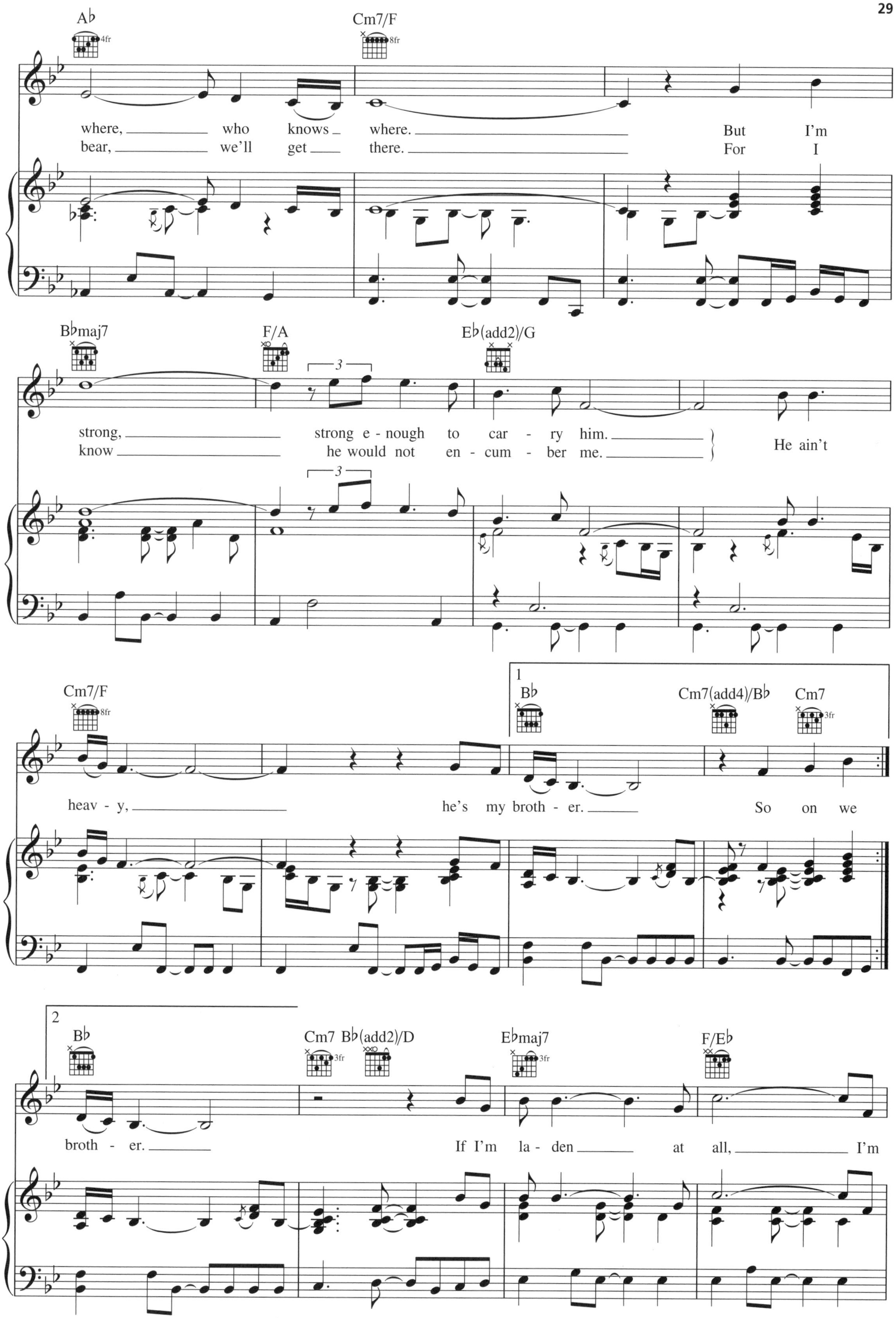
A♭
Cm7/F
where, who knows where. But I'm
bear, we'll get there. For I
B♭maj7
F/A
E♭(add2)/G
strong, strong e-nough to car-ry him.
know he would not en-cum-ber me.
He ain't
Cm7/F
1
B♭
Cm7(add4)/B♭
Cm7
heav-y, he's my broth-er. So on we
2
B♭
Cm7
B♭(add2)/D
E♭maj7
F/E♭
broth-er. If I'm la-den at all, I'm

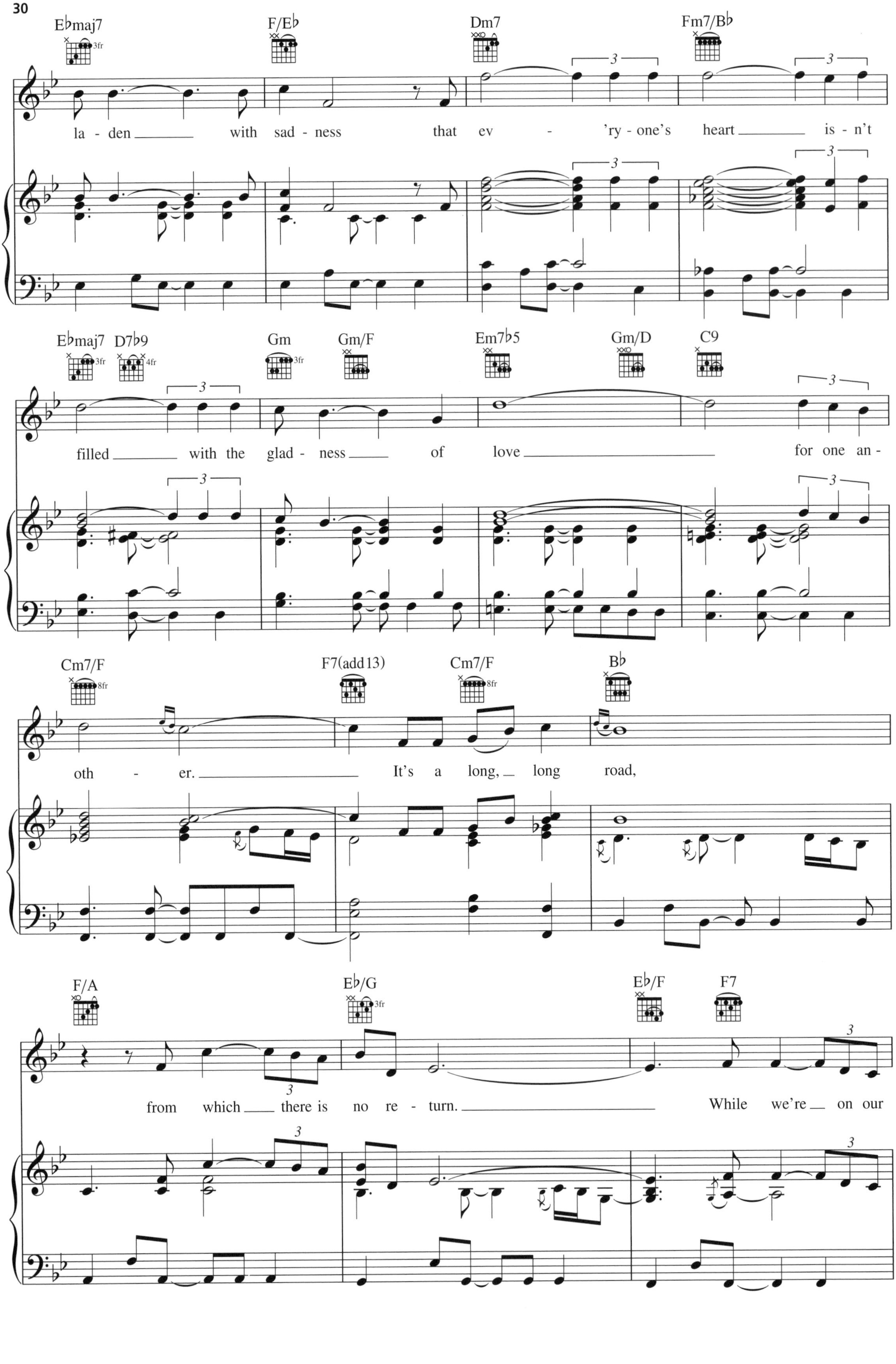
E♭maj7 F/E♭ Dm7 Fm7/B♭
la - den with sad - ness that ev - 'ry - one's heart is - n't
E♭maj7 D7♭9 Gm Gm/F Em7♭5 Gm/D C9
filled with the glad - ness of love for one an -
Cm7/F F7(add13) Cm7/F B♭
oth - er. It's a long, long road,
F/A E♭/G E♭/F F7
from which there is no re - turn. While we're on our
3fr
4fr
8fr

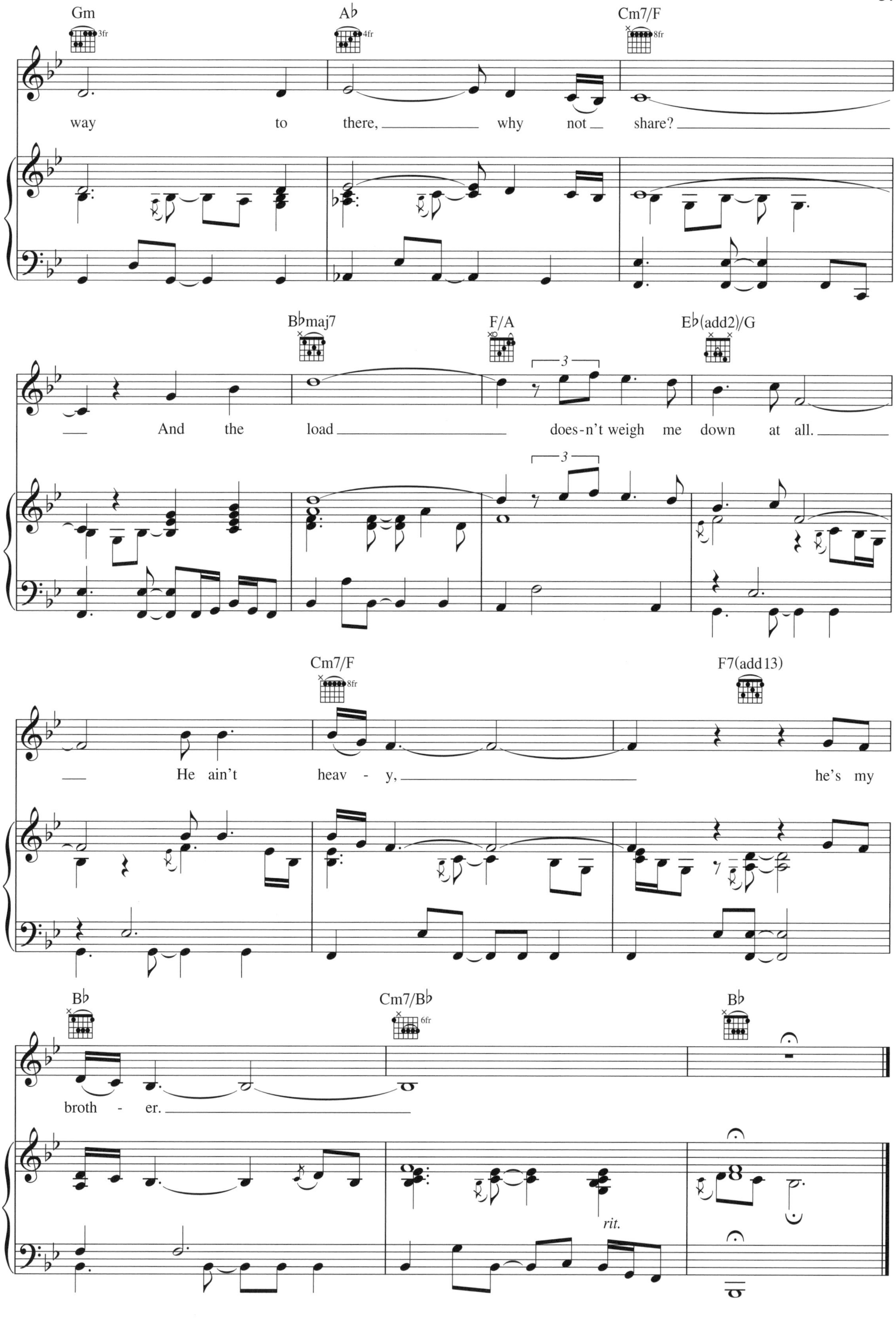
Gm
3fr
A♭
4fr
Cm7/F
8fr
way to there, why not share?
B♭maj7
F/A
E♭(add2)/G
3
And the load does-n't weigh me down at all.
3
Cm7/F
8fr
F7(add13)
He ain't heav - y, he's my
B♭
Cm7/B♭
6fr
B♭
broth - er.
rit.

I FEEL LIKE I'M FIXIN' TO DIE RAG

Words and Music by
JOE McDONALD

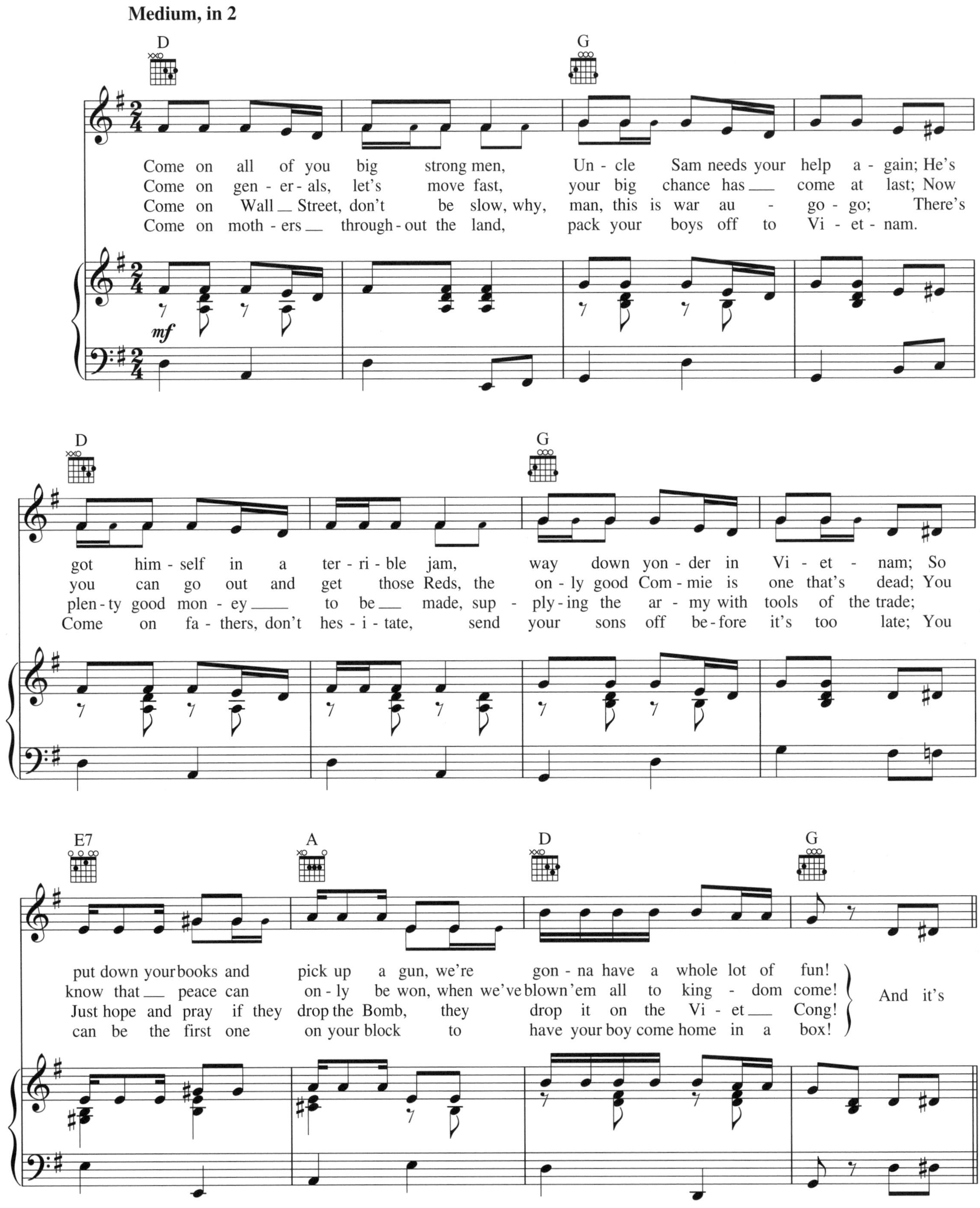

© 1965 Alkatraz Corner Music Co.
Copyright Renewed
All Rights Reserved Used by Permission

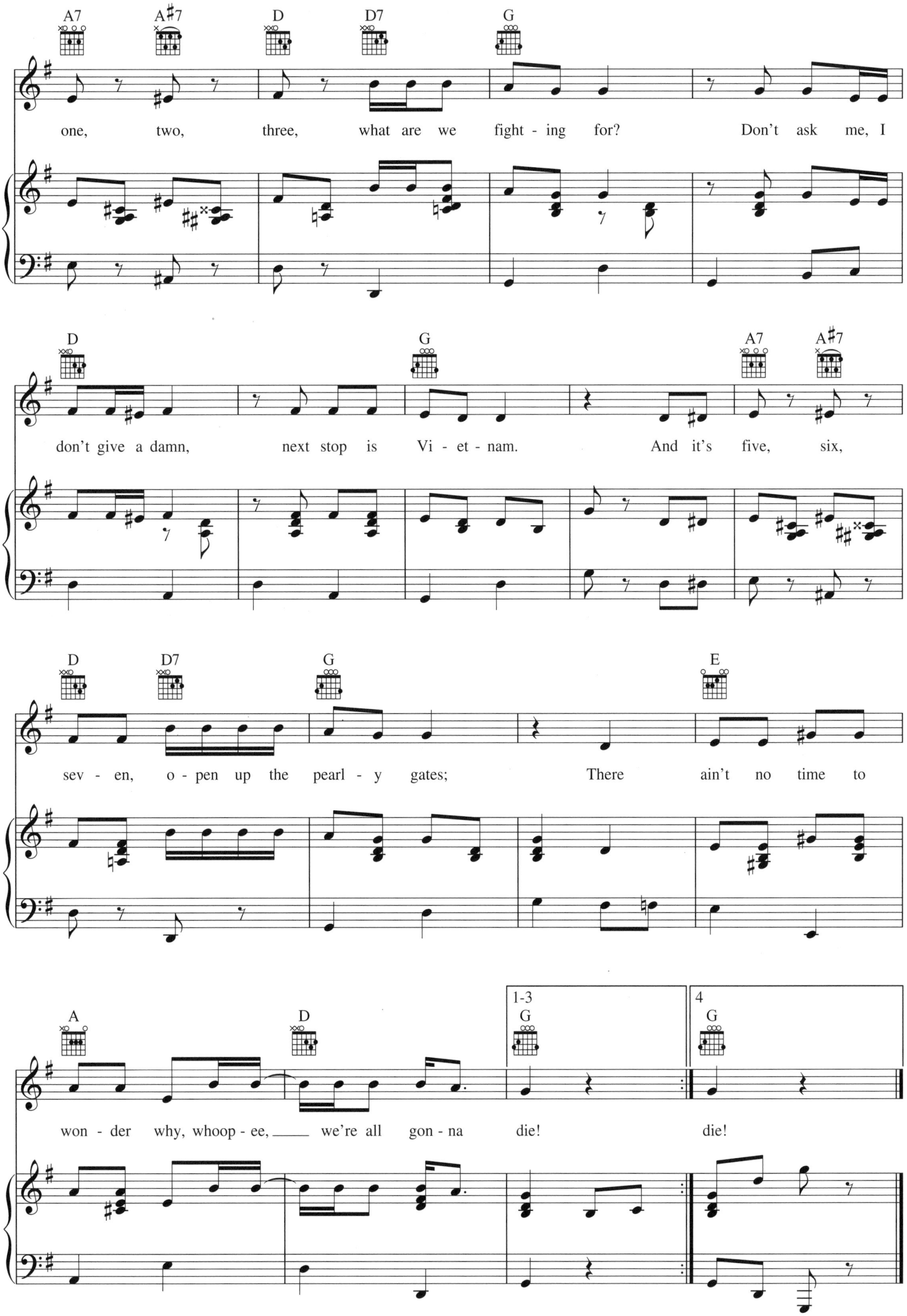
A7 A#7 D D7 G
one, two, three, what are we fight - ing for? Don't ask me, I
D G A7 A#7
don't give a damn, next stop is Vi - et - nam. And it's five, six,
D D7 G E
sev - en, o - pen up the pearl - y gates; There ain't no time to
A D 1-3 G 4 G
won - der why, whoop - ee, we're all gon - na die! die!

IF I HAD A HAMMER
(The Hammer Song)

Words and Music by LEE HAYS
and PETE SEEGER

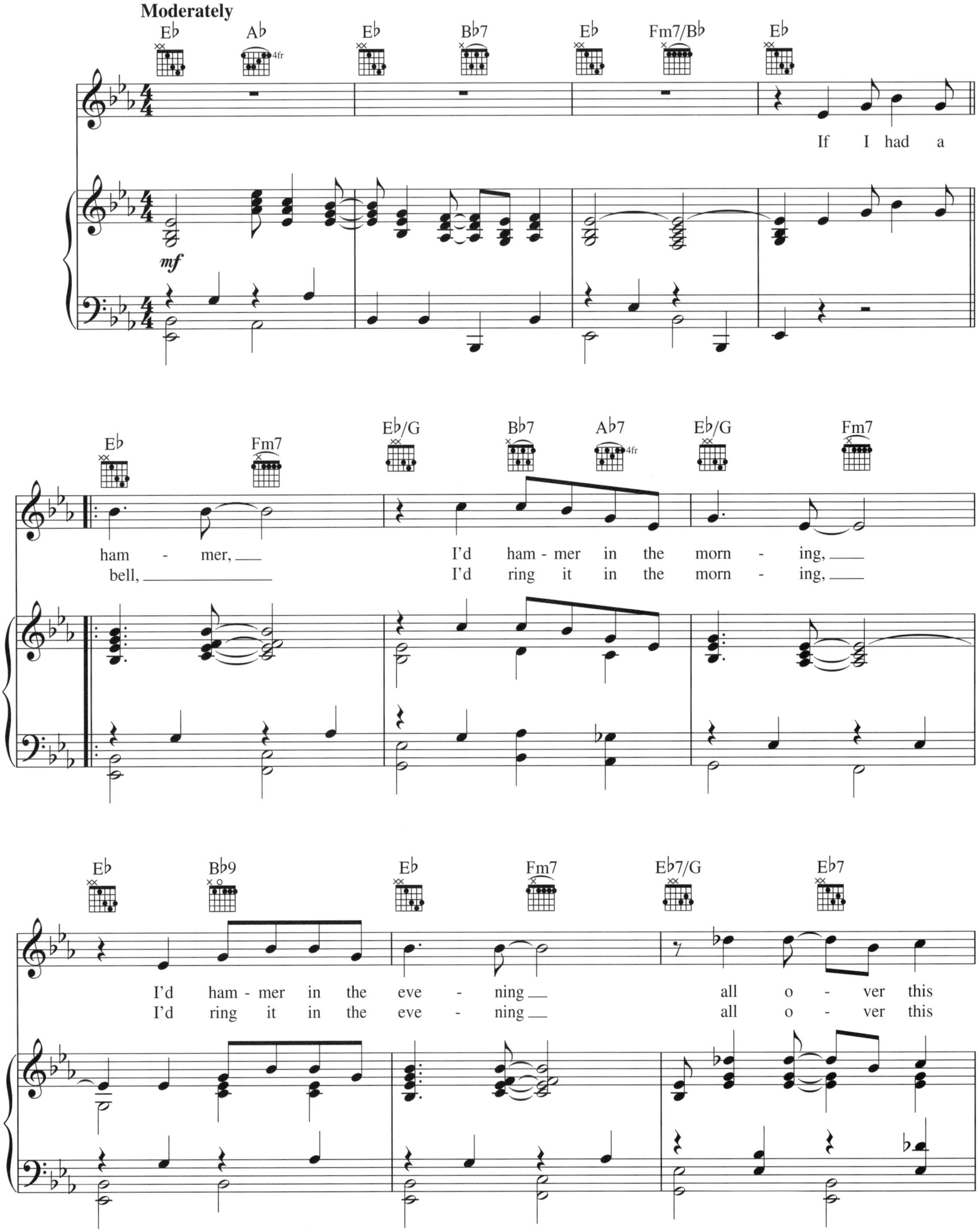

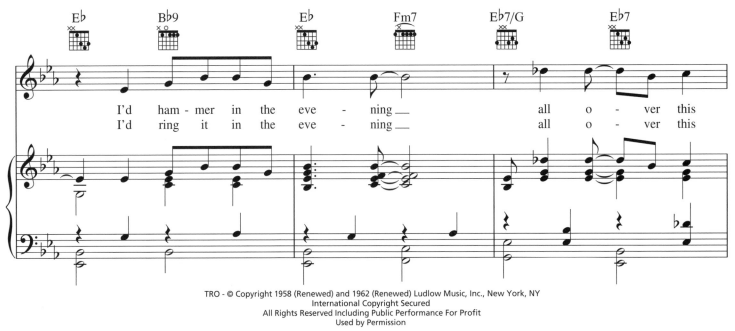

TRO - © Copyright 1958 (Renewed) and 1962 (Renewed) Ludlow Music, Inc., New York, NY
International Copyright Secured
All Rights Reserved Including Public Performance For Profit
Used by Permission

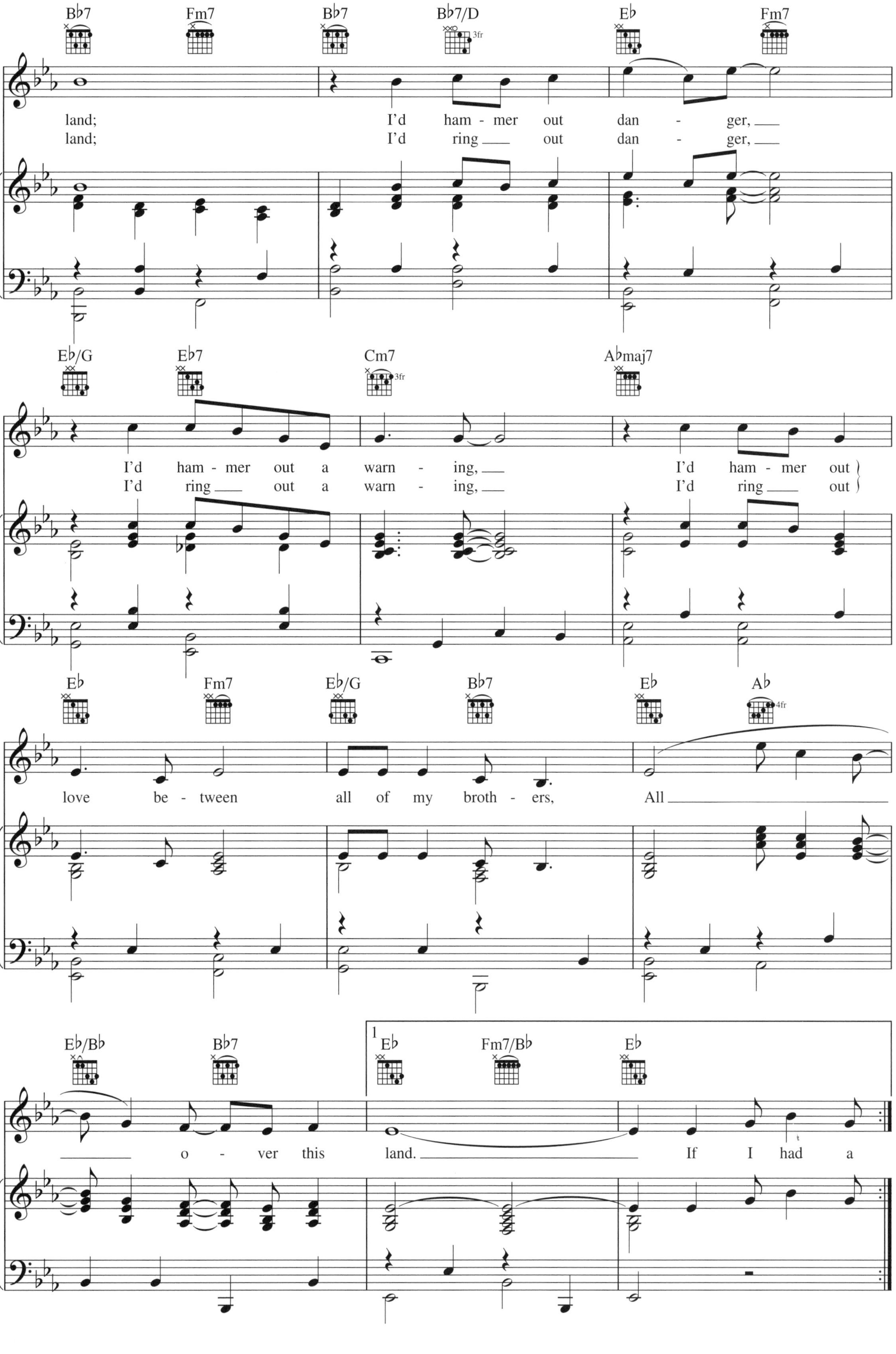
B♭7
Fm7
B♭7
B♭7/D
E♭
Fm7
land; I'd ham - mer out dan - ger,
land; I'd ring out dan - ger,
E♭/G
E♭7
Cm7
A♭maj7
I'd ham - mer out a warn - ing, I'd ham - mer out
I'd ring out a warn - ing, I'd ring out
E♭
Fm7
E♭/G
B♭7
E♭
A♭
love be - tween all of my broth - ers, All
E♭/B♭
B♭7
1
E♭
Fm7/B♭
E♭
o - ver this land. If I had a

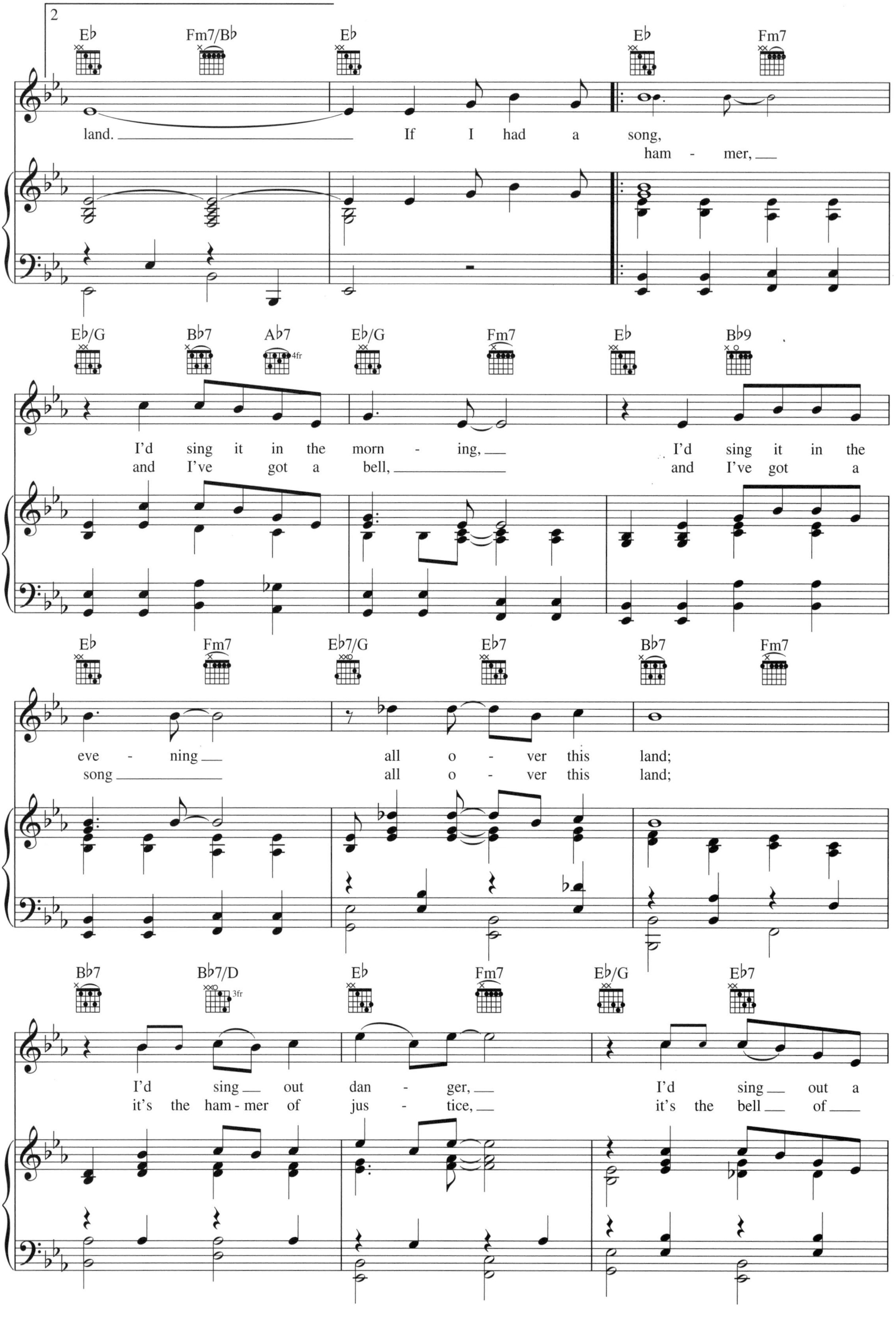
2
Eb
Fm7/Bb
Fm7
land.
If I had a song,
ham - mer,
Eb/G
Bb7
Ab7
Bb9
I'd sing it in the morn - ing,
and I've got a bell,
I'd sing it in the
and I've got a
Eb7/G
Eb7
eve - ning all o - ver this land;
song all o - ver this land;
Bb7/D
I'd sing out dan - ger,
it's the ham - mer of jus - tice,
I'd sing out a
it's the bell of

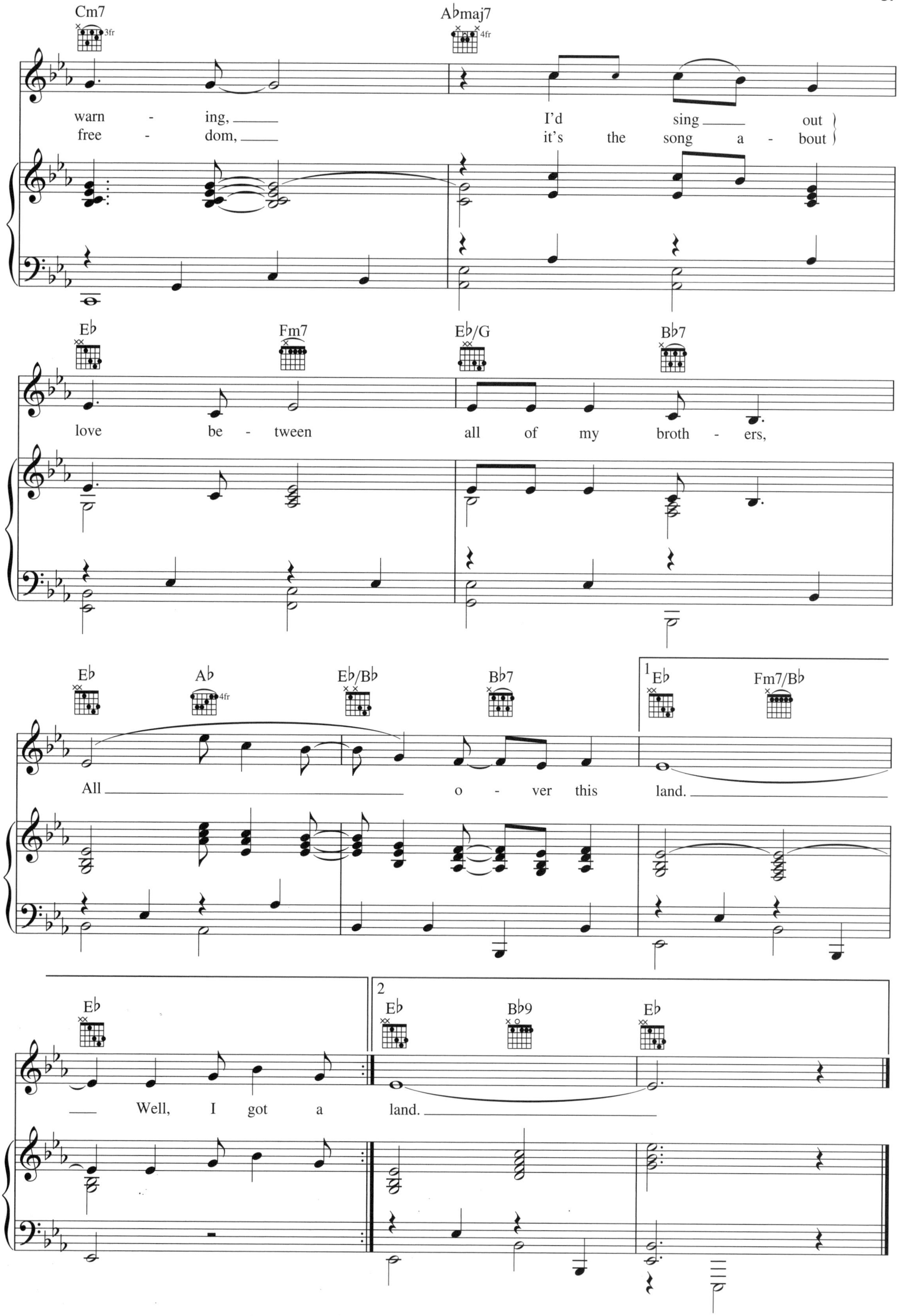
Cm7
A♭maj7
warn - ing,
I'd sing out
free - dom,
it's the song a - bout
E♭
Fm7
E♭/G
B♭7
love be - tween all of my broth - ers,
E♭
A♭
E♭/B♭
B♭7
1 E♭
Fm7/B♭
All o - ver this land.
E♭
2 E♭
B♭9
E♭
Well, I got a land.

IMAGINE

Words and Music by
JOHN LENNON

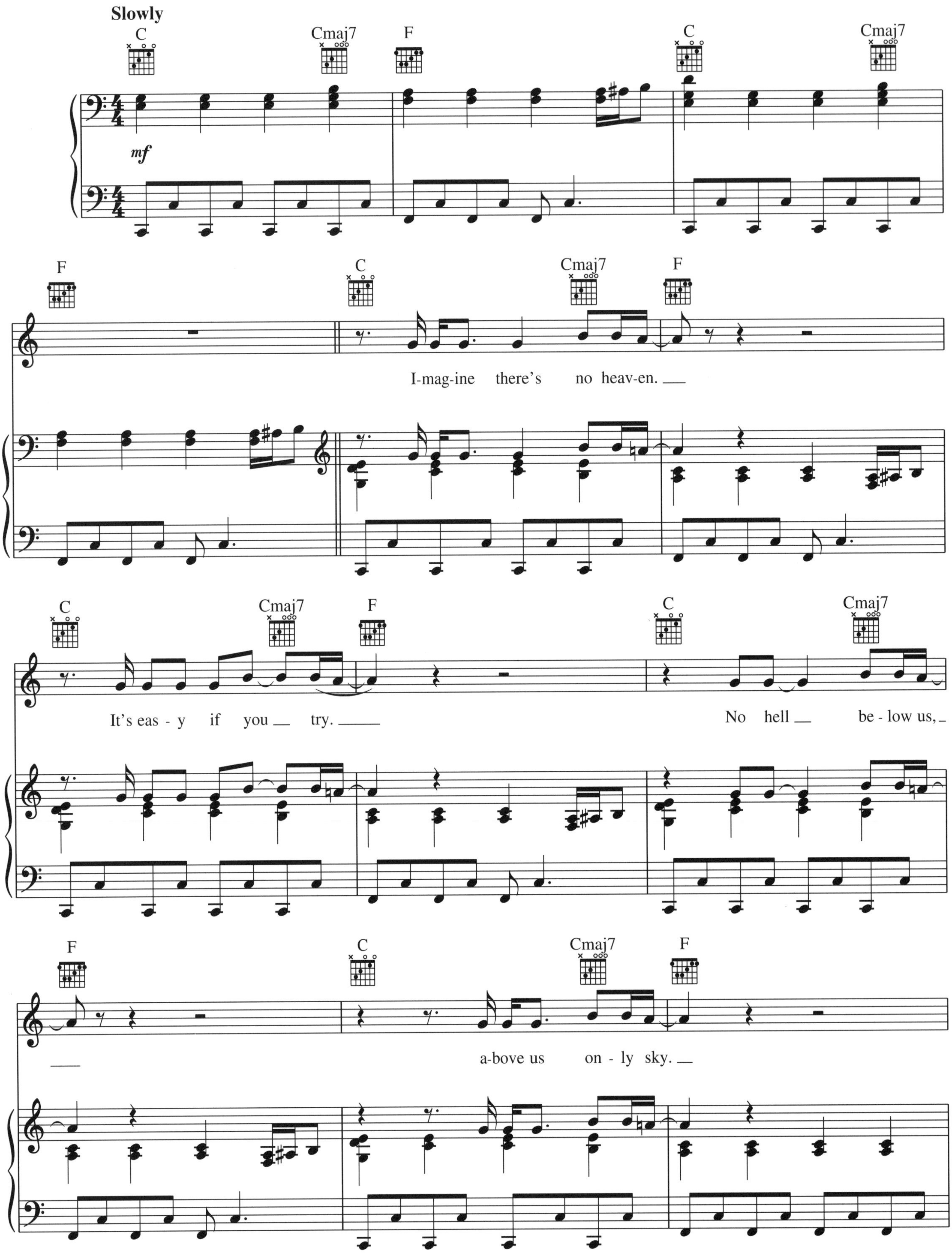

© 1971 (Renewed 1999) LENONO.MUSIC
All Rights Controlled and Administered by EMI BLACKWOOD MUSIC INC.
All Rights Reserved International Copyright Secured Used by Permission

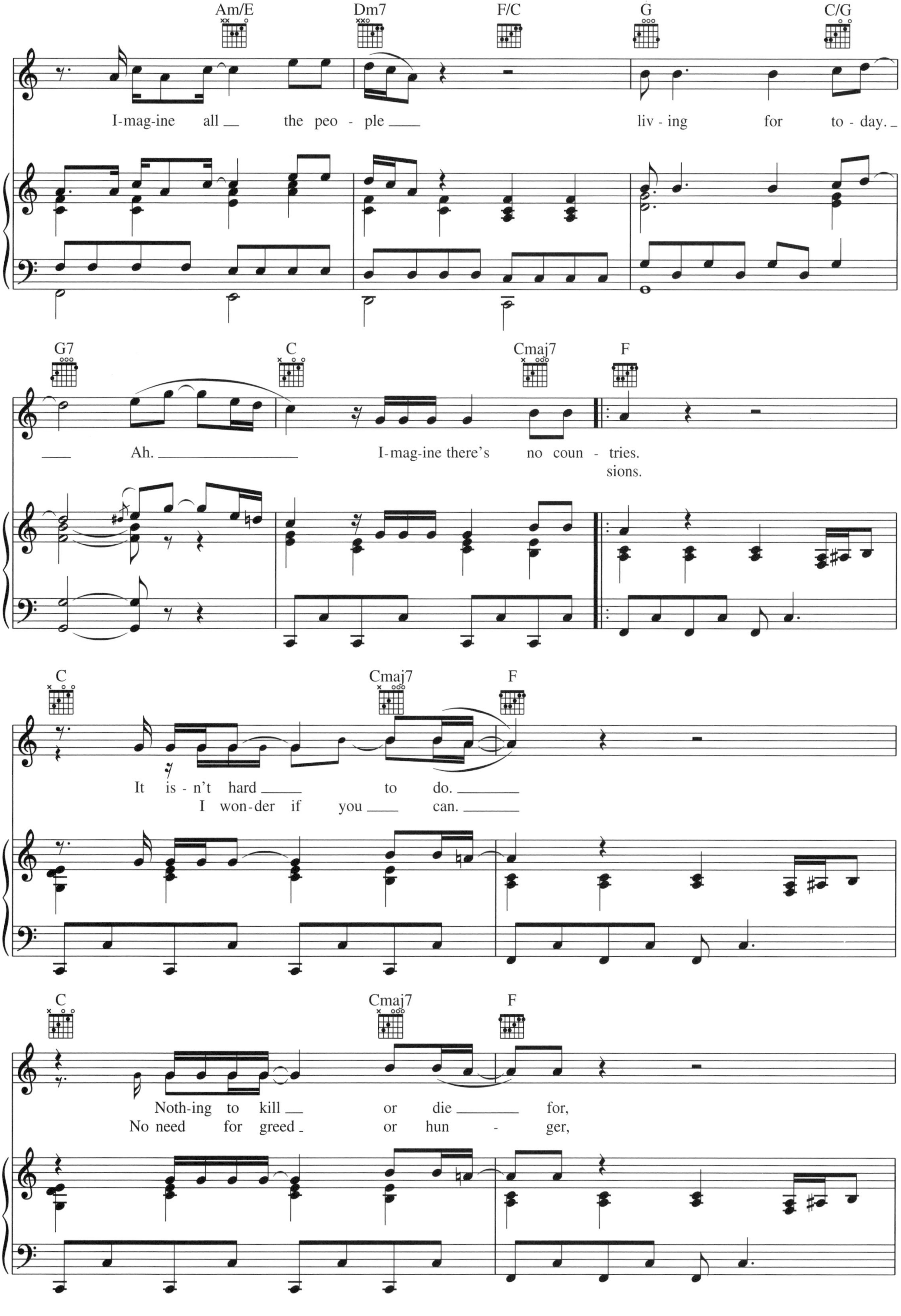
Am/E Dm7 F/C G C/G
I-mag-ine all the peo-ple liv-ing for to-day.
G7 C Cmaj7 F
Ah. I-mag-ine there's no coun-tries.
sions.
C Cmaj7 F
It is-n't hard to do.
I won-der if you can.
C Cmaj7 F
Noth-ing to kill or die for,
No need for greed or hun-ger,

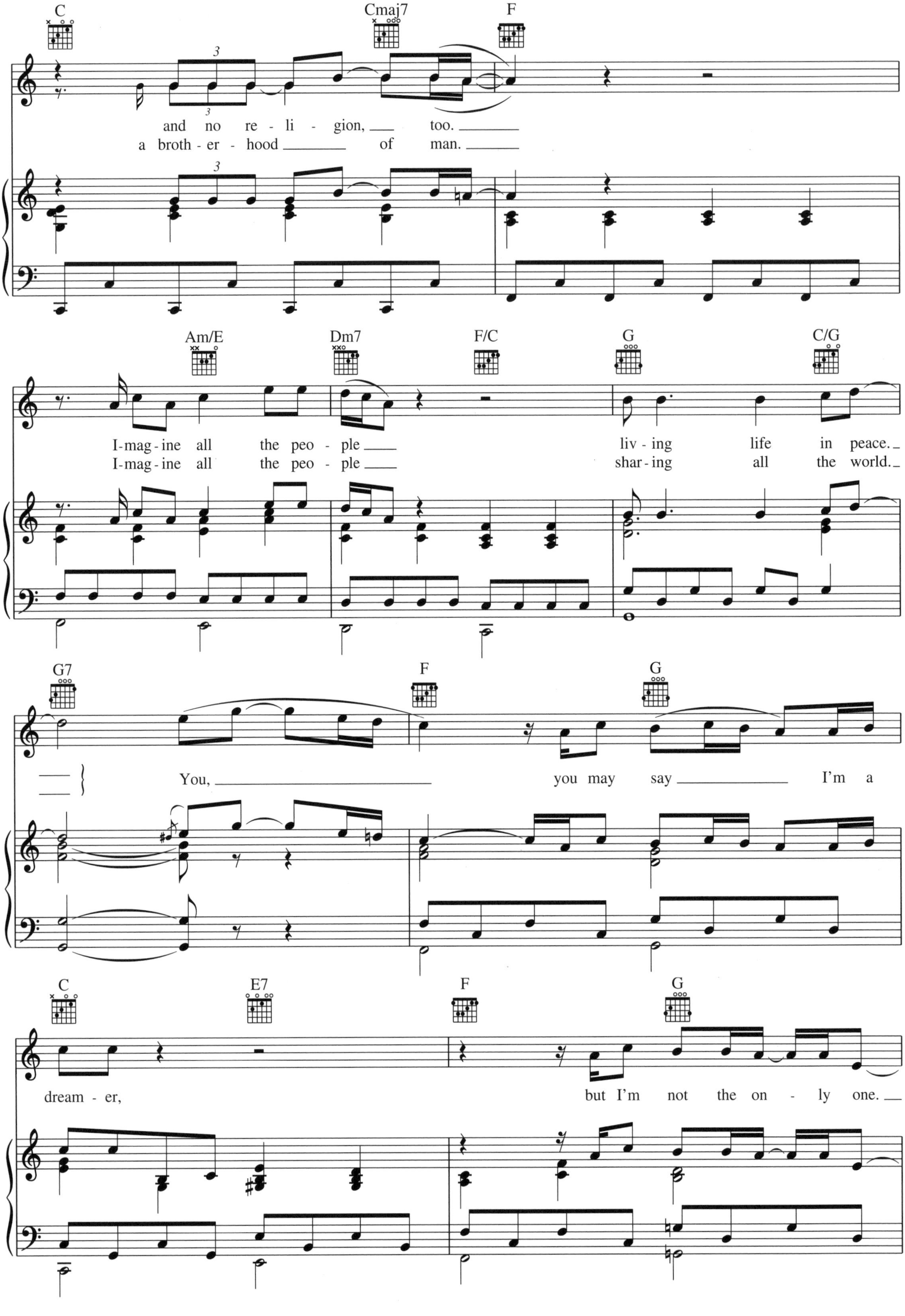
C
Cmaj7
F
and no re - li - gion, too.
a broth - er - hood of man.
Am/E
Dm7
F/C
G
C/G
I-mag - ine all the peo - ple
I-mag - ine all the peo - ple
liv - ing life in peace.
shar - ing all the world.
G7
F
G
You, you may say I'm a
C
E7
F
G
dream - er, but I'm not the on - ly one.

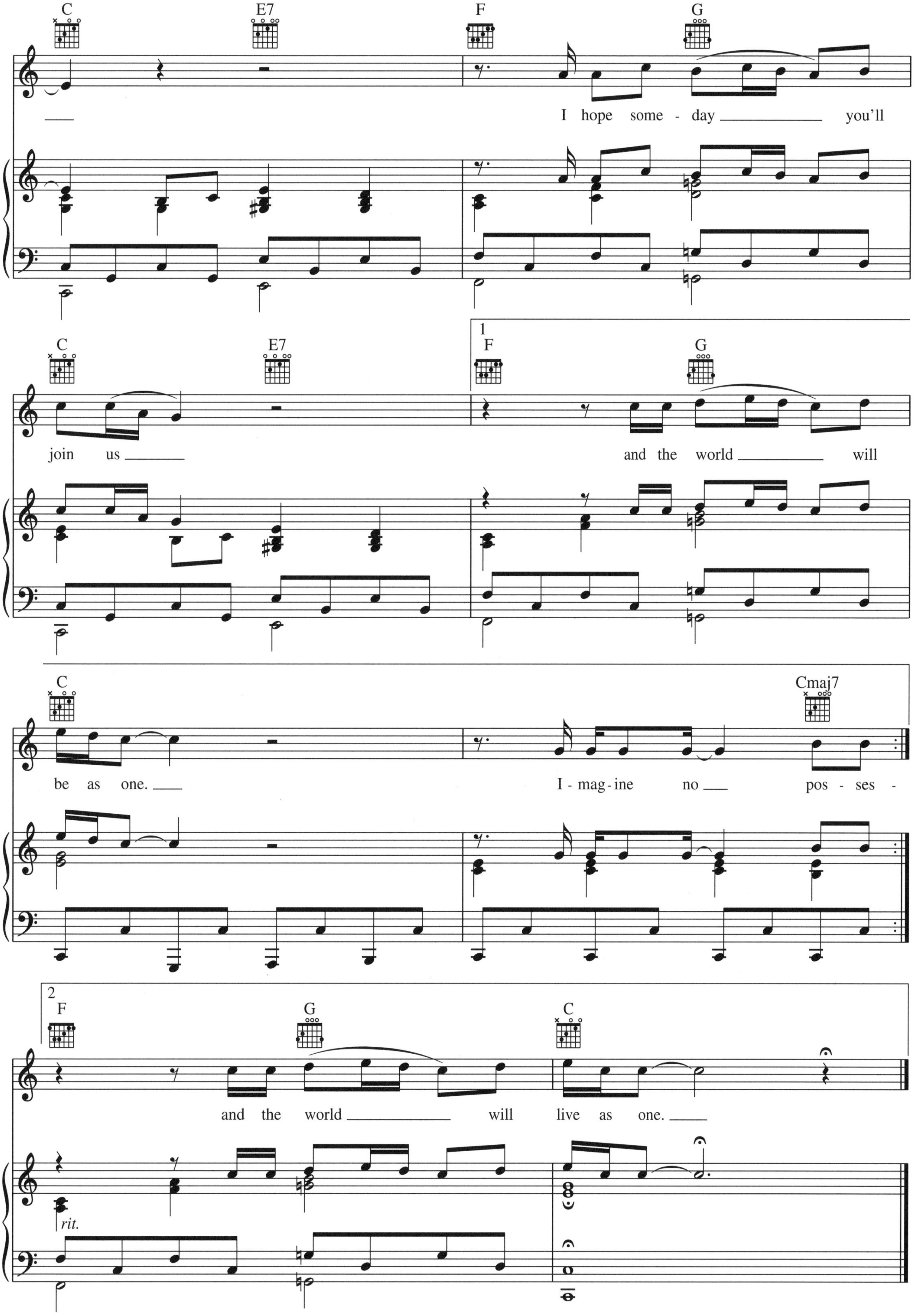
C E7 F G
I hope some - day you'll
C E7
1
F G
join us and the world will
C Cmaj7
be as one. I - mag - ine no pos - ses -
2
F G C
and the world will live as one.
rit.

IN THE GHETTO
(The Vicious Circle)

Words and Music by
MAC DAVIS

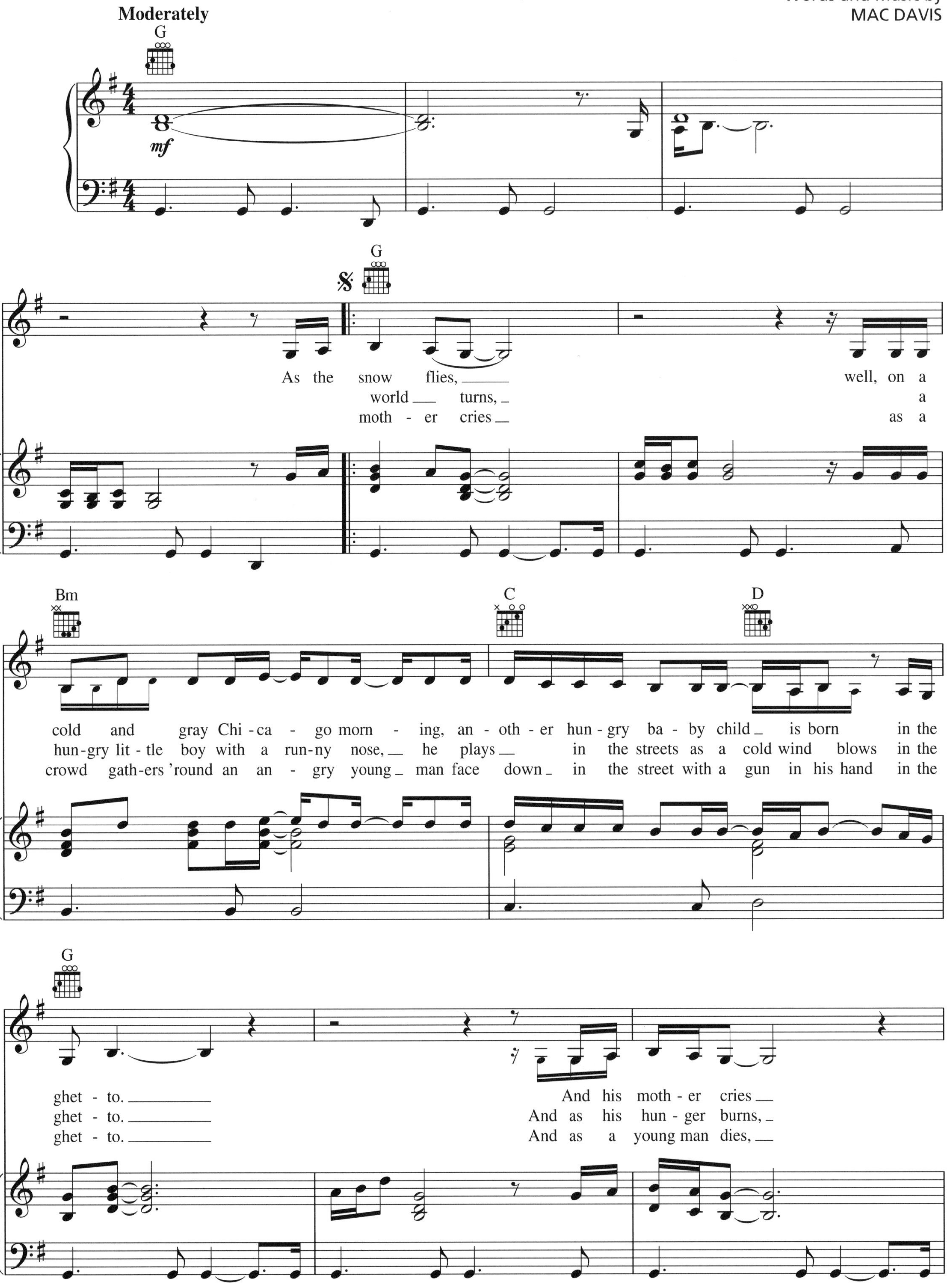

Copyright © 1978 Sony/ATV Songs LLC and Elvis Presley Music, Inc.
All Rights on behalf of Sony/ATV Songs LLC Administered by Sony/ATV Music Publishing, 8 Music Square West, Nashville, TN 37203
International Copyright Secured All Rights Reserved

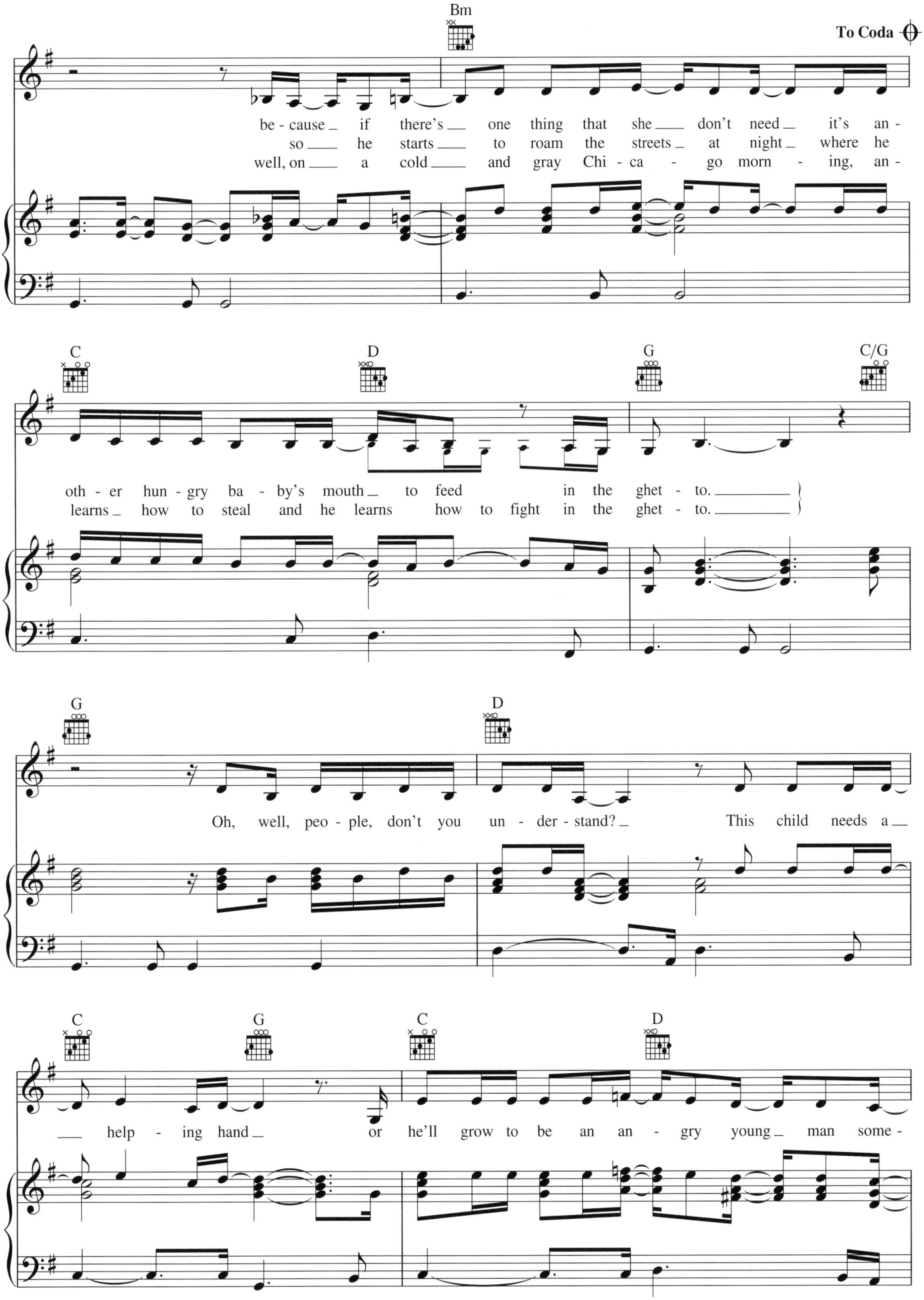
Bm
To Coda
be - cause if there's one thing that she don't need it's an -
so he starts to roam the streets at night where he
well, on a cold and gray Chi - ca - go morn - ing, an -
C D G C/G
oth - er hun - gry ba - by's mouth to feed in the ghet - to.
learns how to steal and he learns how to fight in the ghet - to.
G D
Oh, well, peo - ple, don't you un - der - stand? This child needs a
C G C D
help - ing hand or he'll grow to be an an - gry young man some -

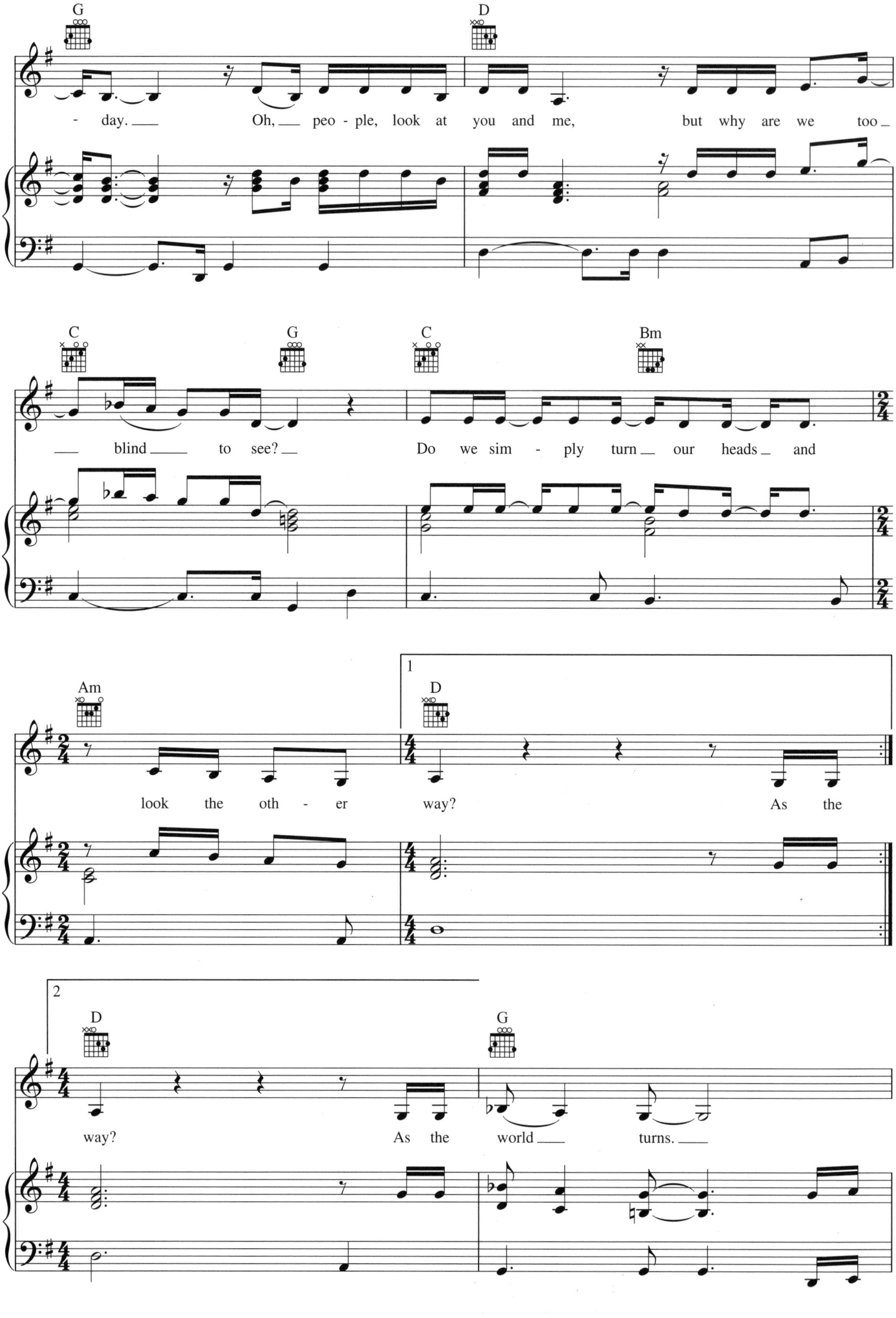
G
D
- day. Oh, peo - ple, look at you and me, but why are we too
C
G
C
Bm
blind to see? Do we sim - ply turn our heads and
Am
1
D
look the oth - er way? As the
2
D
G
way? As the world turns.

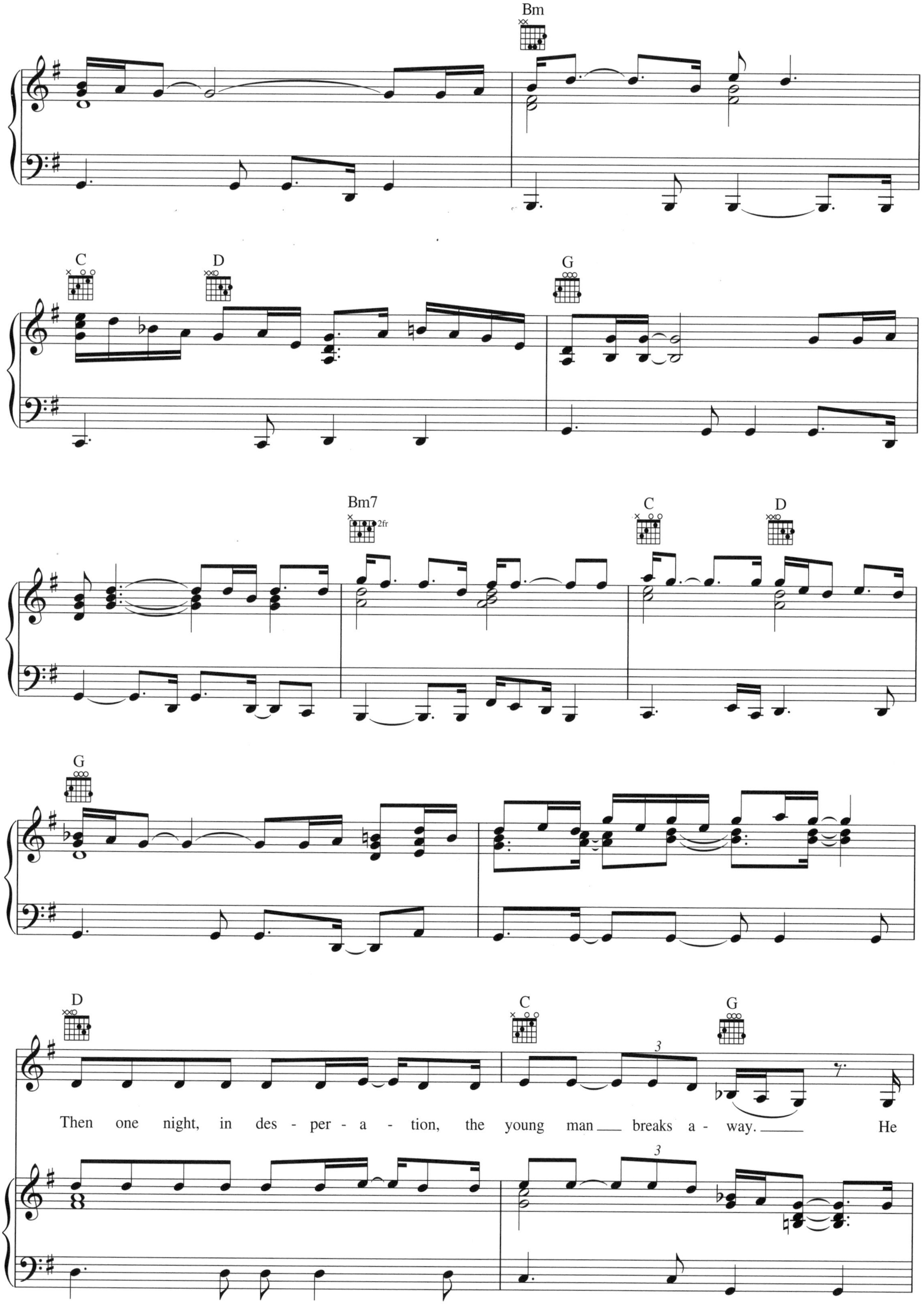
Bm
C
D
G
Bm7
2fr
C
D
G
D
C
G
Then one night, in des - per - a - tion, the young man breaks a - way. He

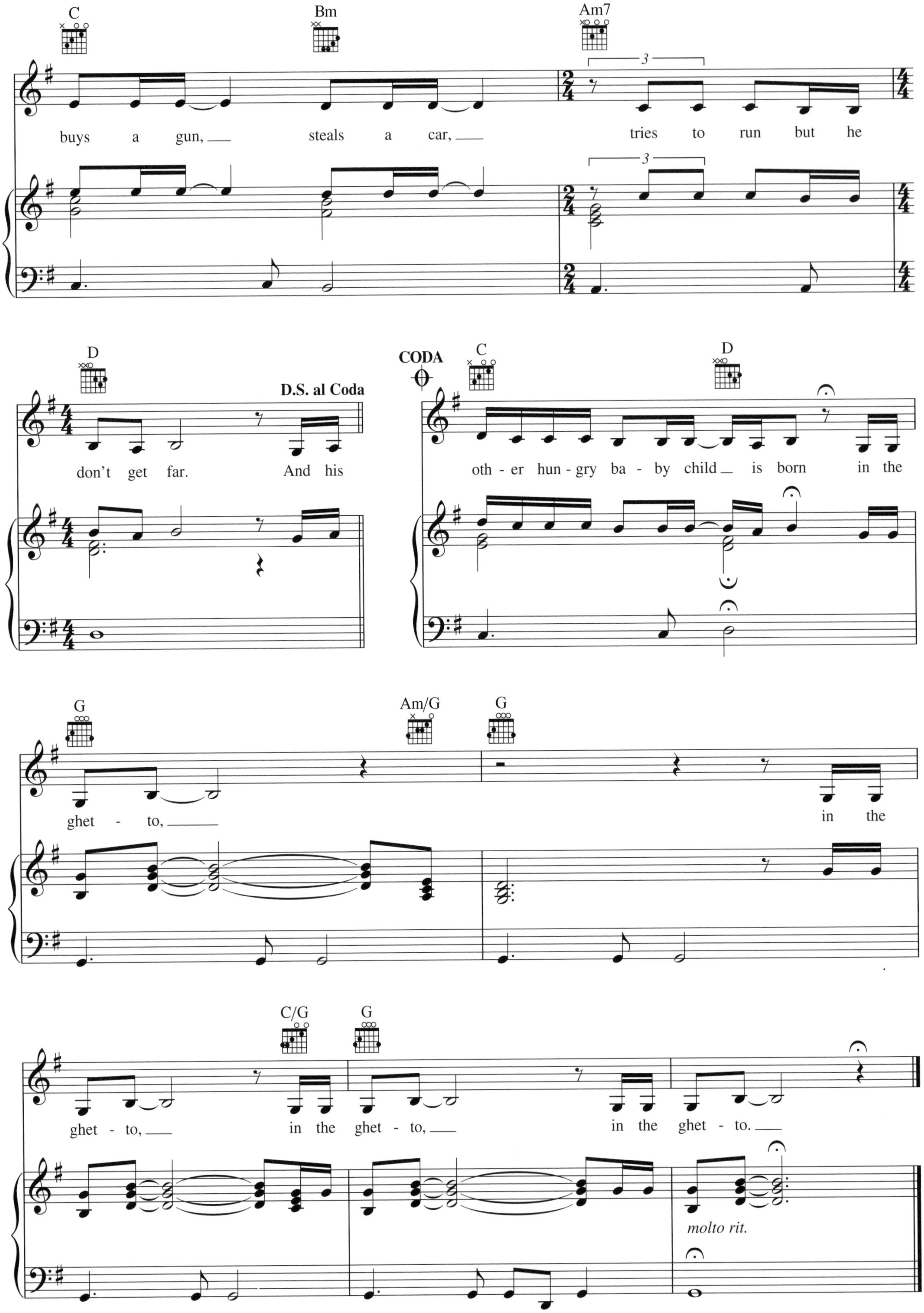
C
Bm
Am7
buys a gun, steals a car, tries to run but he
D
D.S. al Coda
don't get far. And his
CODA
C
D
oth - er hun - gry ba - by child is born in the
G
Am/G
G
ghet - to, in the
C/G
G
ghet - to, in the ghet - to, in the ghet - to.
molto rit.

LET IT BE

Words and Music by JOHN LENNON
and PAUL McCARTNEY

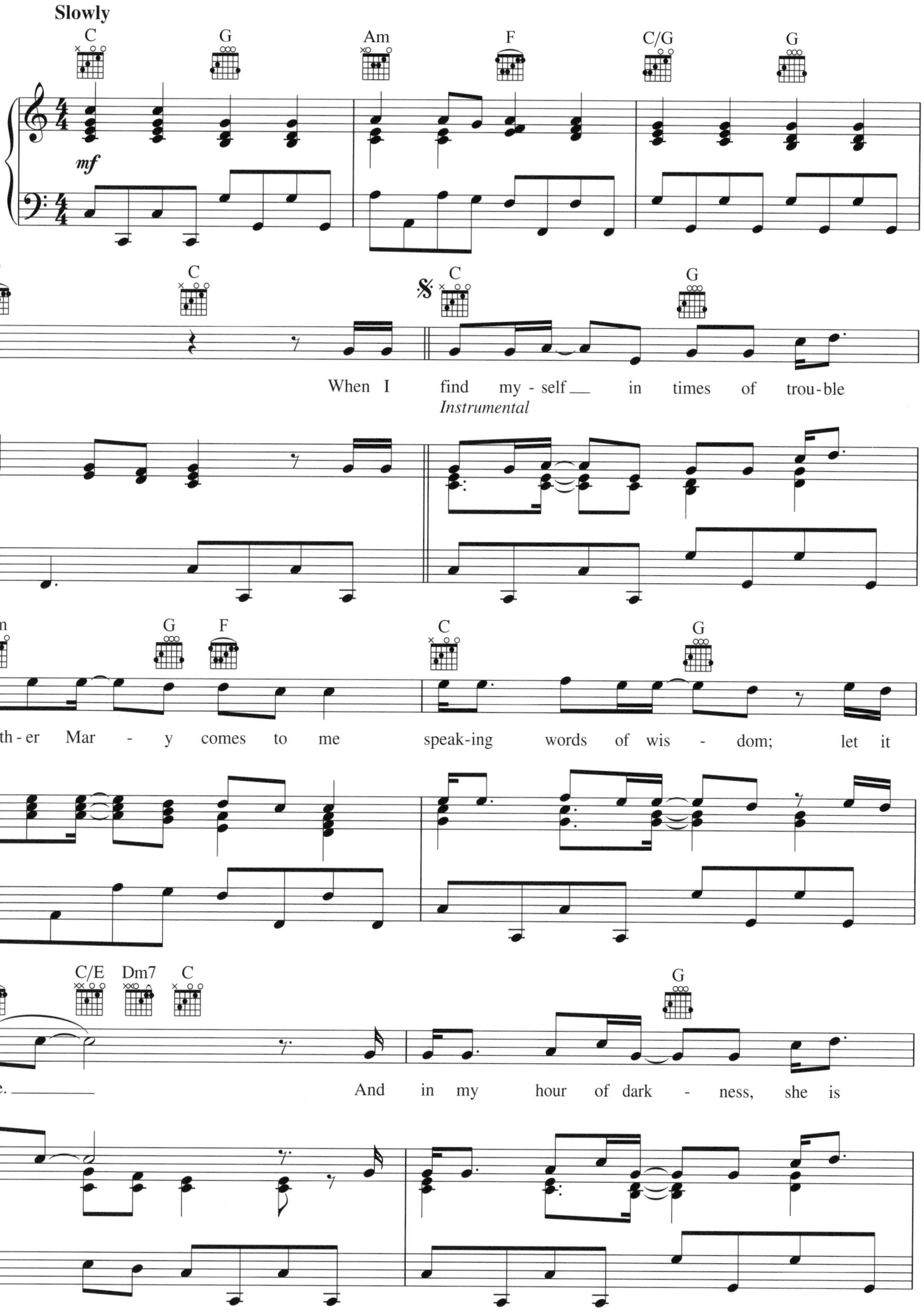

Copyright © 1970 Sony/ATV Songs LLC
Copyright Renewed
All Rights Administered by Sony/ATV Music Publishing, 8 Music Square West, Nashville, TN 37203
International Copyright Secured All Rights Reserved

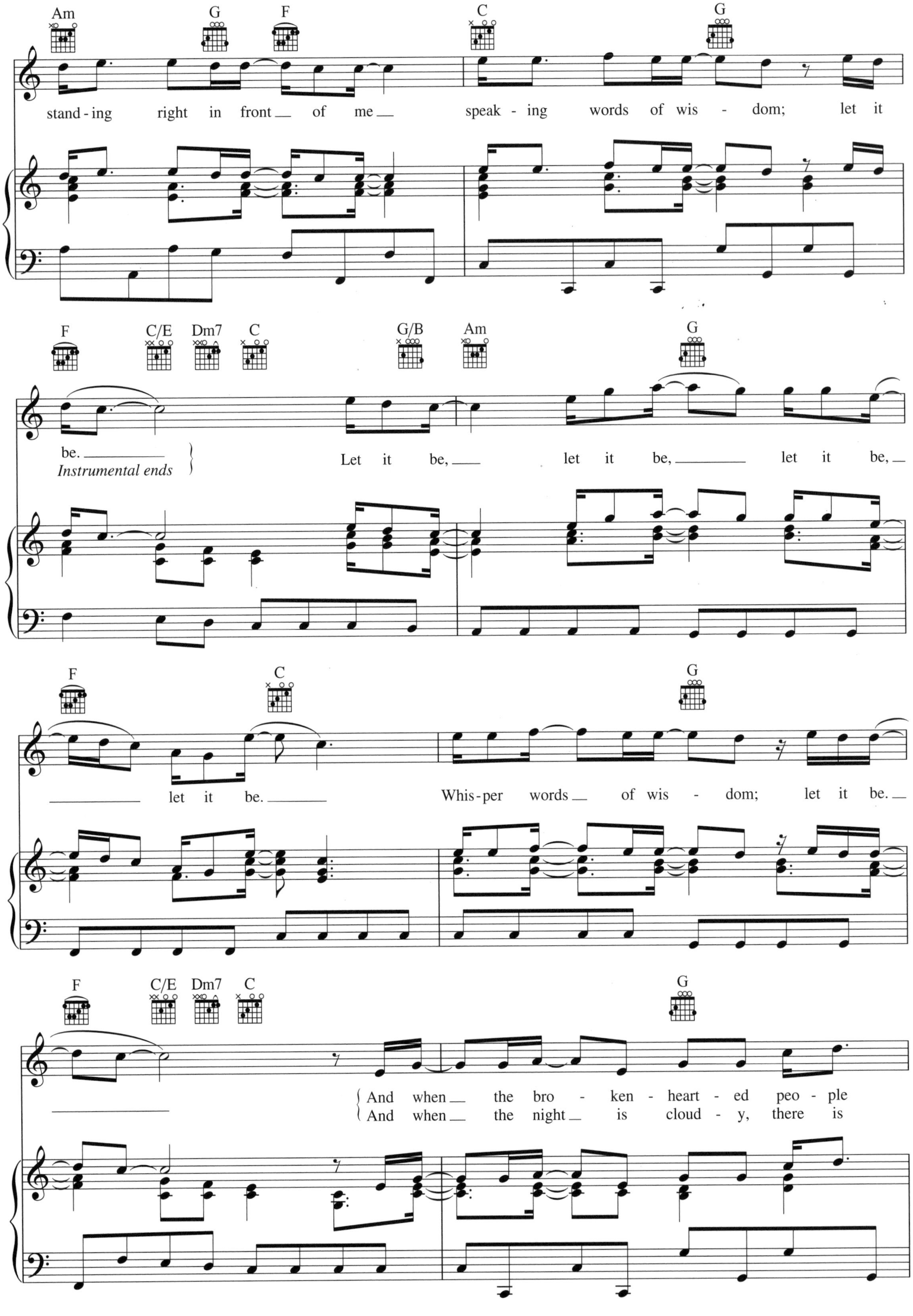
Am G F C G
standing right in front of me speaking words of wisdom; let it
F C/E Dm7 C G/B Am G
be.
Instrumental ends
Let it be, let it be, let it be,
F C G
let it be. Whisper words of wisdom; let it be.
F C/E Dm7 C G
And when the broken-hearted people
And when the night is cloudy, there is

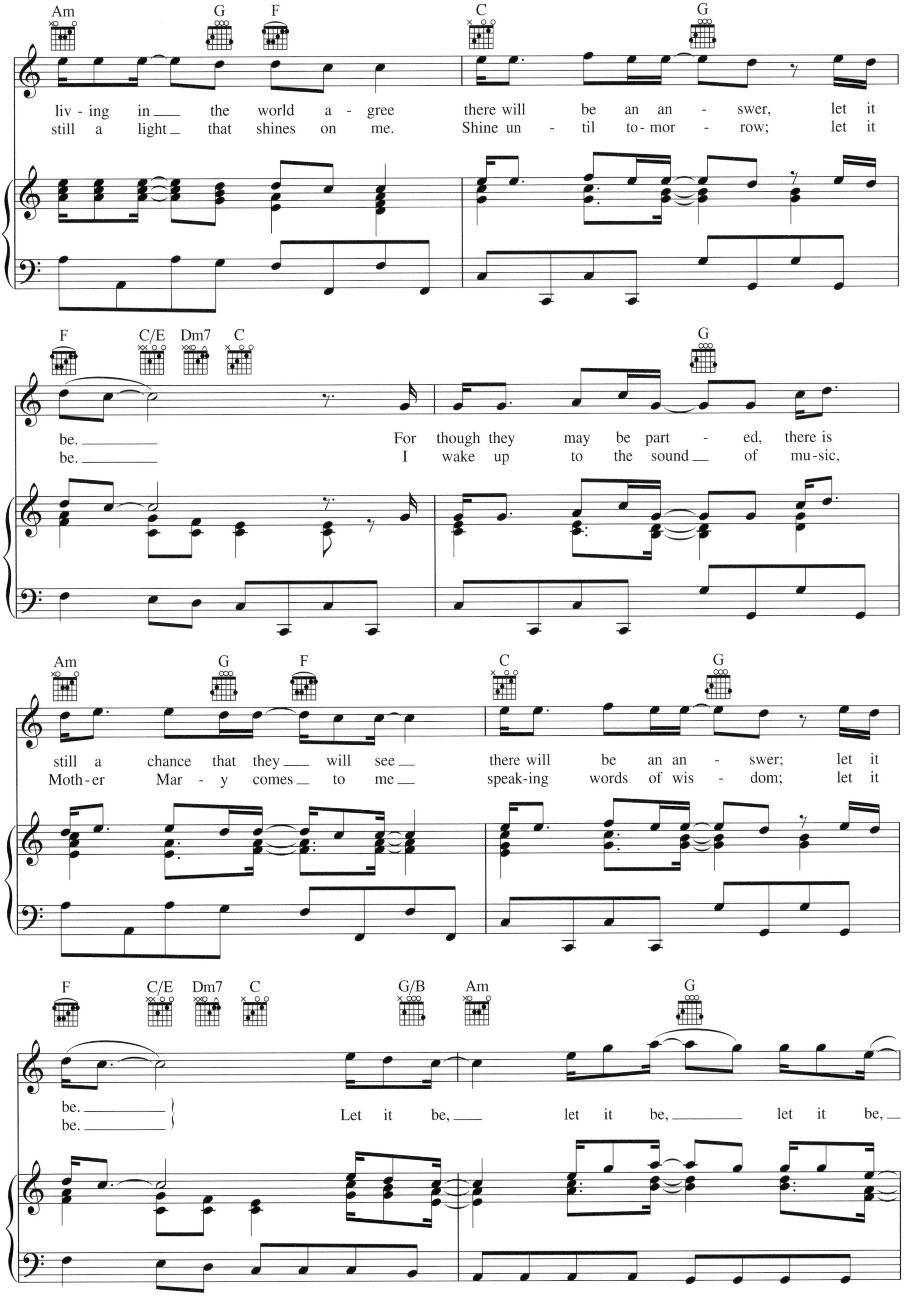
Am G F C G
liv - ing in the world a - gree there will be an an - swer, let it
still a light that shines on me. Shine un - til to - mor - row; let it
F C/E Dm7 C G
be. For though they may be part - ed, there is
be. I wake up to the sound of mu - sic,
Am G F C G
still a chance that they will see there will be an an - swer; let it
Moth - er Mar - y comes to me speak - ing words of wis - dom; let it
F C/E Dm7 C G/B Am G
be.
be.
Let it be, let it be, let it be,

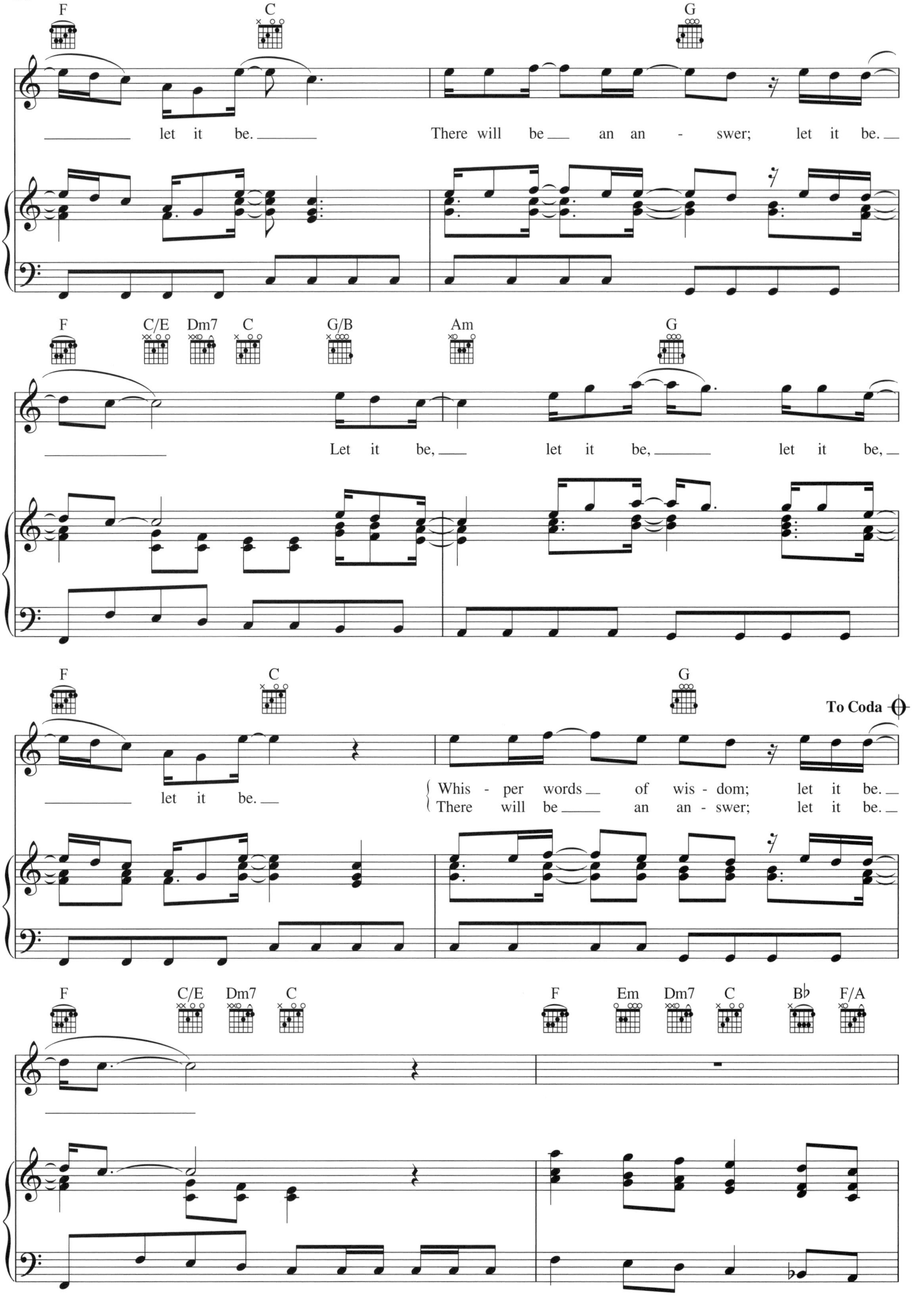
F C G
let it be. There will be an an - swer; let it be.
F C/E Dm7 C G/B Am G
Let it be, let it be, let it be,
F C G
To Coda
let it be.
Whis - per words of wis - dom; let it be.
There will be an an - swer; let it be.
F C/E Dm7 C F Em Dm7 C B♭ F/A

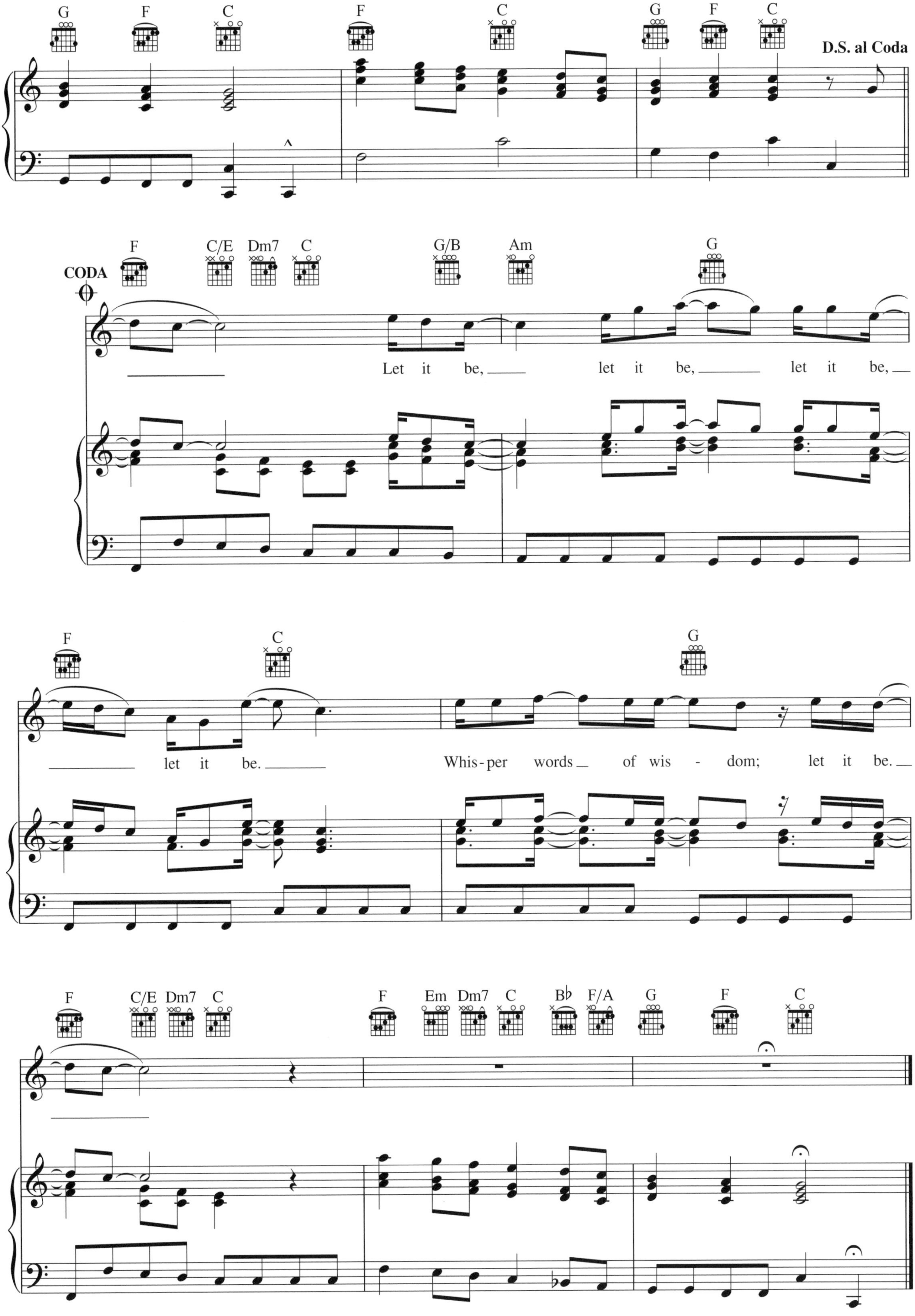
G F C F C G F C
D.S. al Coda
CODA
F C/E Dm7 C G/B Am G
Let it be, let it be, let it be,
F C G
let it be. Whis-per words of wis - dom; let it be.
F C/E Dm7 C F Em Dm7 C B♭ F/A G F C

JOY TO THE WORLD

Words and Music by
HOYT AXTON

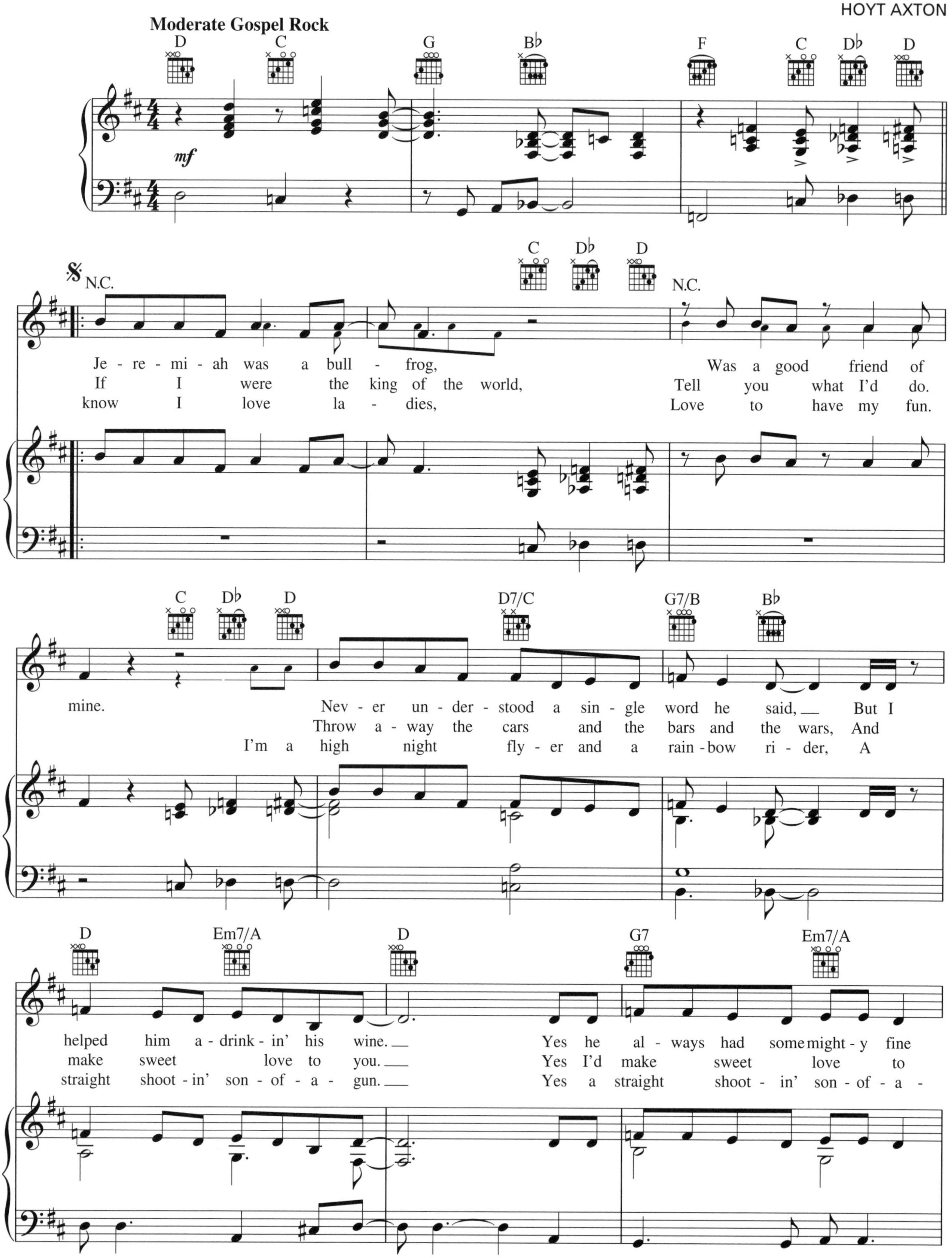

Copyright © 1970 IRVING MUSIC, INC.
Copyright Renewed
All Rights Reserved Used by Permission

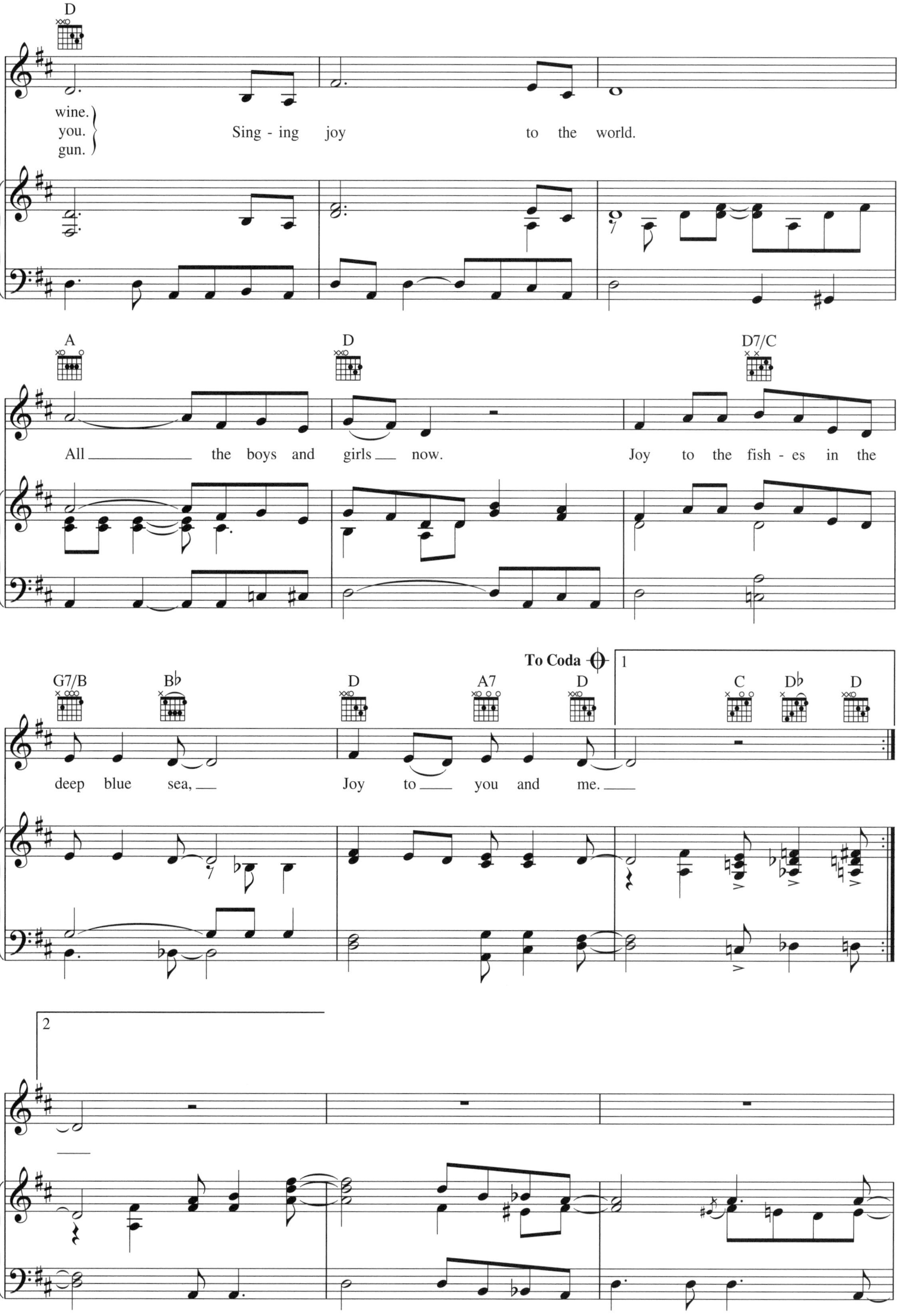
D
wine.
you.
gun.
Sing - ing joy to the world.
A
D
D7/C
All the boys and girls now. Joy to the fish - es in the
To Coda
1
G7/B
B♭
D
A7
D
C
D♭
D
deep blue sea, Joy to you and me.
2

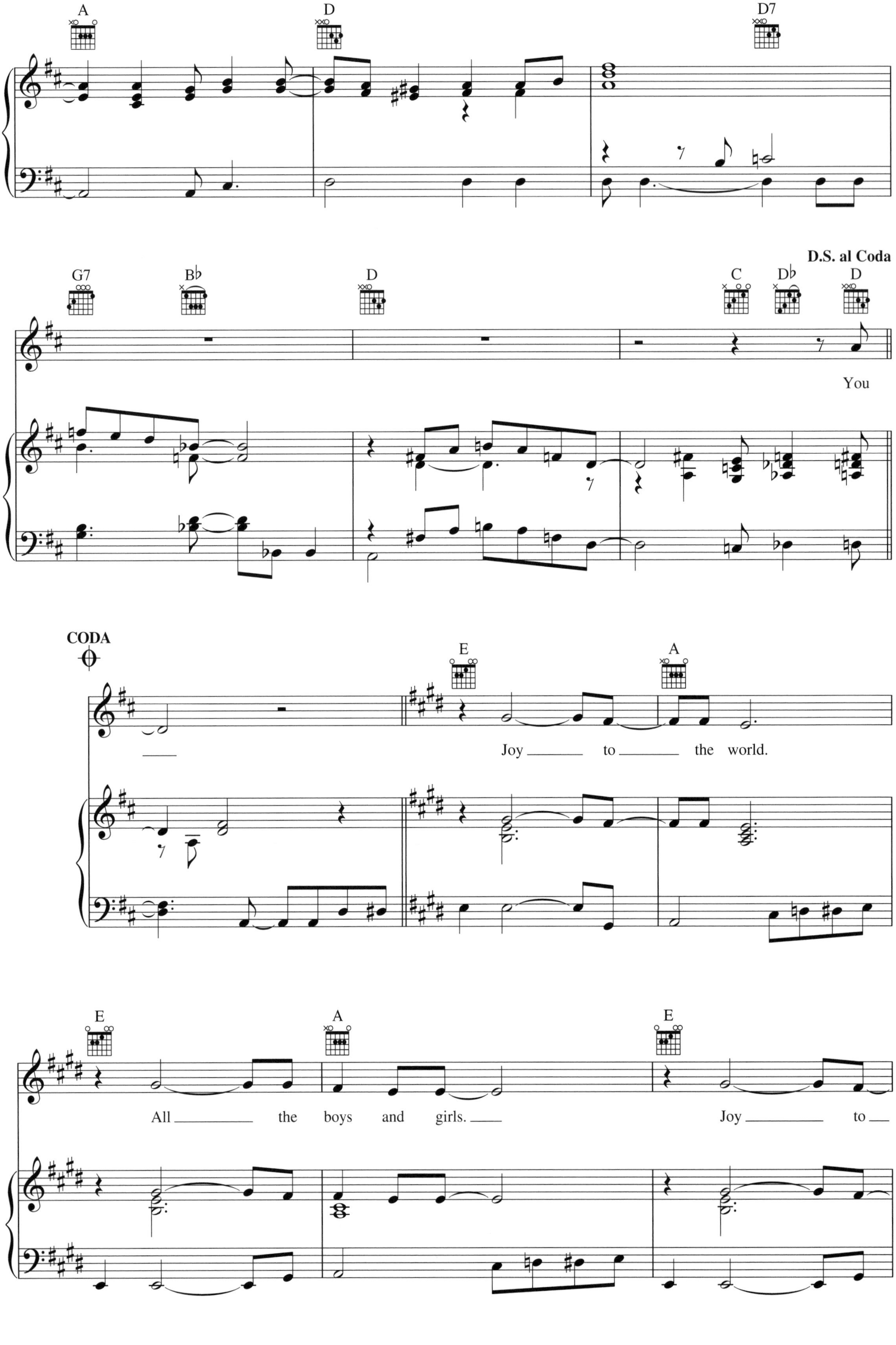
A
D
D7
G7
B♭
D
D.S. al Coda
C
D♭
D
You
CODA
E
A
Joy to the world.
E
A
E
All the boys and girls.
Joy to

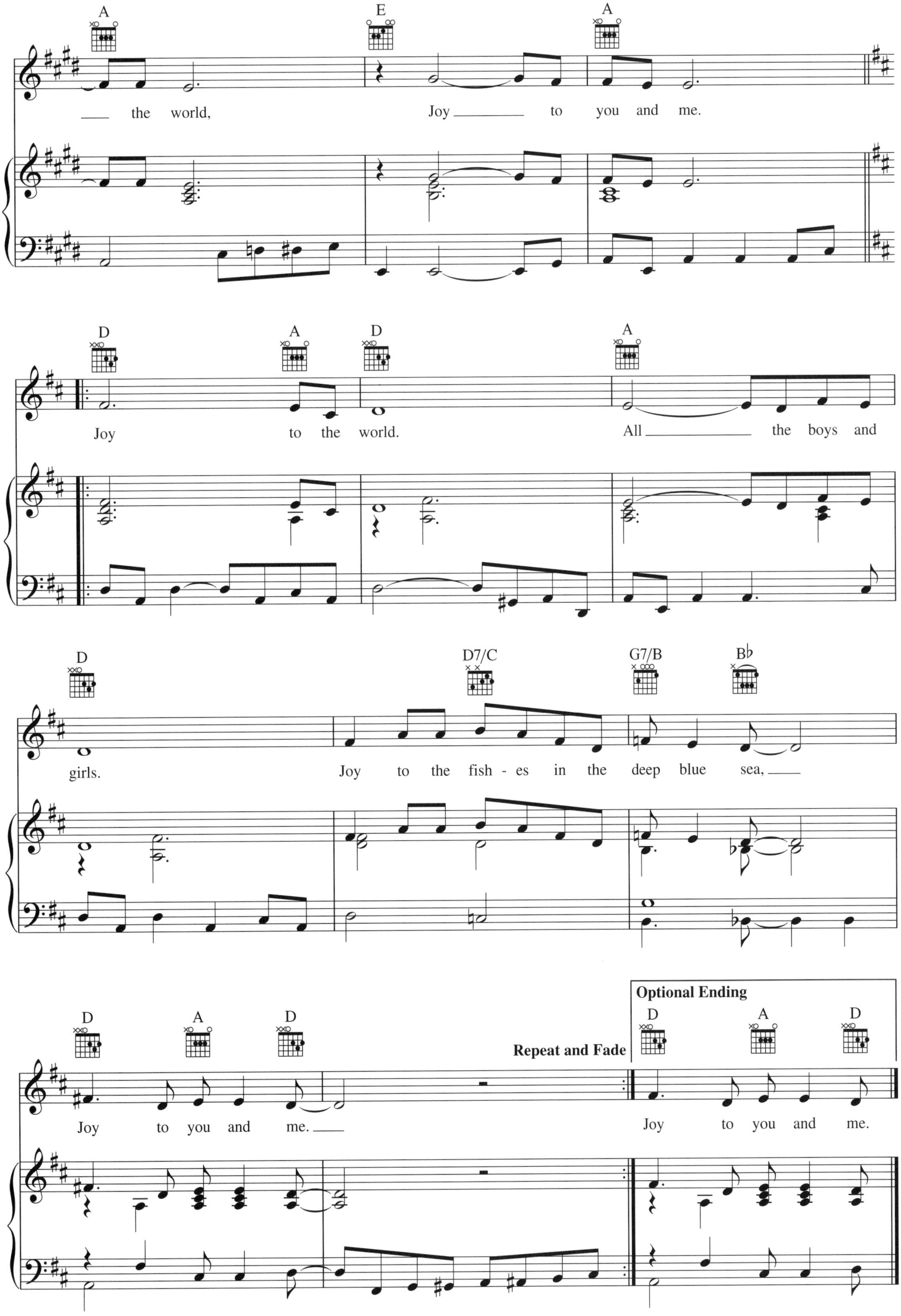
A
E
A
the world,
Joy to you and me.
D
A
D
A
Joy to the world.
All the boys and
D
D7/C
G7/B
B♭
girls.
Joy to the fish - es in the deep blue sea,
D
A
D
Repeat and Fade
Joy to you and me.
Optional Ending
D
A
D
Joy to you and me.

LET ME BE

Words and Music by
P.F. SLOAN

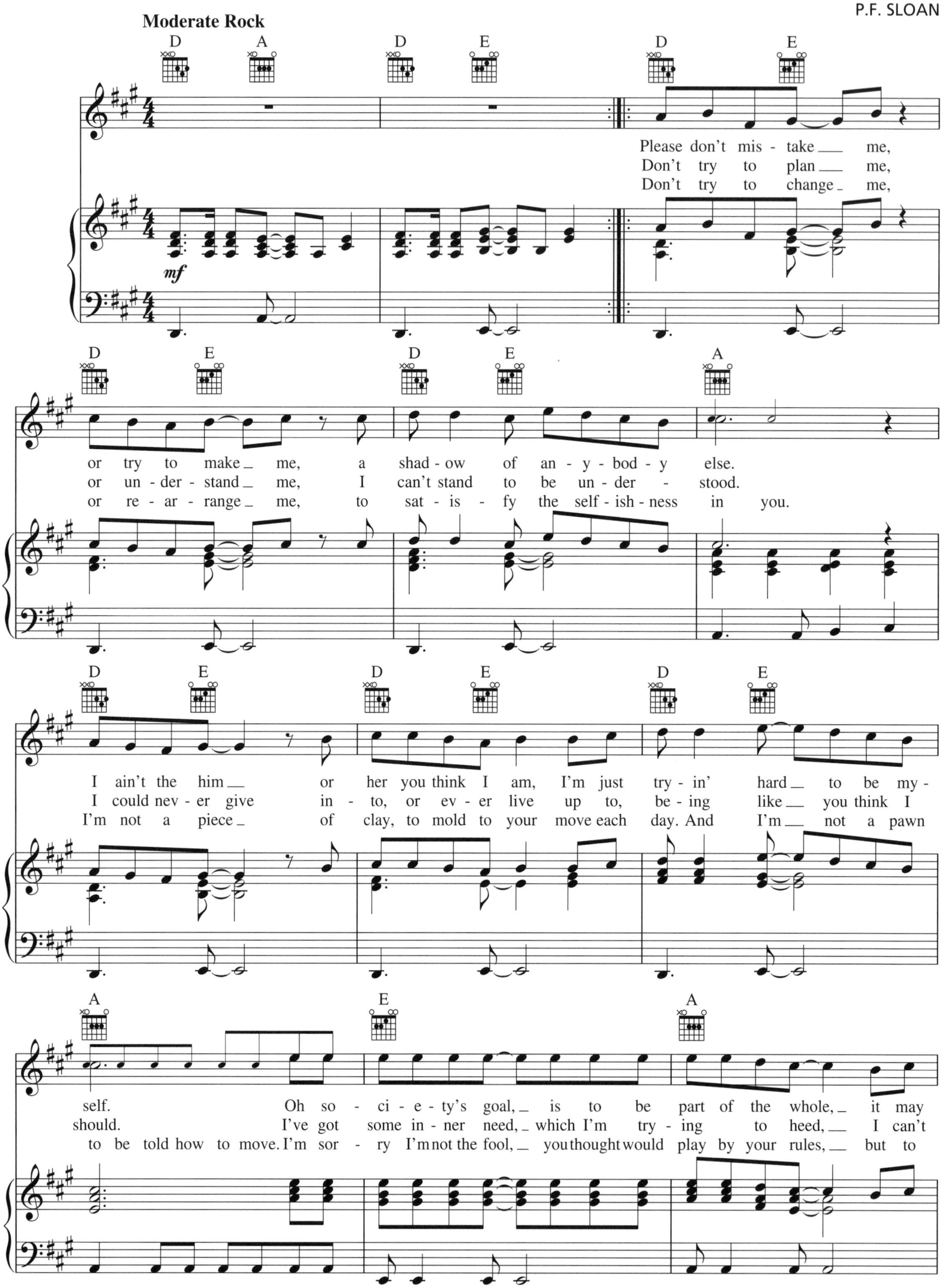

Copyright © 1965 UNIVERSAL MUSIC CORP.
Copyright Renewed
All Rights Reserved Used by Permission

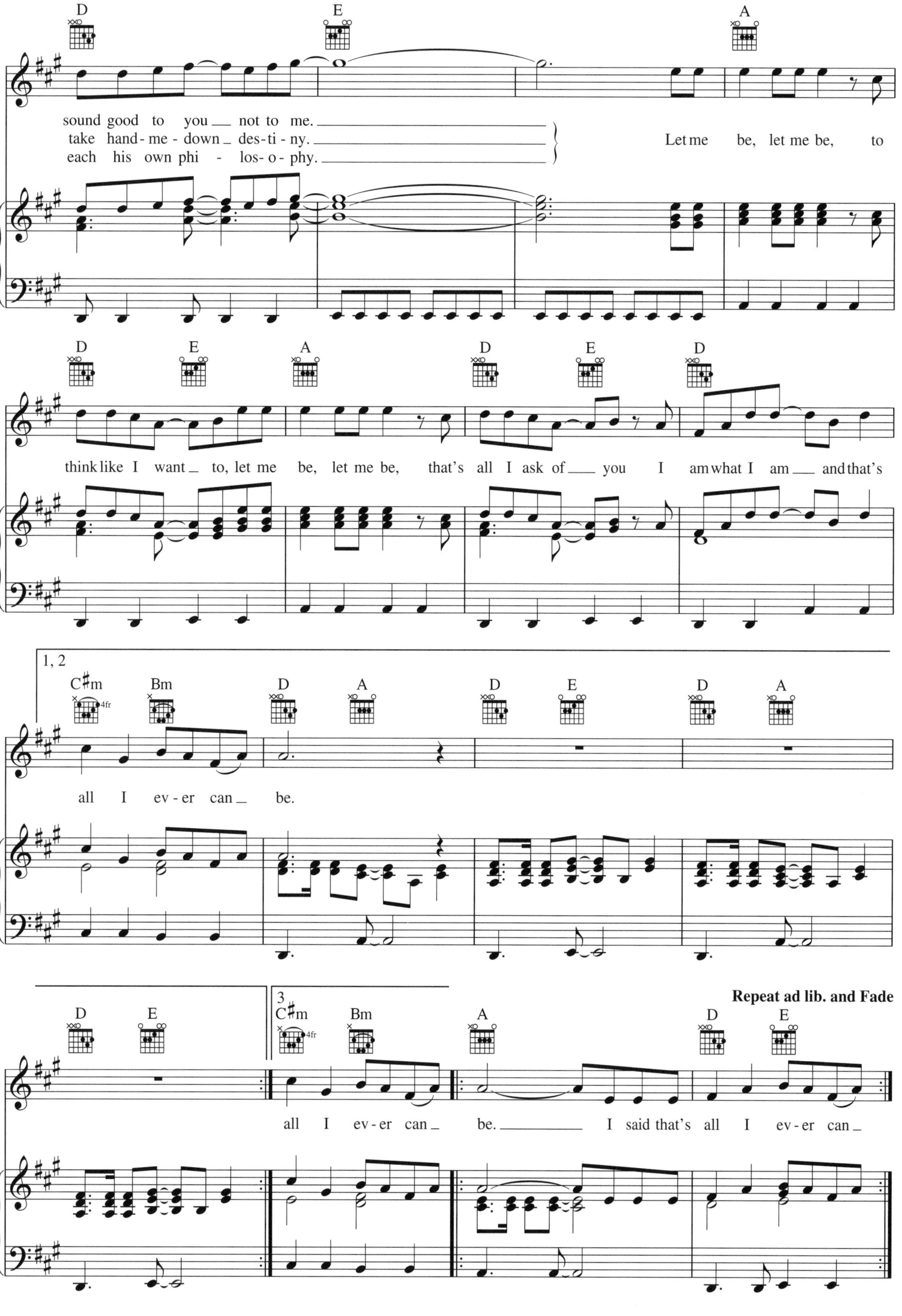
D E A
sound good to you not to me.
take hand-me-down destiny.
each his own philosophy.
Let me be, let me be, to
D E A D E D
think like I want to, let me be, let me be, that's all I ask of you I am what I am and that's
1, 2
C♯m Bm D A D E D A
all I ev-er can be.
D E
3
C♯m Bm A D E
Repeat ad lib. and Fade
all I ev-er can be. I said that's all I ev-er can

LONDON CALLING

Words and Music by JOE STRUMMER,
MICK JONES, PAUL SIMONON
and TOPPER HEADON

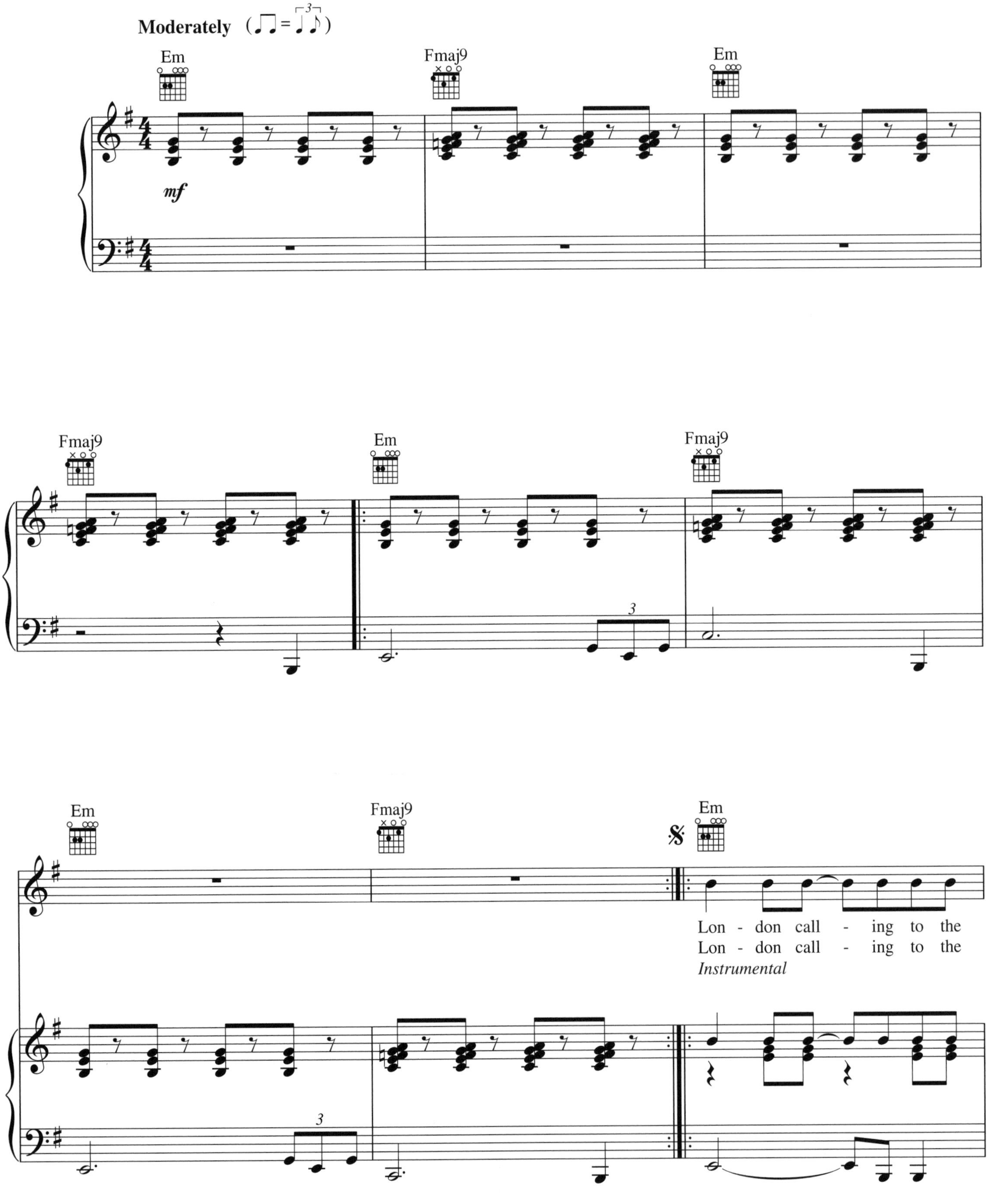

Copyright © 1979 UNIVERSAL MUSIC PUBLISHING LTD.
All Rights for the U.S. and Canada Controlled and Administered by UNIVERSAL - POLYGRAM INTERNATIONAL PUBLISHING, INC.
All Rights Reserved Used by Permission

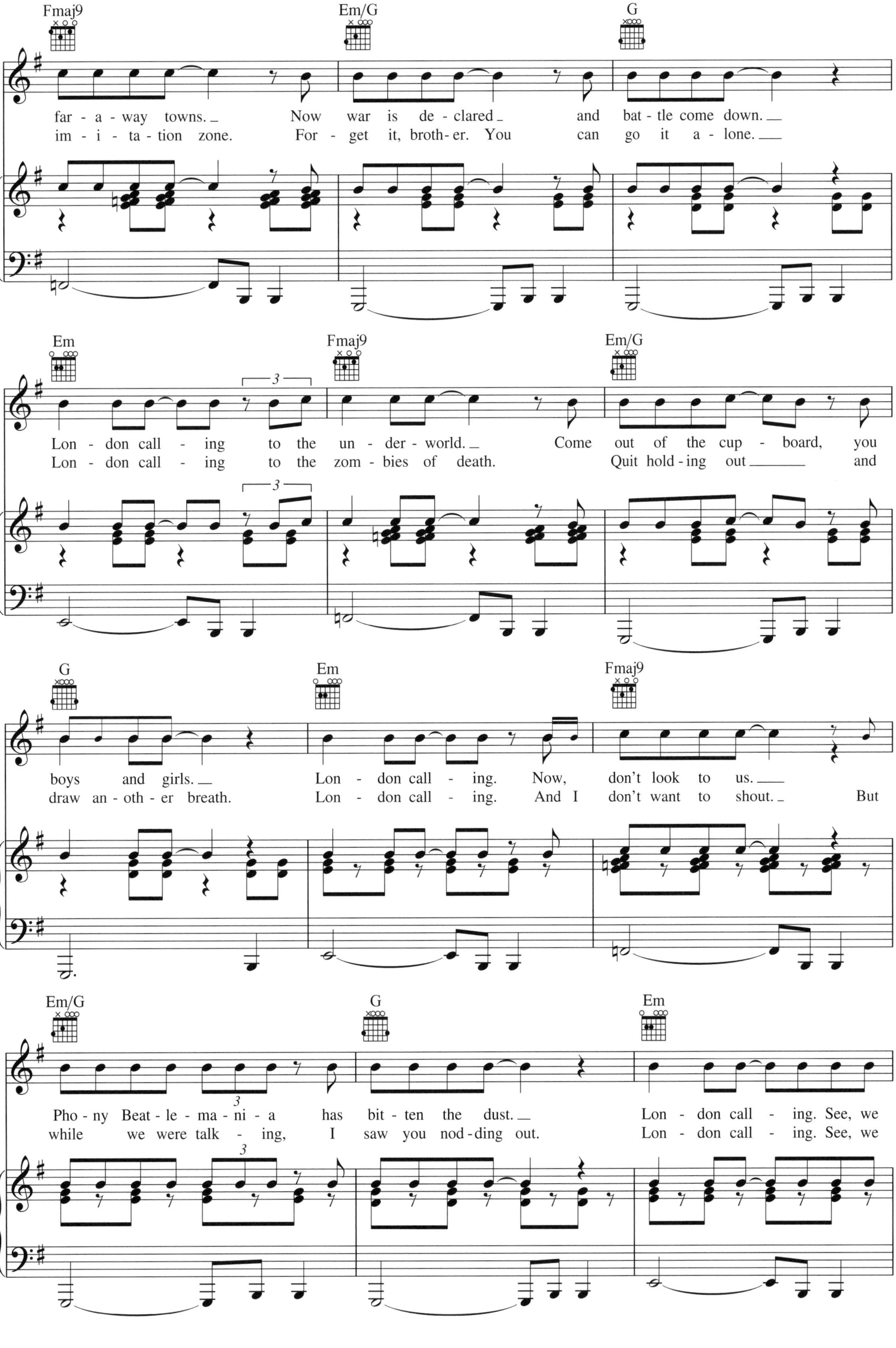
Fmaj9
Em/G
G
far - a - way towns. _ Now war is de - clared _ and bat - tle come down. _
im - i - ta - tion zone. For - get it, broth - er. You can go it a - lone. _
Em
Fmaj9
Em/G
Lon - don call - ing to the un - der - world. _ Come out of the cup - board, you
Lon - don call - ing to the zom - bies of death. Quit hold - ing out _ and
G
Em
Fmaj9
boys and girls. _ Lon - don call - ing. Now, don't look to us. _
draw an - oth - er breath. Lon - don call - ing. And I don't want to shout. _ But
Em/G
G
Em
Pho - ny Beat - le - ma - ni - a has bit - ten the dust. _ Lon - don call - ing. See, we
while we were talk - ing, I saw you nod - ding out. Lon - don call - ing. See, we

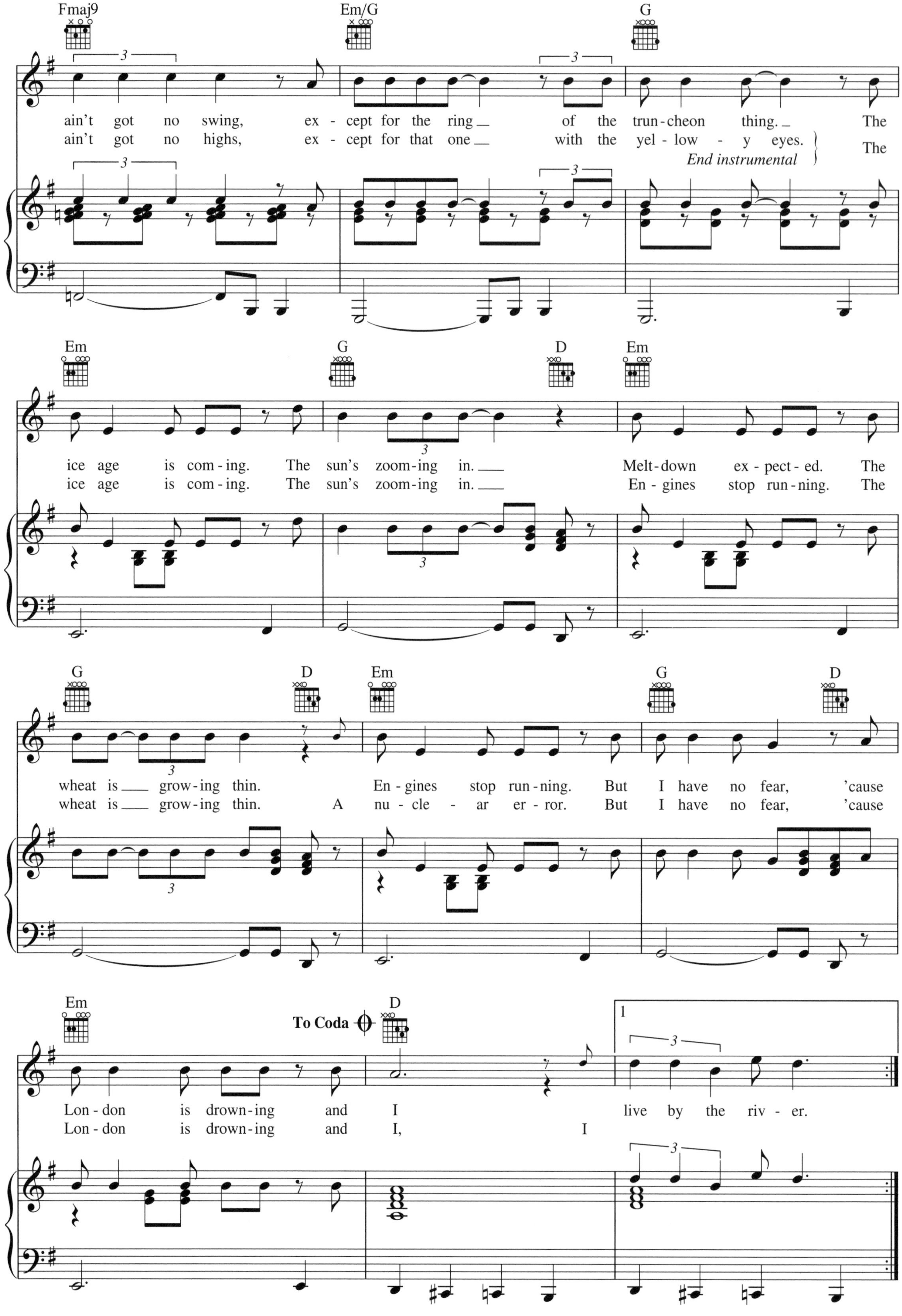
Fmaj9
Em/G
G
ain't got no swing, ex - cept for the ring of the trun-cheon thing. The
ain't got no highs, ex - cept for that one with the yel - low - y eyes. The
End instrumental
Em
G
D
Em
ice age is com - ing. The sun's zoom-ing in. Melt-down ex - pect - ed. The
ice age is com - ing. The sun's zoom-ing in. En - gines stop run-ning. The
G
D
Em
G
D
wheat is grow-ing thin. En - gines stop run-ning. But I have no fear, 'cause
wheat is grow-ing thin. A nu - cle - ar er - ror. But I have no fear, 'cause
Em
To Coda
D
1
Lon - don is drown-ing and I live by the riv - er.
Lon - don is drown-ing and I, I

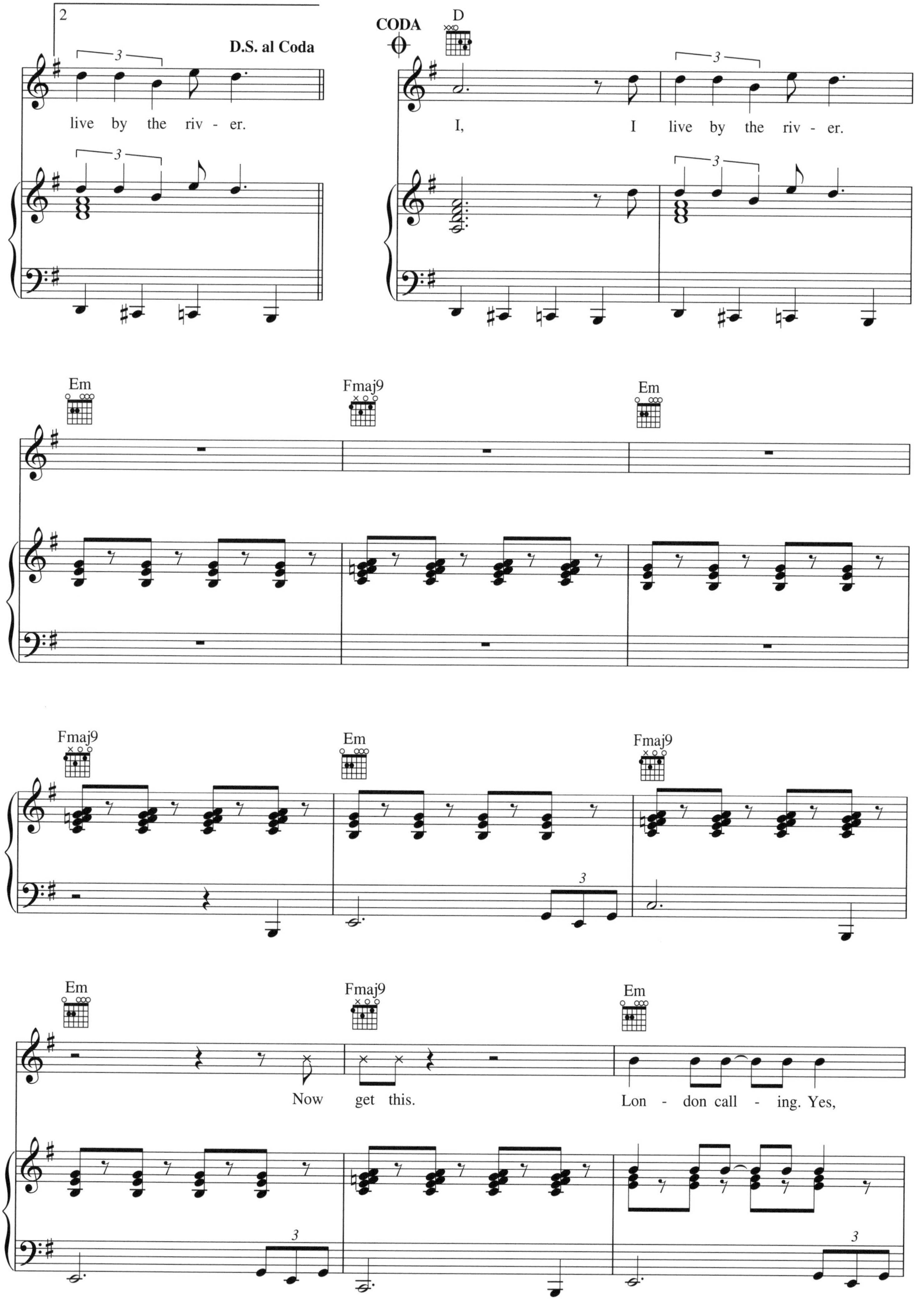
2
D.S. al Coda
live by the riv - er.
CODA
D
I, I live by the riv - er.
Em
Fmaj9
Em
Fmaj9
Em
Fmaj9
Em
Fmaj9
Em
Now get this. Lon - don call - ing. Yes,

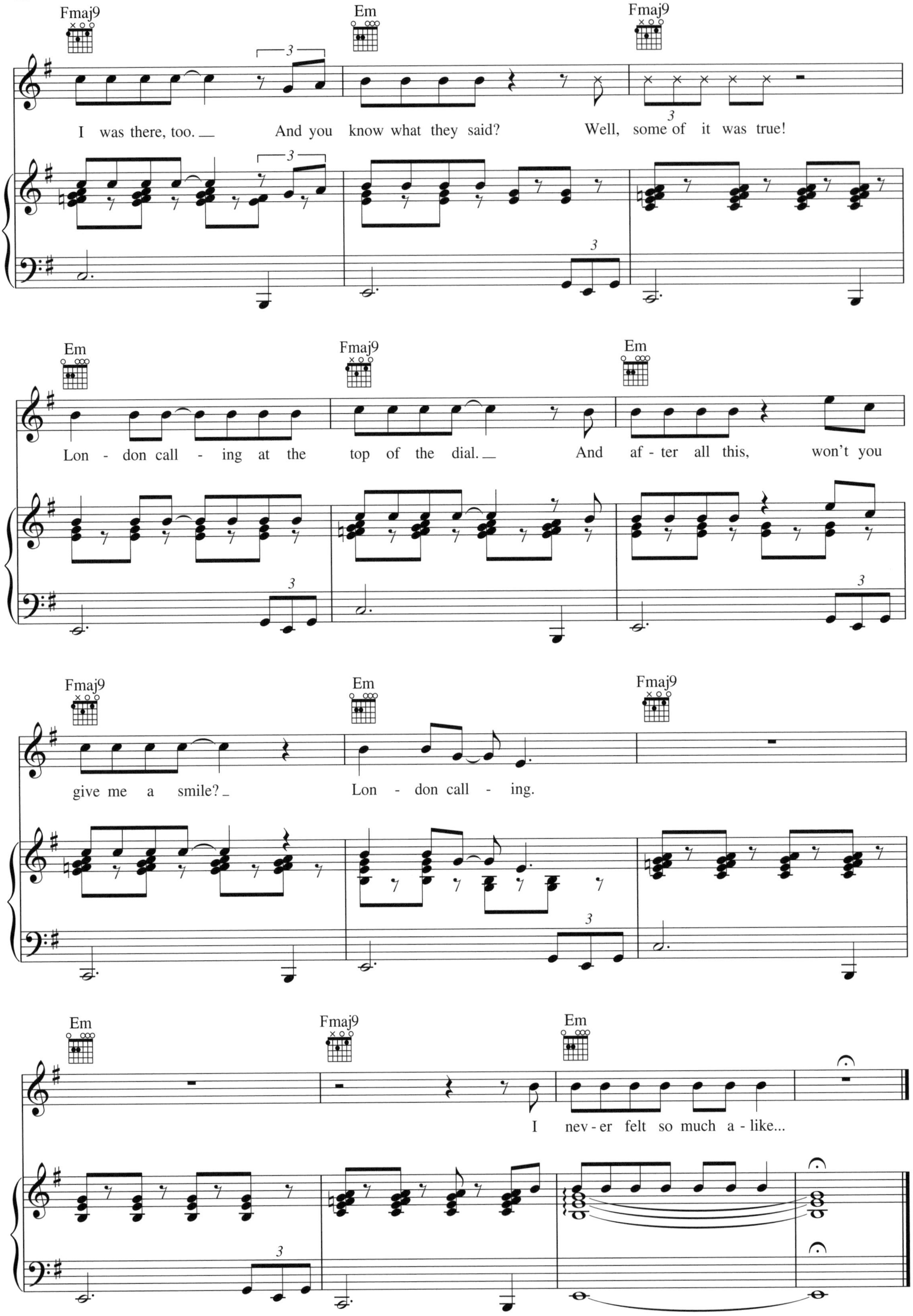
Fmaj9
Em
Fmaj9
I was there, too. And you know what they said? Well, some of it was true!
Em
Fmaj9
Em
Lon - don call - ing at the top of the dial. And af - ter all this, won't you
Fmaj9
Em
Fmaj9
give me a smile? Lon - don call - ing.
Em
Fmaj9
Em
I nev - er felt so much a - like...

ONE TIN SOLDIER

from BILLY JACK

Words and Music by DENNIS LAMBERT
and BRIAN POTTER

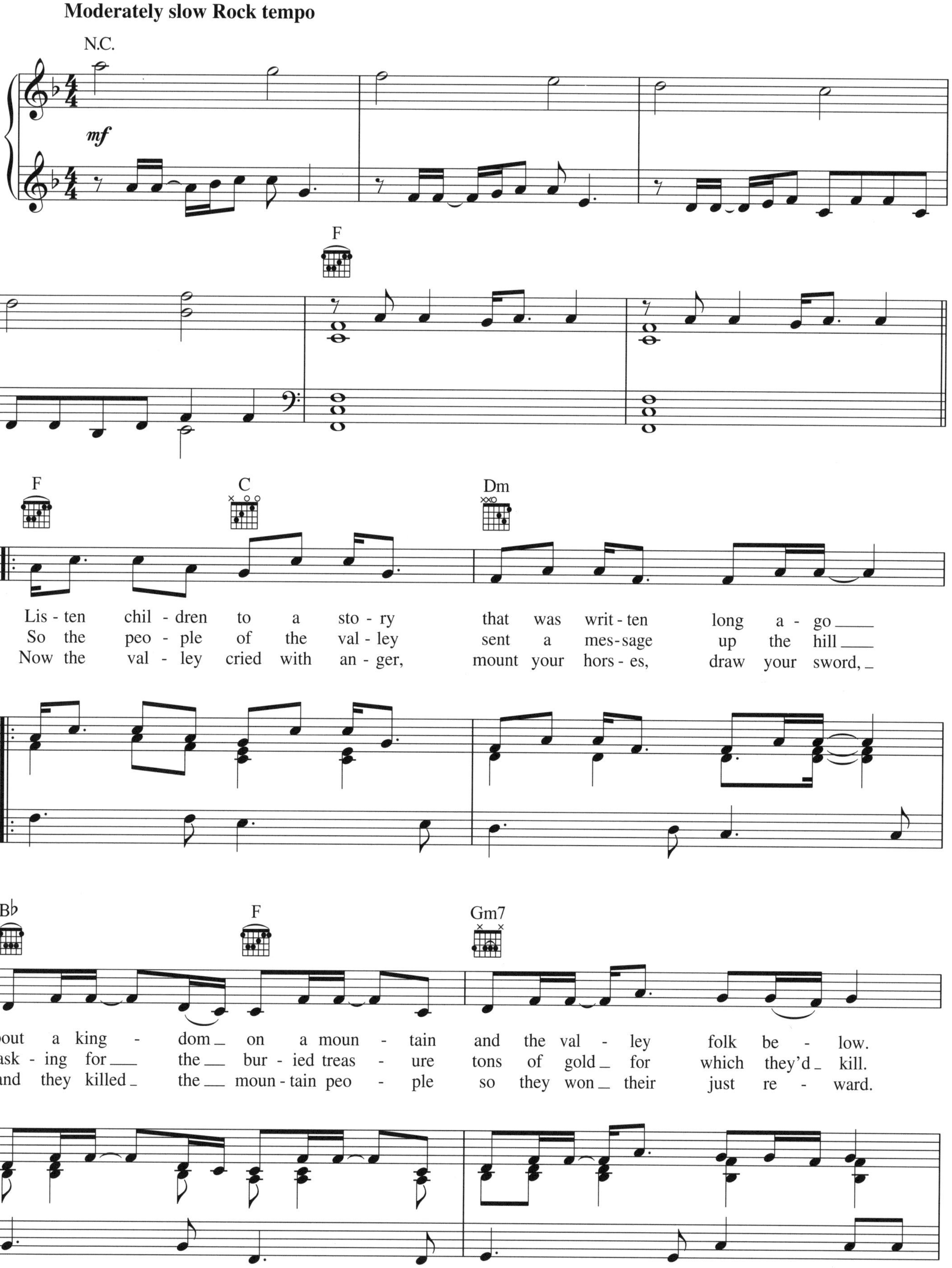

Copyright © 1969, 1974 SONGS OF UNIVERSAL, INC.
Copyright Renewed
All Rights Reserved Used by Permission

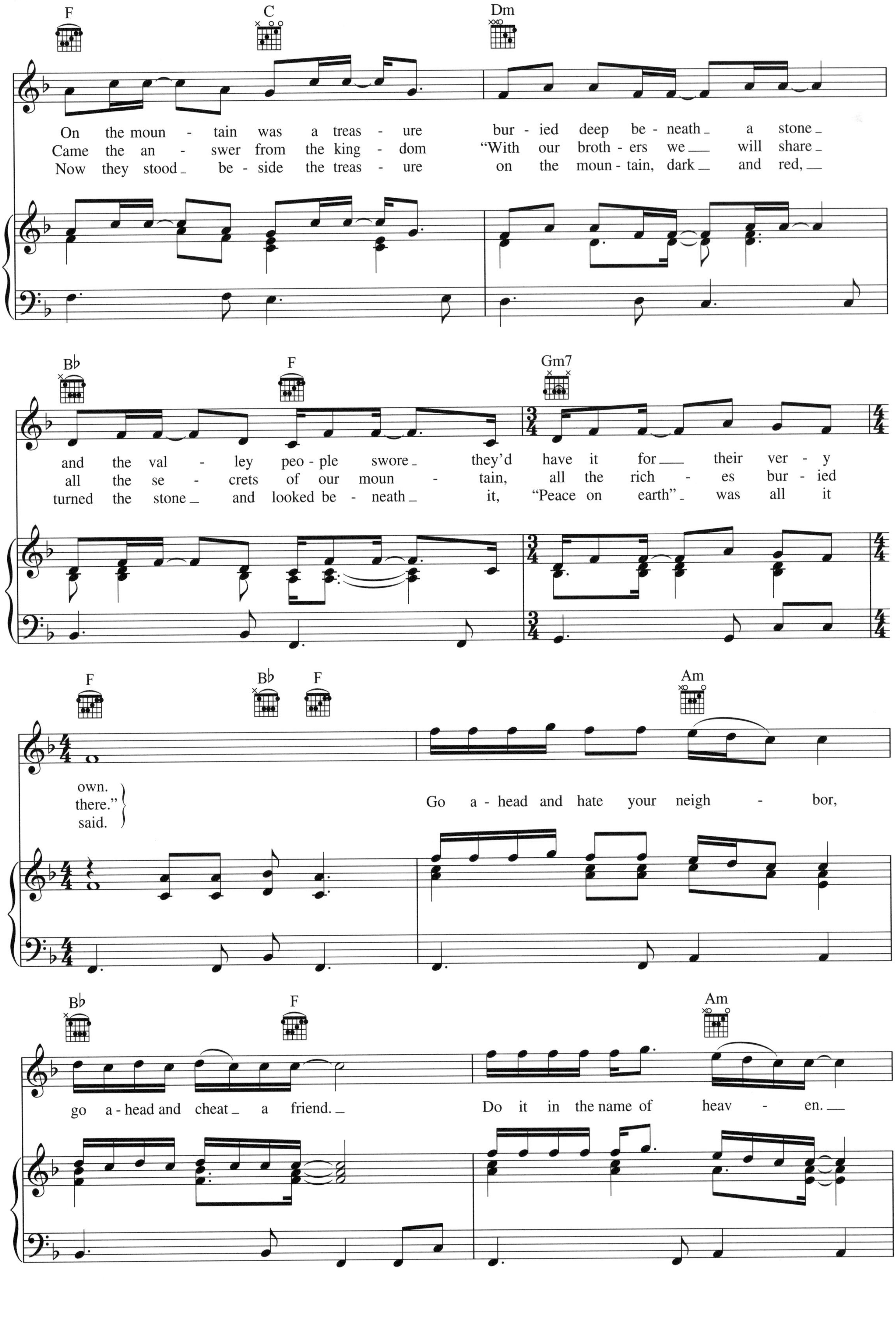
F C Dm
On the moun - tain was a treas - ure bur - ied deep be - neath a stone
Came the an - swer from the king - dom "With our broth - ers we will share
Now they stood be - side the treas - ure on the moun - tain, dark and red,
B♭ F Gm7
and the val - ley peo - ple swore they'd have it for their ver - y
all the se - crets of our moun - tain, all the rich - es bur - ied
turned the stone and looked be - neath it, "Peace on earth" was all it
F B♭ F Am
own.
there."
said.
Go a - head and hate your neigh - bor,
B♭ F Am
go a - head and cheat a friend.
Do it in the name of heav - en.

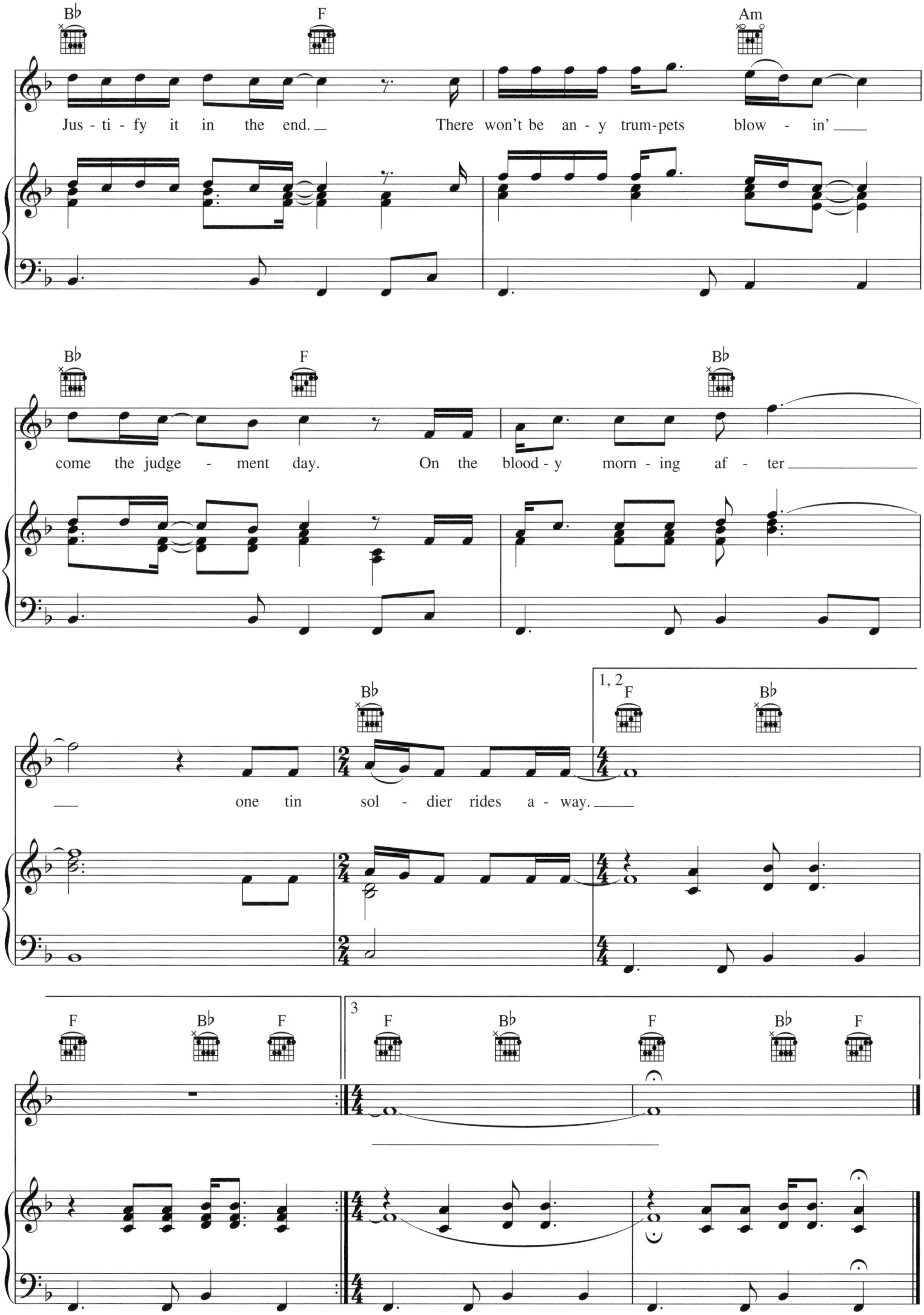
B♭ F Am
Jus - ti - fy it in the end. There won't be an - y trum-pets blow - in'
B♭ F B♭
come the judge - ment day. On the blood - y morn - ing af - ter
B♭ 1, 2 F B♭
one tin sol - dier rides a - way.
F B♭ F 3 F B♭ F B♭ F

PEOPLE GOT TO BE FREE

Words and Music by FELIX CAVALIERE
and EDWARD BRIGATI, JR.

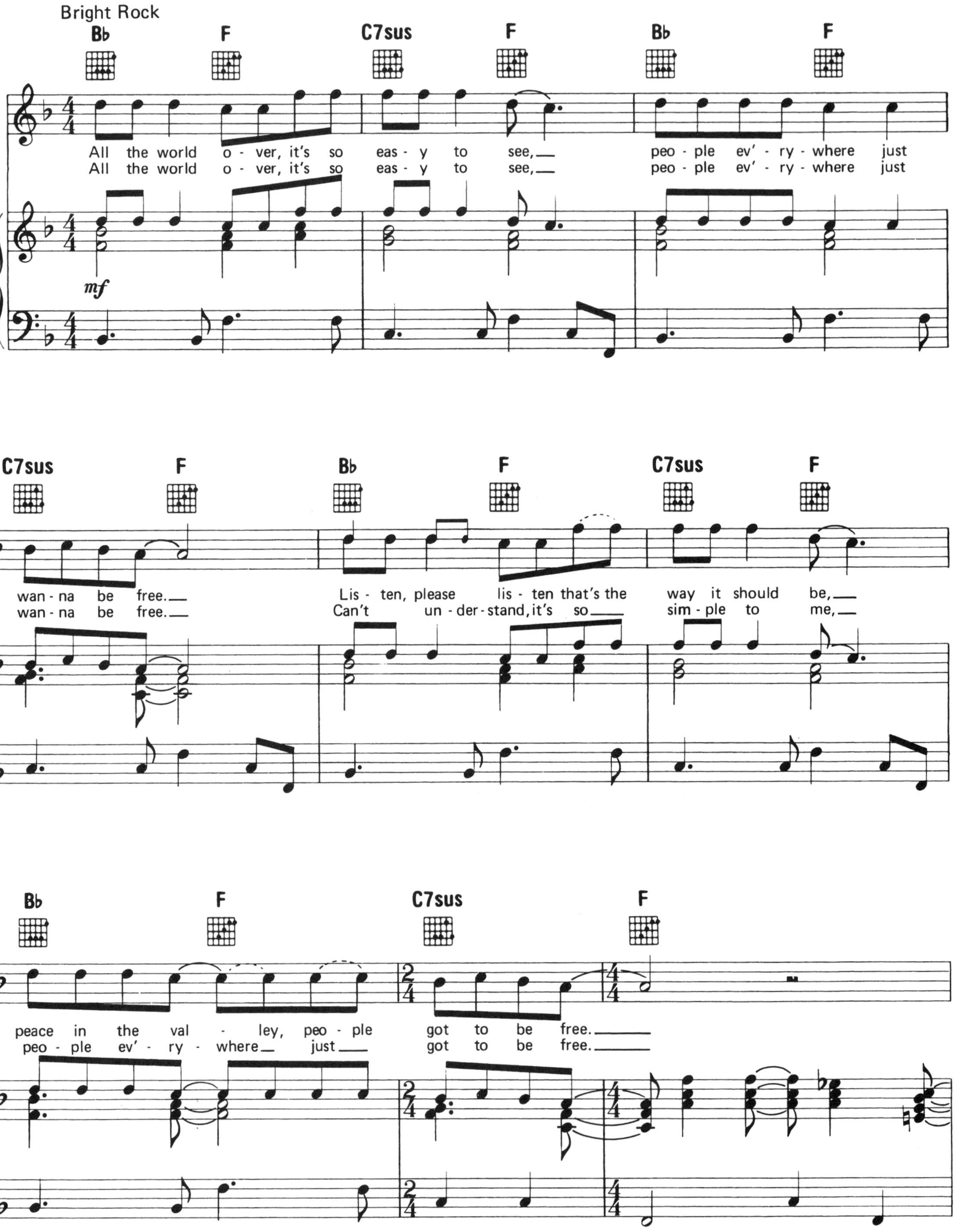

© 1968 (Renewed 1996) EMI JEMAXAL MUSIC INC. and DELICIOUS APPLE MUSIC CORP.
All Rights Reserved International Copyright Secured Used by Permission

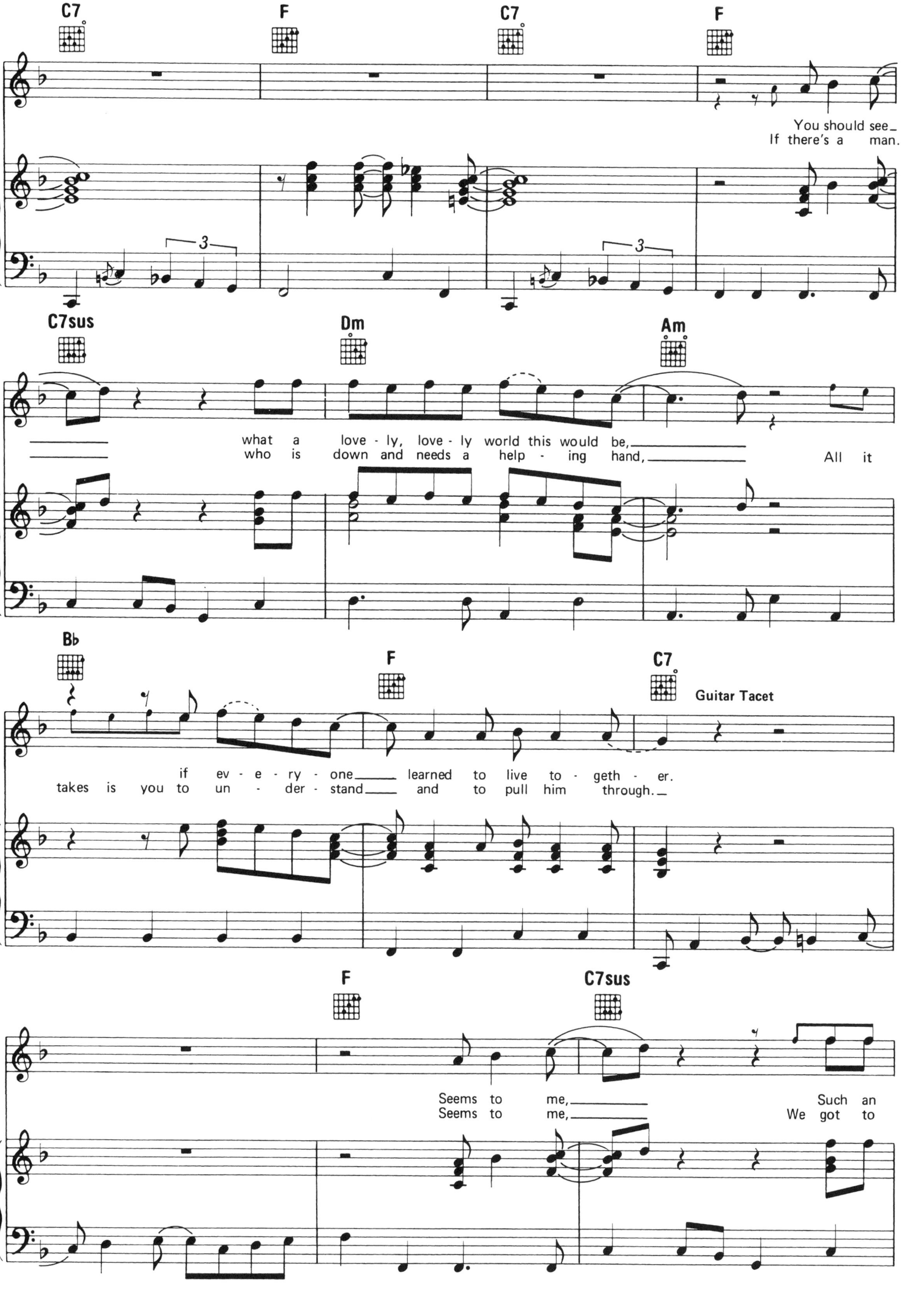
C7
F
C7
F
You should see
If there's a man.
C7sus
Dm
Am
what a lovely, lovely world this would be,
who is down and needs a helping hand,
All it
Bb
F
C7
Guitar Tacet
if everyone learned to live together.
takes is you to understand and to pull him through.
F
C7sus
Seems to me,
Seems to me,
Such an
We got to

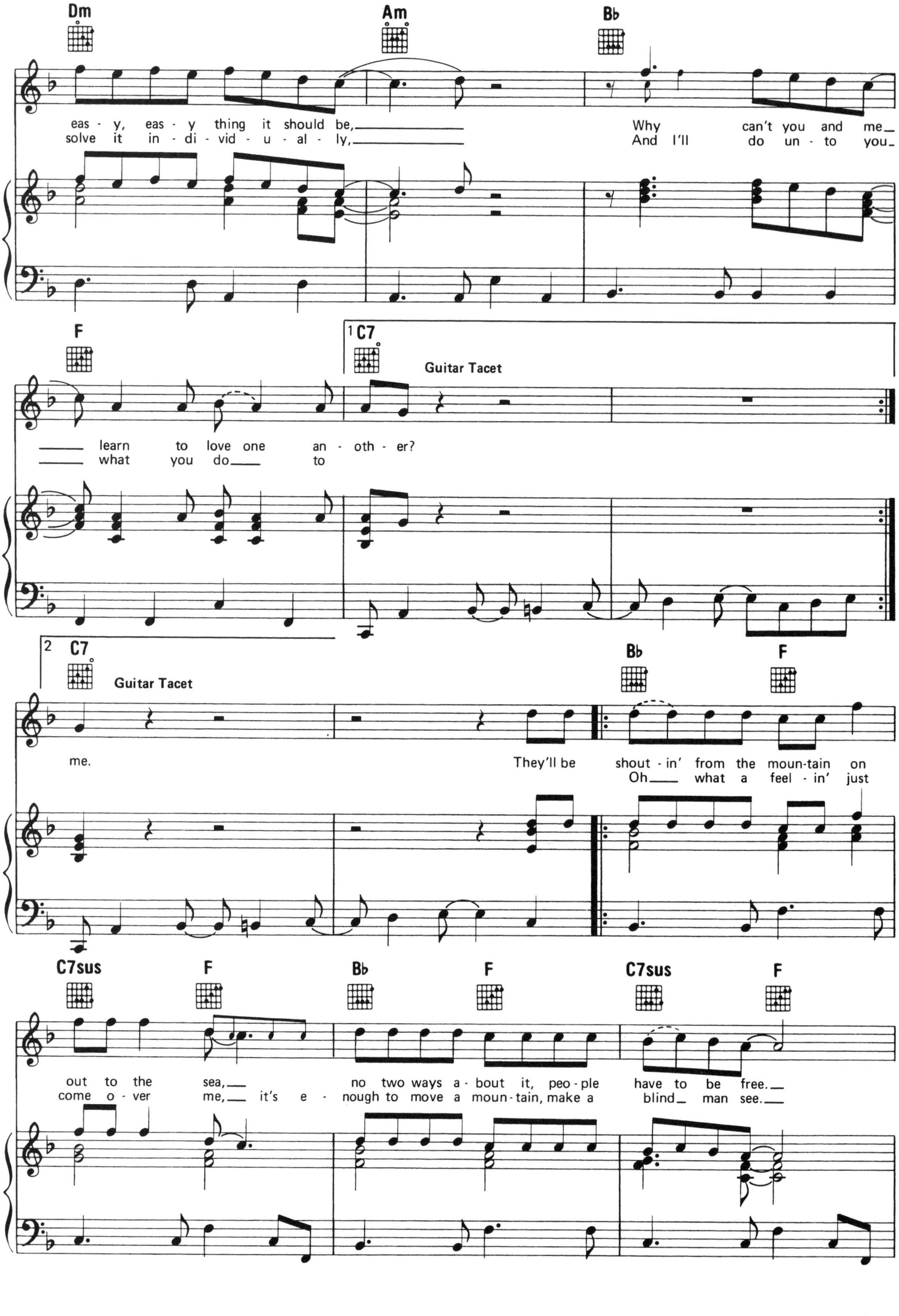
Dm
Am
Bb
eas - y, eas - y thing it should be,
solve it in - di - vid - u - al - ly,
Why can't you and me
And I'll do un - to you
F
1 C7
Guitar Tacet
learn to love one an - oth - er?
what you do to
2 C7
Guitar Tacet
me.
They'll be
Bb
F
shout - in' from the moun-tain on
Oh what a feel - in' just
C7sus
F
Bb
F
C7sus
F
out to the sea,
come o - ver me,
it's e - nough to move a moun-tain, make a
no two ways a - bout it, peo-ple
have to be free.
blind man see.

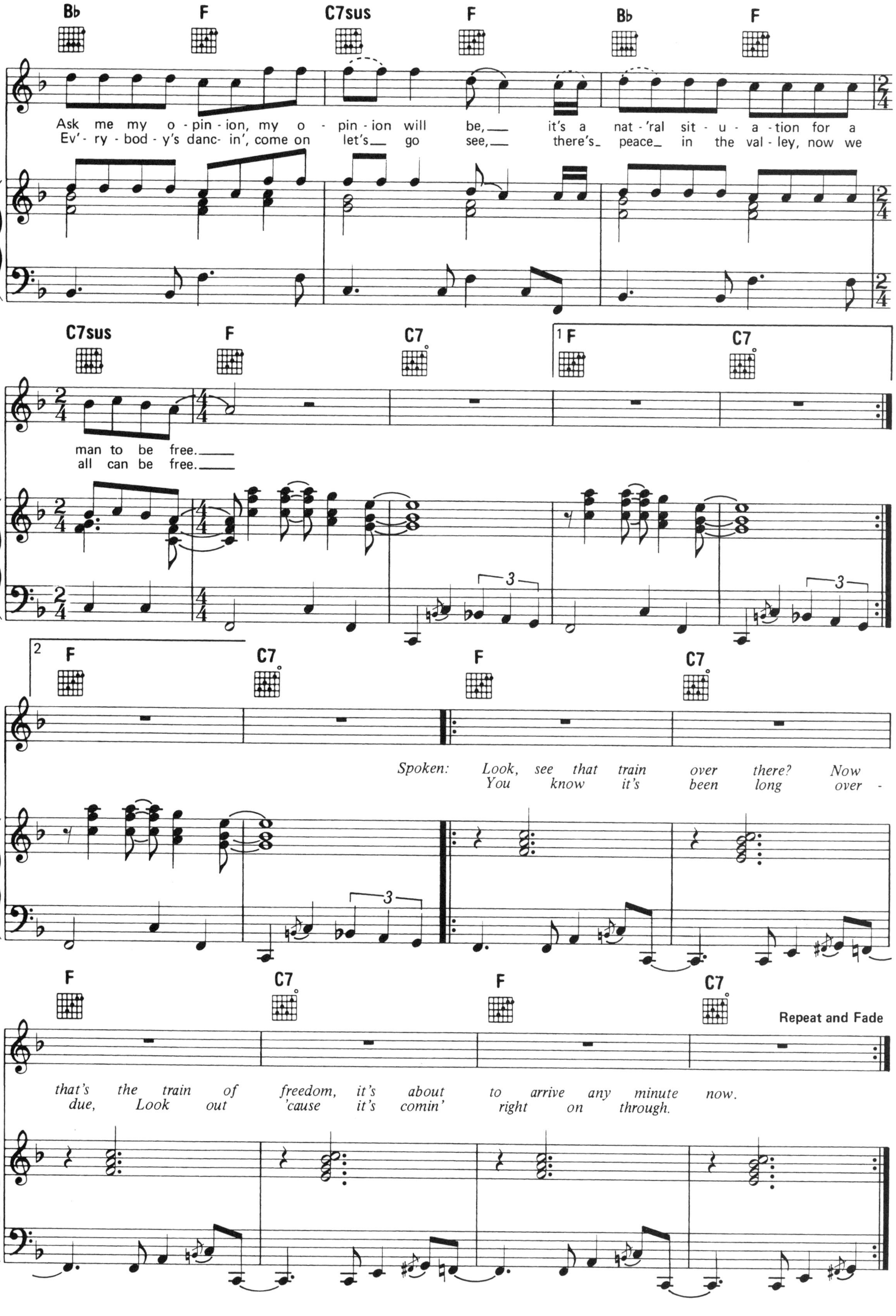
Bb F C7sus F Bb F
Ask me my o - pin - ion, my o - pin - ion will be, it's a nat - 'ral sit - u - a - tion for a
Ev' - ry - bod - y's danc - in', come on let's go see, there's peace in the val - ley, now we
C7sus F C7
man to be free.
all can be free.
1 F C7
2 F C7 F C7
Spoken: Look, see that train over there? Now
You know it's been long over -
F C7 F C7
that's the train of freedom, it's about to arrive any minute now.
due, Look out 'cause it's comin' right on through.
Repeat and Fade

POWER TO THE PEOPLE

Words and Music by
JOHN LENNON

32 bars per minute

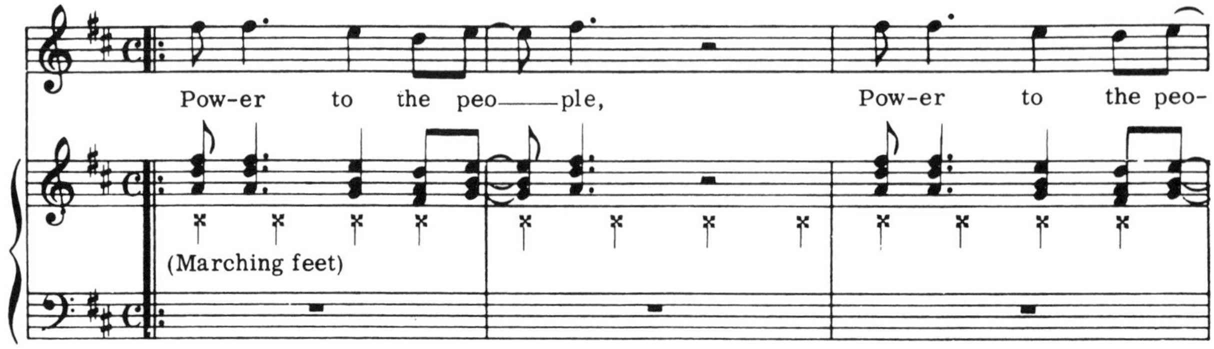
Pow-er to the peo—ple, Pow-er to the peo-
(Marching feet)

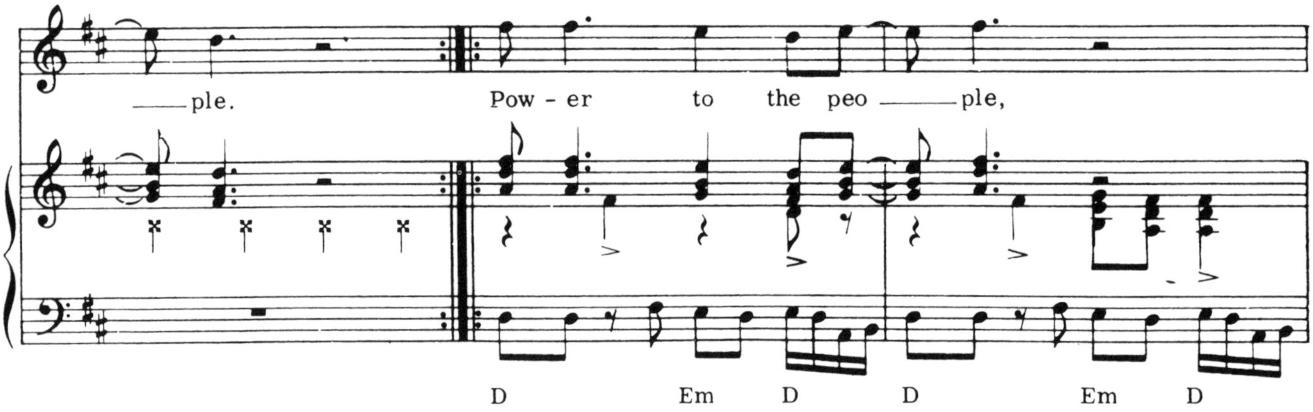
—ple. Pow - er to the peo—ple,
D Em D D Em D

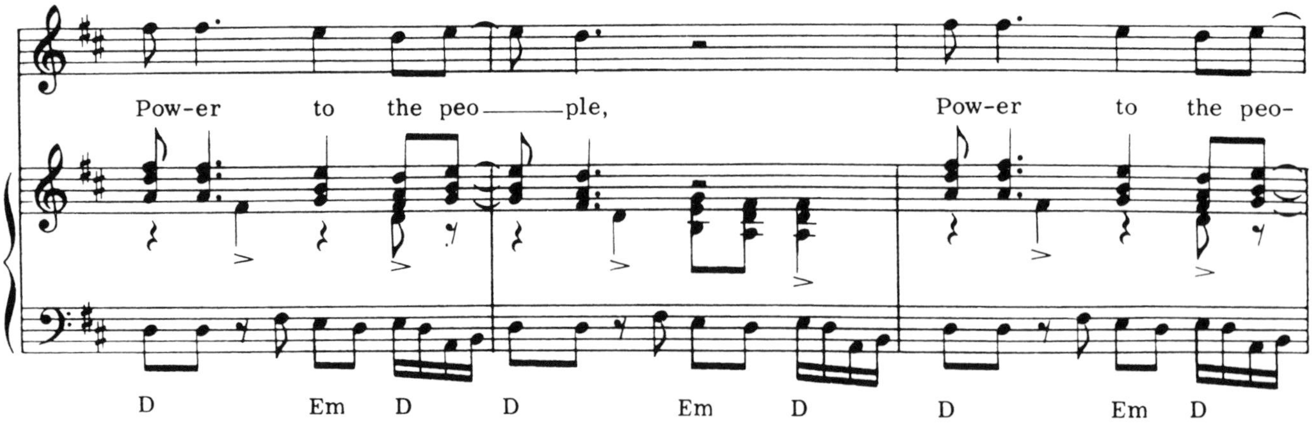
Pow-er to the peo—ple, Pow-er to the peo-
D Em D D Em D D Em D

© 1971 (Renewed 1999) LENONO.MUSIC
All Rights Controlled and Administered by EMI BLACKWOOD MUSIC INC.
All Rights Reserved International Copyright Secured Used by Permission

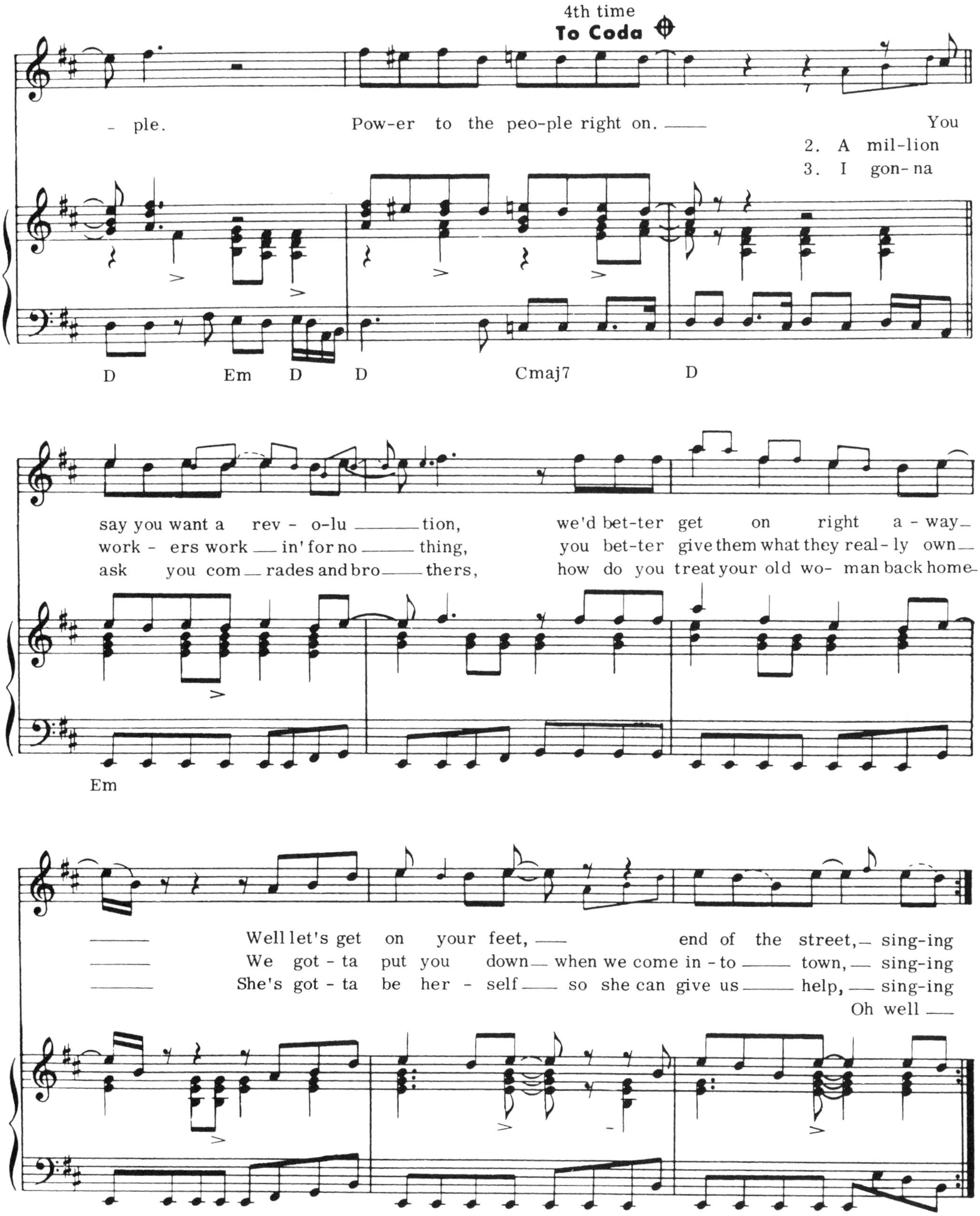
4th time
To Coda
- ple.
Pow-er to the peo-ple right on.
You
2. A mil-lion
3. I gon-na
D
Em
D
D
Cmaj7
D
say you want a rev - o-lu tion,
we'd bet-ter get on right a - way
work - ers work in' for no thing,
you bet-ter give them what they real - ly own
ask you com rades and bro thers,
how do you treat your old wo- man back home
Em
Well let's get on your feet,
end of the street, sing-ing
We got - ta put you down when we come in - to town, sing-ing
She's got - ta be her - self so she can give us help, sing-ing
Oh well

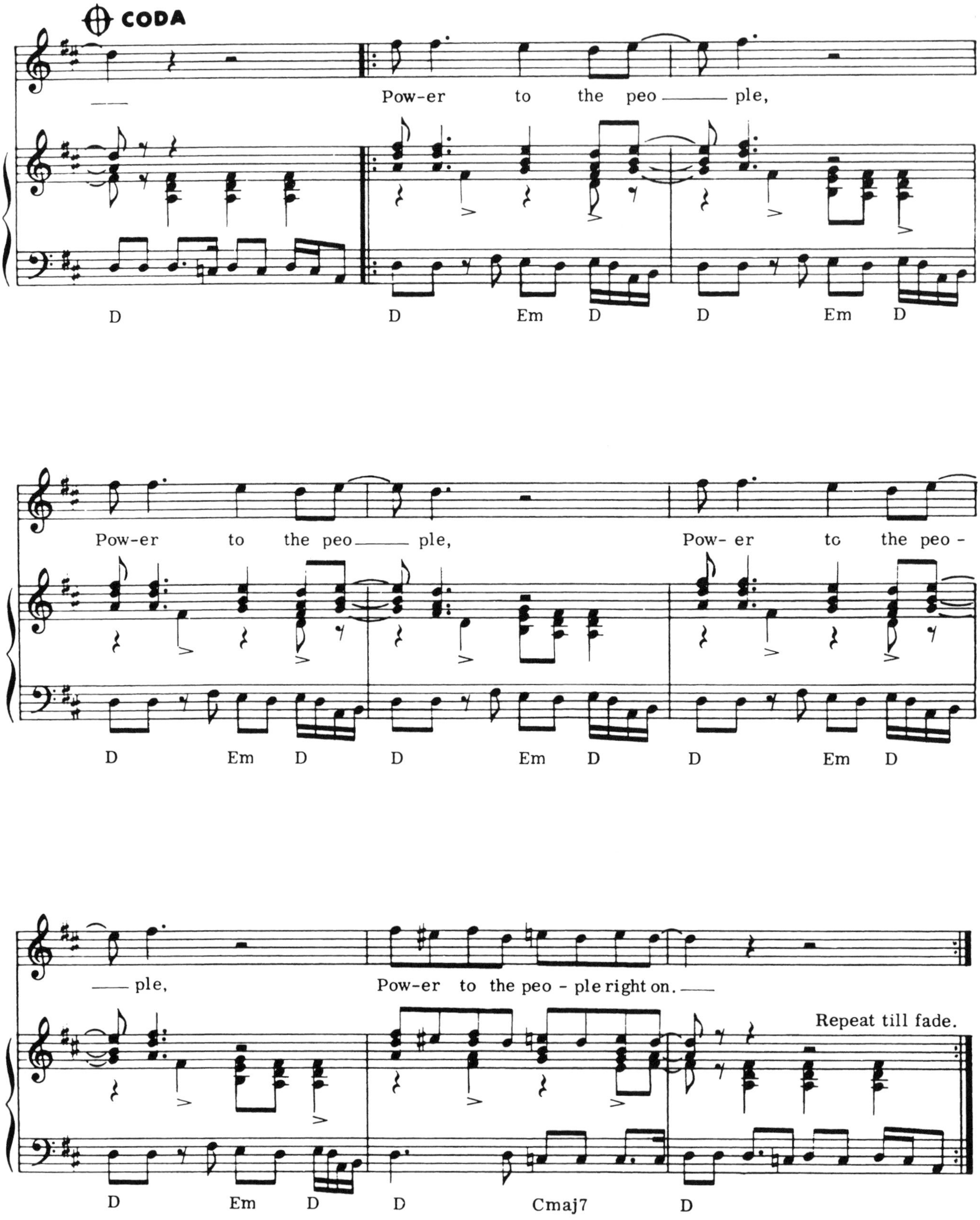
CODA
Pow-er to the peo — ple,
D
D Em D D Em D
Pow-er to the peo — ple, Pow- er to the peo -
D Em D D Em D D Em D
— ple, Pow-er to the peo - ple right on. —
Repeat till fade.
D Em D D Cmaj7 D

SHARE THE LAND

Words and Music by
BURTON CUMMINGS

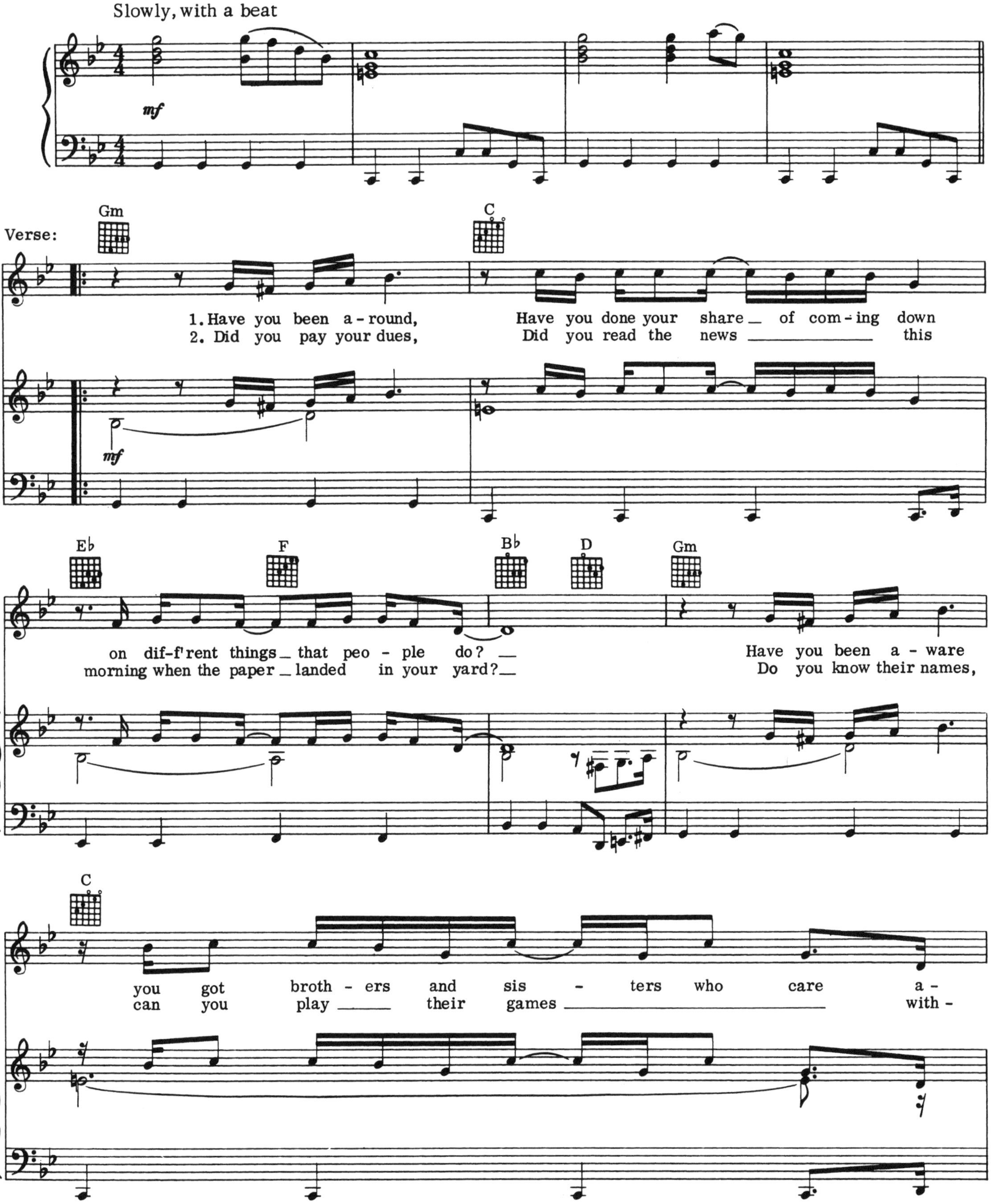

© 1970 (Renewed 1998) SHILLELAGH MUSIC (SOCAN/BMI)/Administered by BUG MUSIC
All Rights Reserved Used by Permission

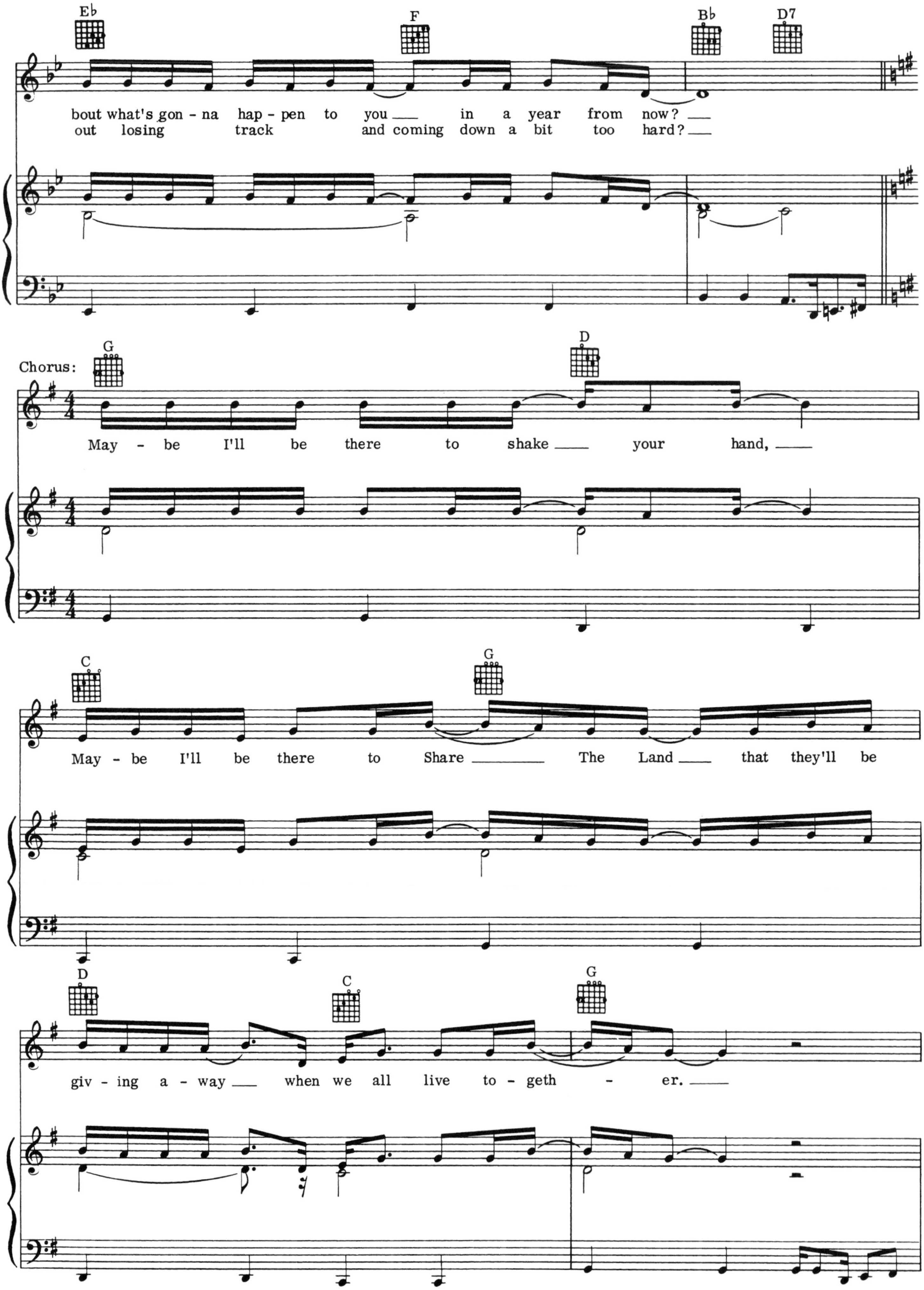
Eb
F
Bb
D7
bout what's gon - na hap - pen to you in a year from now?
out losing track and coming down a bit too hard?
Chorus:
G
D
May - be I'll be there to shake your hand,
C
G
May - be I'll be there to Share The Land that they'll be
D
C
G
giv - ing a - way when we all live to - geth - er.

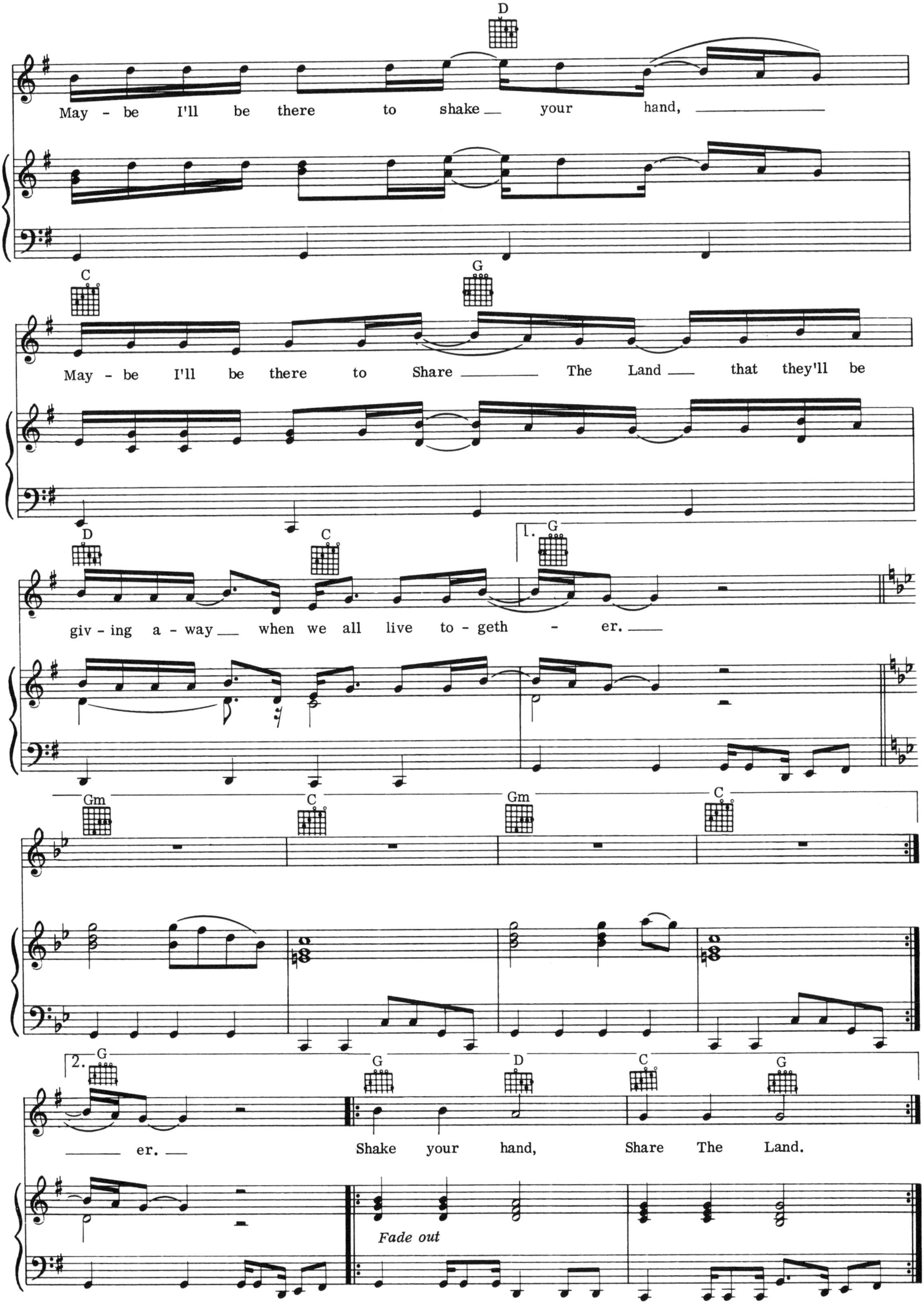
D
May - be I'll be there to shake your hand,
C G
May - be I'll be there to Share The Land that they'll be
D C 1. G
giv - ing a - way when we all live to - geth - er.
Gm C Gm C
2. G G D C G
er. Shake your hand, Share The Land.
Fade out

REVOLUTION

Words and Music by JOHN LENNON
and PAUL McCARTNEY

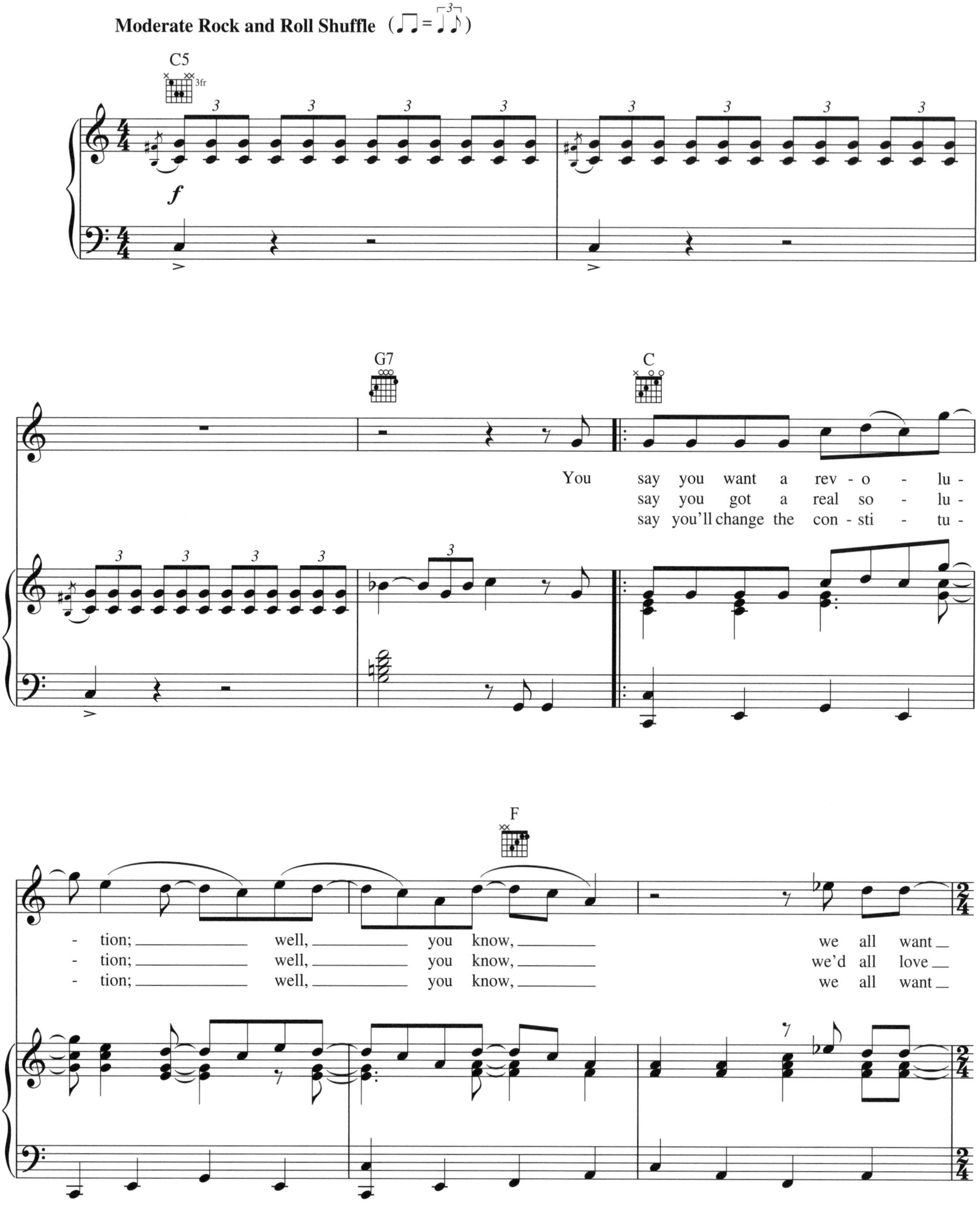
Moderate Rock and Roll Shuffle
C5
G7
C
You say you want a rev - o - lu - tion; well, you know, we all want
say you got a real so - lu - tion; well, you know, we'd all love
say you'll change the con - sti - tu - tion; well, you know, we all want
F

Copyright © 1968 Sony/ATV Songs LLC
Copyright Renewed
All Rights Administered by Sony/ATV Music Publishing, 8 Music Square West, Nashville, TN 37203
International Copyright Secured All Rights Reserved

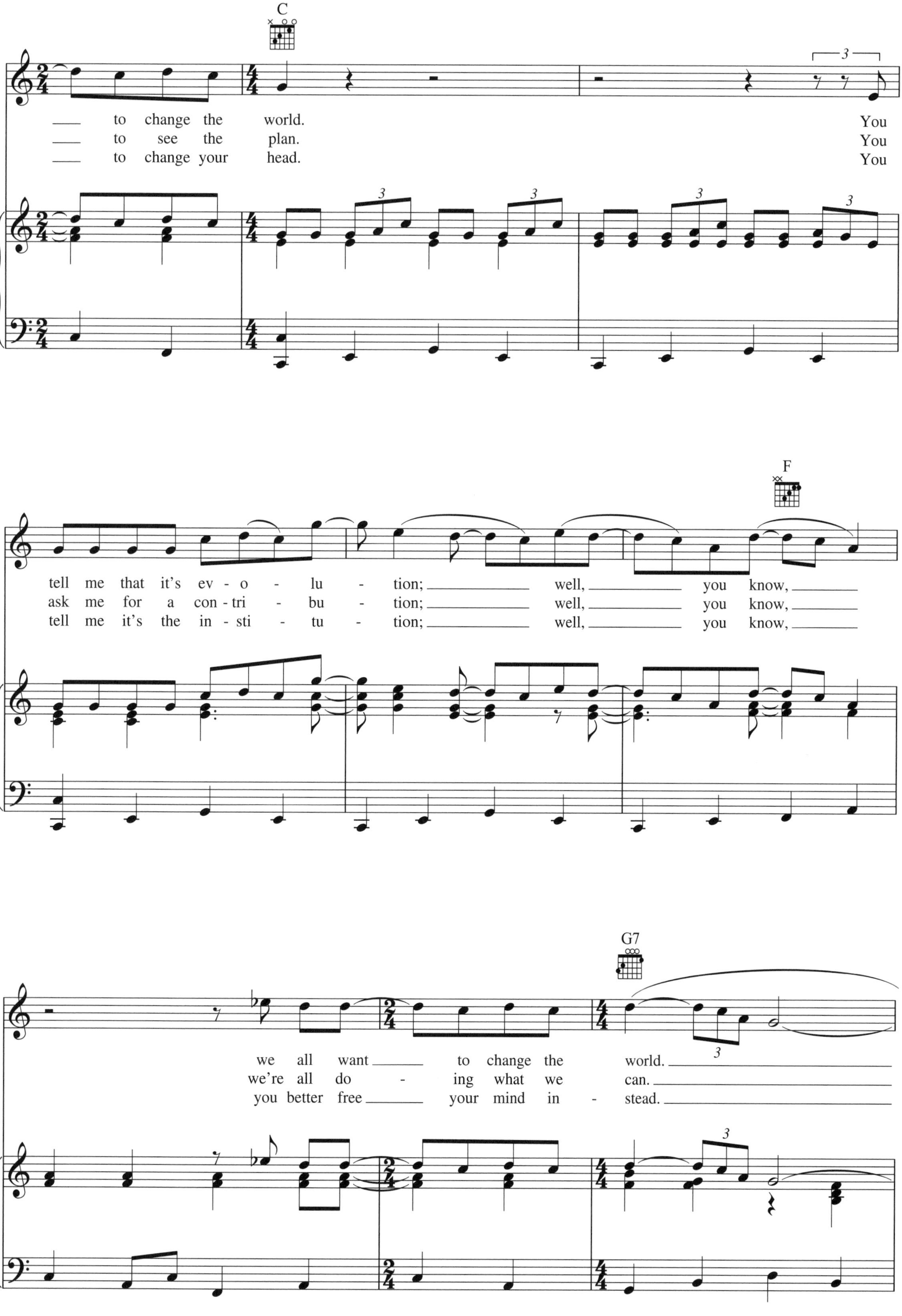
C
to change the world. You
to see the plan. You
to change your head. You
F
tell me that it's ev - o - lu - tion; well, you know,
ask me for a con - tri - bu - tion; well, you know,
tell me it's the in - sti - tu - tion; well, you know,
G7
we all want to change the world.
we're all do - ing what we can.
you better free your mind in - stead.

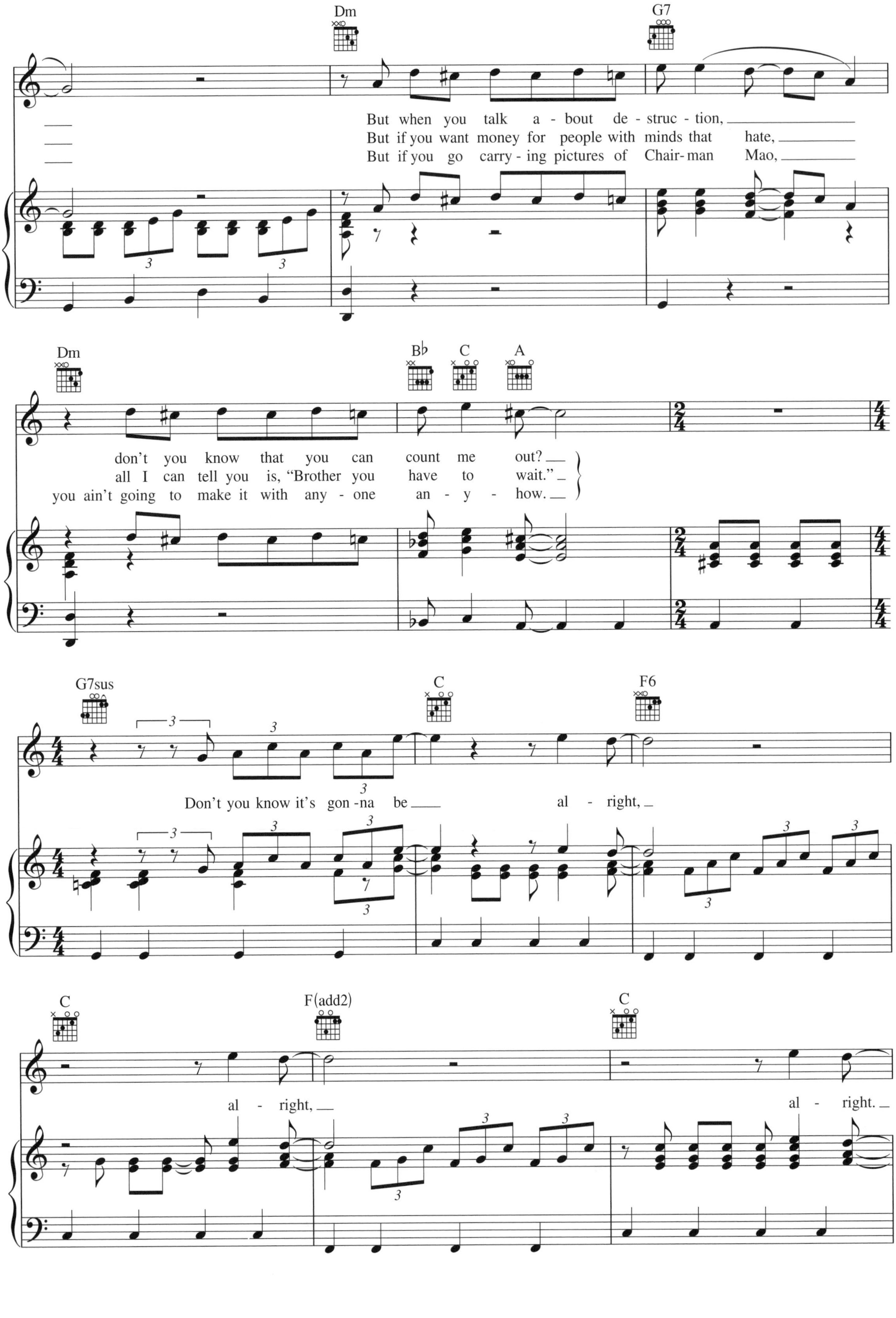
Dm
G7
But when you talk a - bout de - struc - tion,
But if you want money for people with minds that hate,
But if you go carry - ing pictures of Chair - man Mao,
Dm
B♭
C
A
don't you know that you can count me out?
all I can tell you is, "Brother you have to wait."
you ain't going to make it with any - one an - y - how.
G7sus
C
F6
Don't you know it's gon - na be al - right,
C
F(add2)
C
al - right,
al - right.

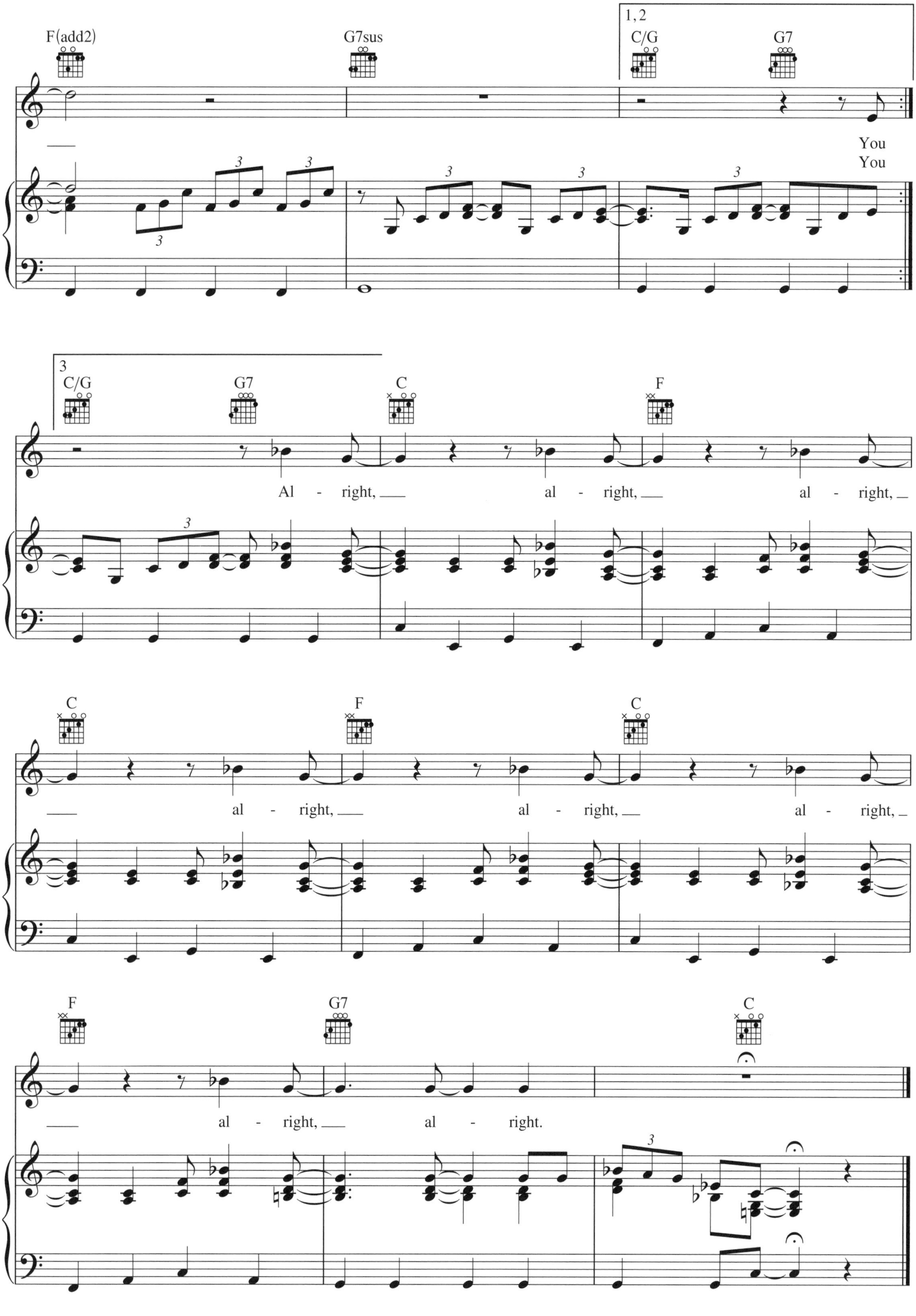
F(add2)
G7sus
1, 2
C/G
G7
You
You
3
C/G
G7
C
F
Al - right,
al - right,
al - right,
C
F
C
al - right,
al - right,
al - right,
F
G7
C
al - right,
al - right.

SAN FRANCISCO
(Be Sure to Wear Some Flowers in Your Hair)

Words and Music by
JOHN PHILLIPS

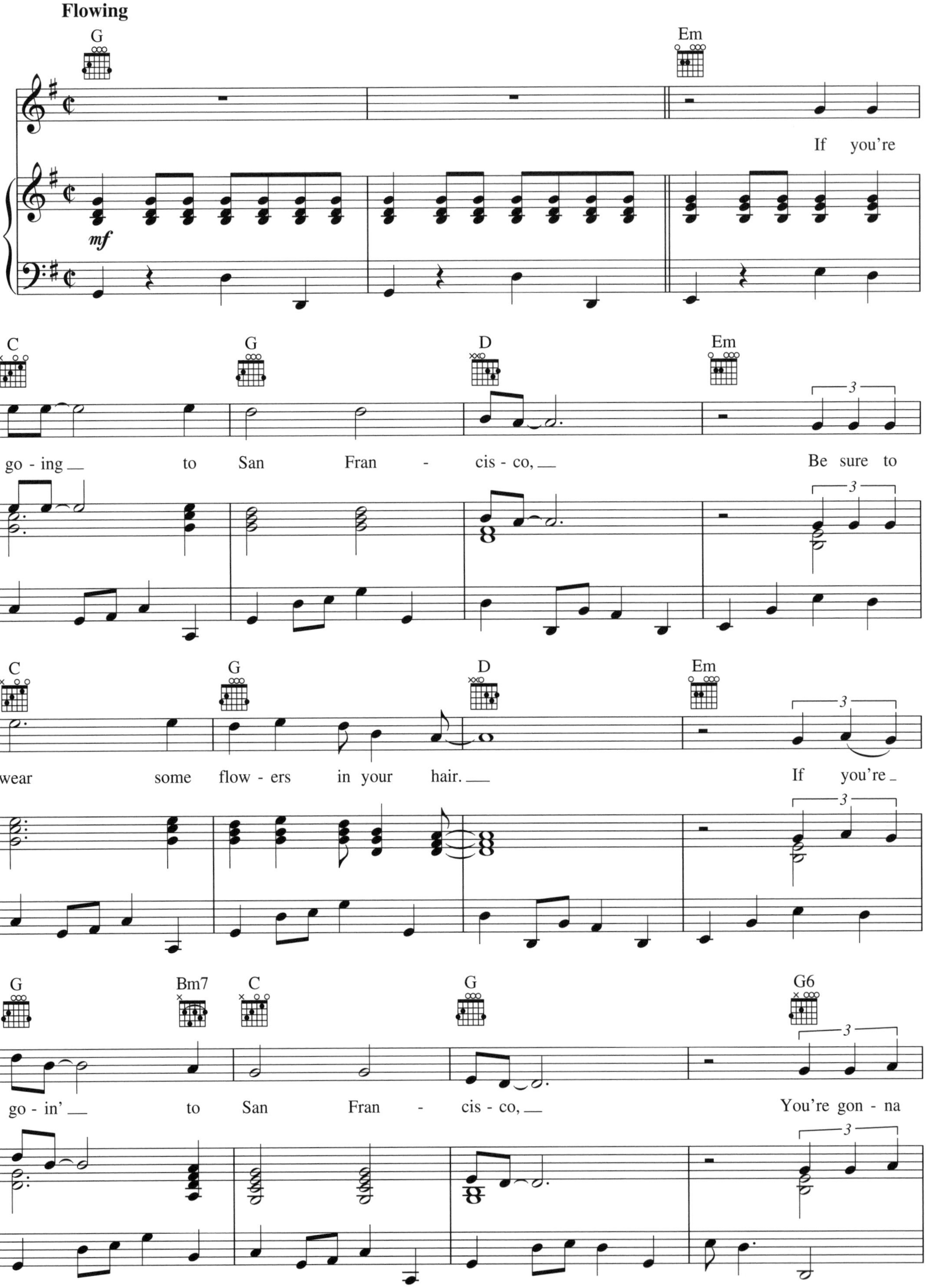

Copyright © 1967 UNIVERSAL MUSIC CORP.
Copyright Renewed
All Rights Reserved Used by Permission

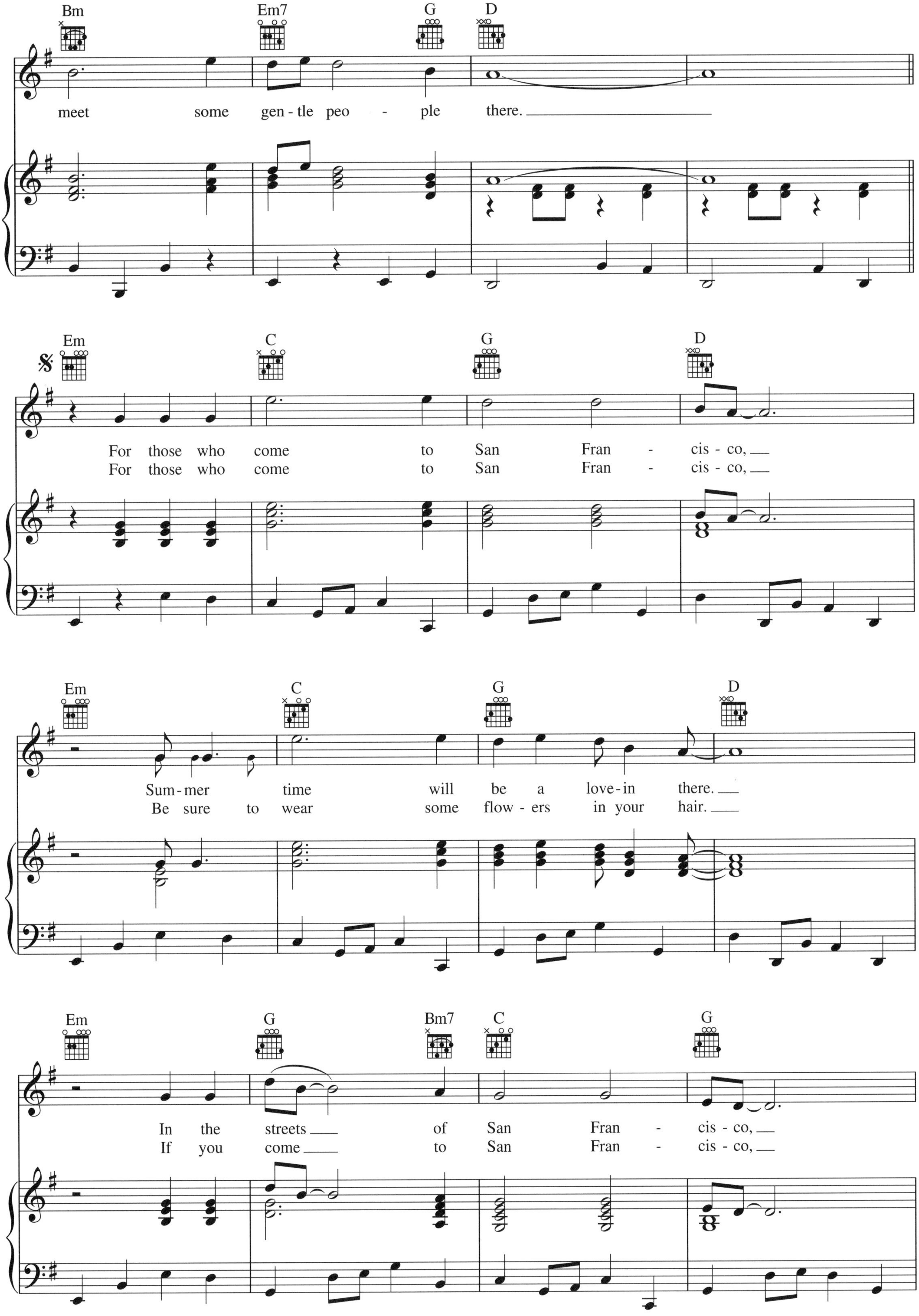
Bm
Em7
G
D
meet some gen - tle peo - ple there.
Em
C
G
D
For those who come to San Fran - cis - co,
For those who come to San Fran - cis - co,
Em
C
G
D
Sum - mer time will be a love - in there.
Be sure to wear some flow - ers in your hair.
Em
G
Bm7
C
G
In the streets of San Fran - cis - co,
If you come to San Fran - cis - co,

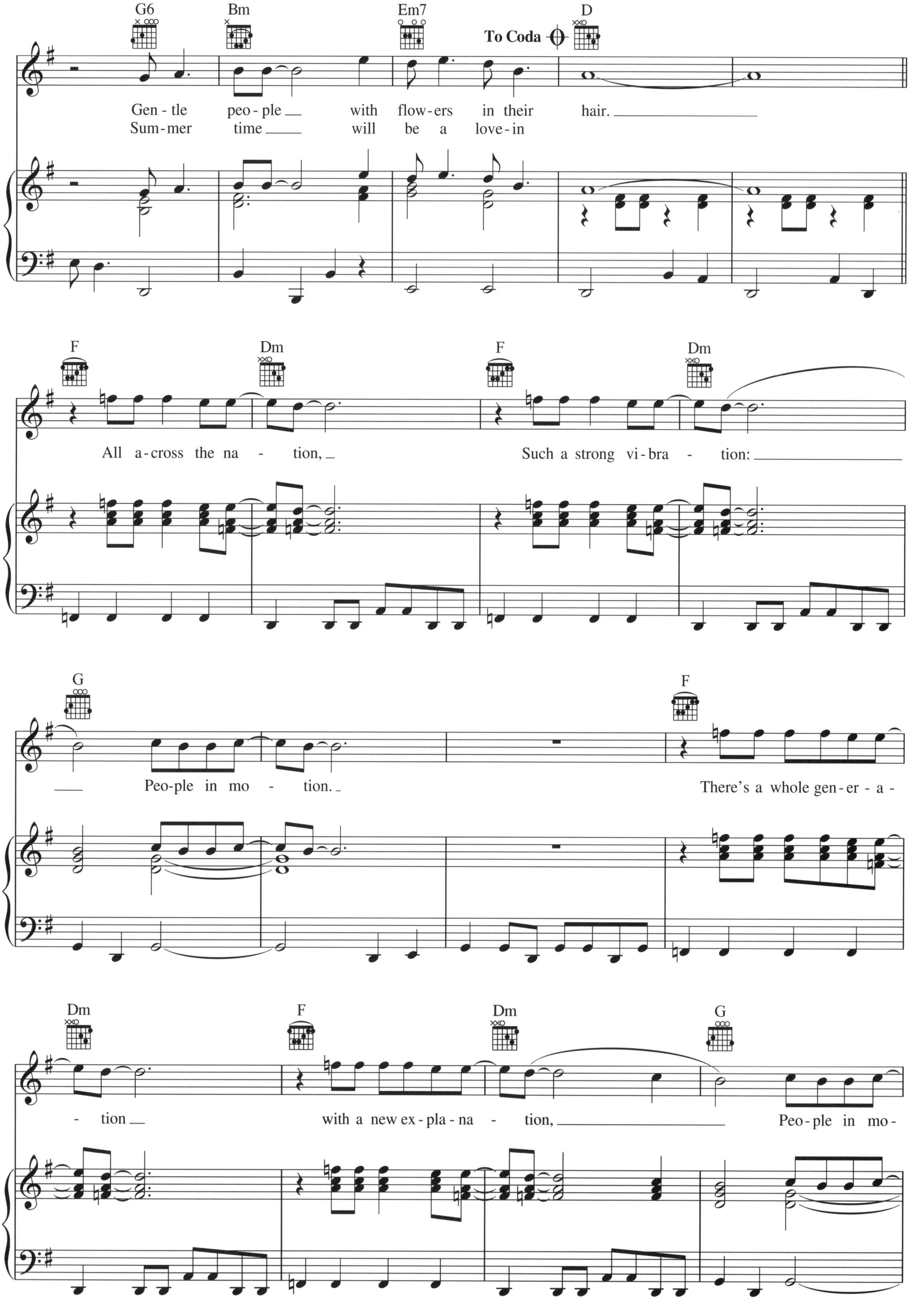
G6
Bm
Em7
To Coda
D
Gen-tle peo-ple with flow-ers in their hair.
Sum-mer time will be a love-in
F
Dm
F
Dm
All a-cross the na - tion,
Such a strong vi-bra - tion:
G
F
Peo-ple in mo - tion.
There's a whole gen-er-a -
Dm
F
Dm
G
- tion
with a new ex-pla-na - tion,
Peo-ple in mo-

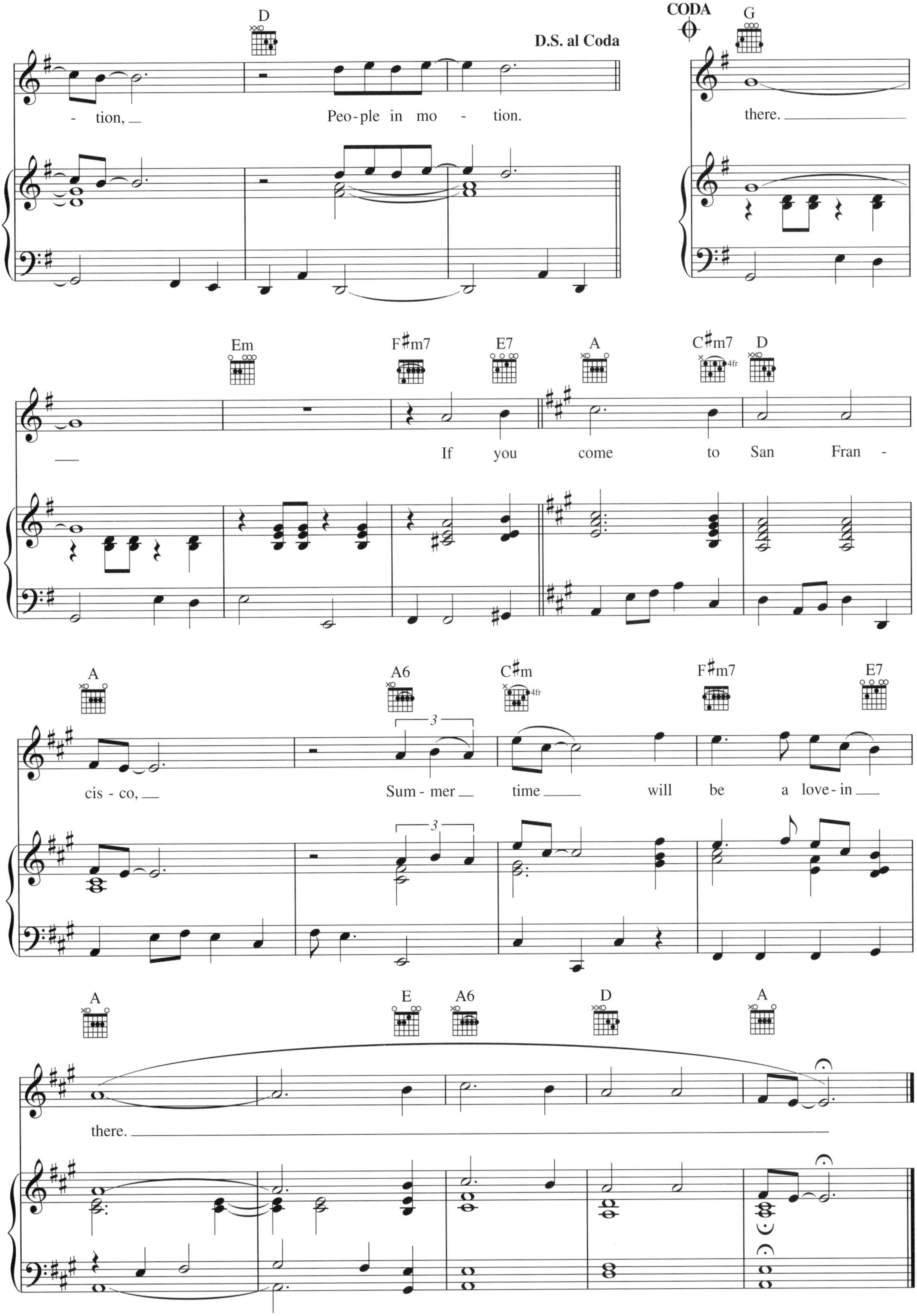
D
D.S. al Coda
CODA
G
tion,
Peo-ple in mo - tion.
there.
Em
F♯m7
E7
A
C♯m7
D
If you come to San Fran -
A
A6
C♯m
F♯m7
E7
cis - co,
Sum - mer time will be a love - in
A
E
A6
D
A
there.

SIGNS

Words and Music by
LES EMMERSON

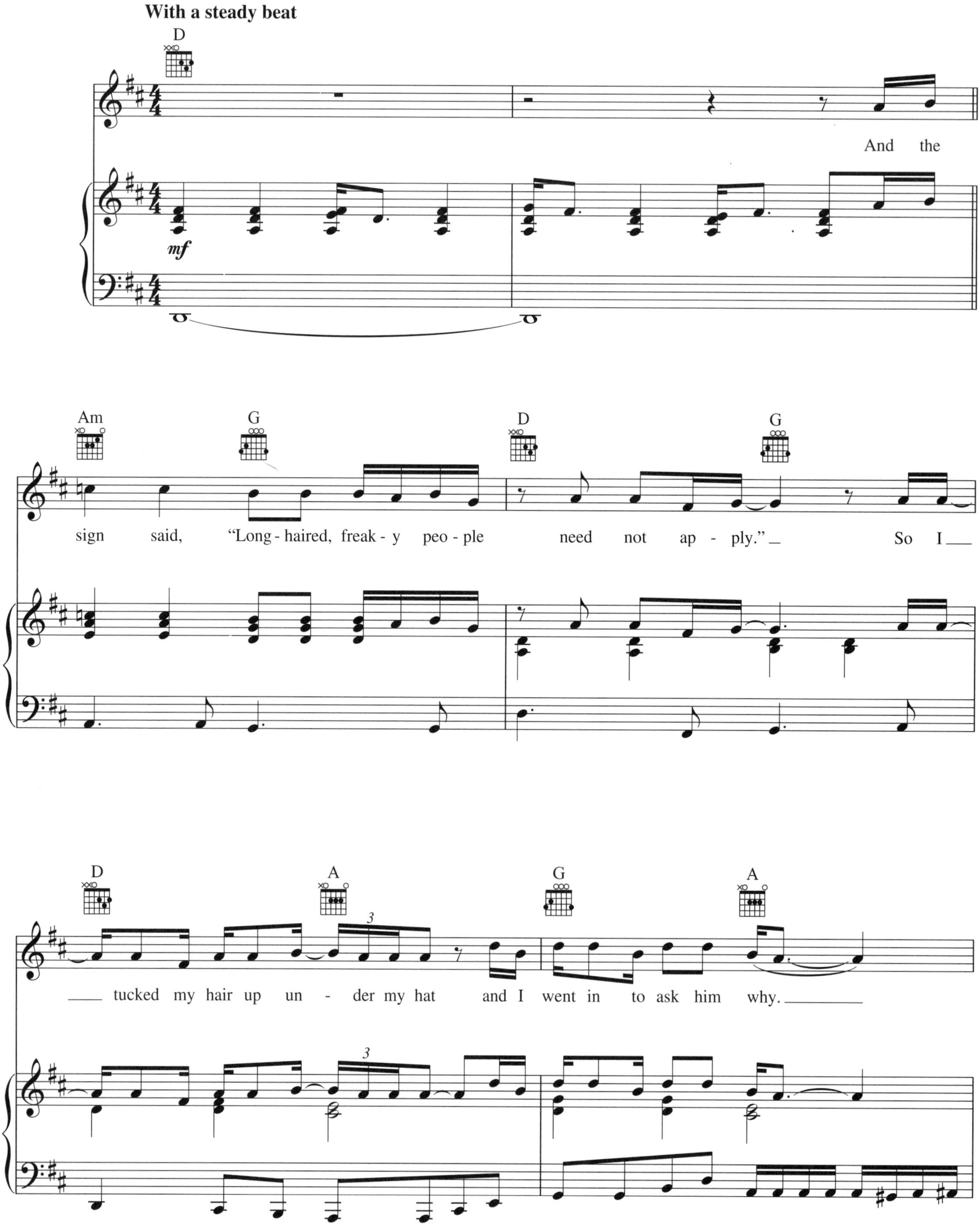
With a steady beat
D
mf
And the
Am G D G
sign said, "Long-haired, freak-y peo-ple need not ap-ply." So I
D A G A
tucked my hair up un-der my hat and I went in to ask him why.
3

Copyright © 1970 Sony/ATV Songs LLC and Galeneye Music
Copyright Renewed
All Rights on behalf of Sony/ATV Songs LLC Administered by Sony/ATV Music Publishing, 8 Music Square West, Nashville, TN 37203
International Copyright Secured All Rights Reserved

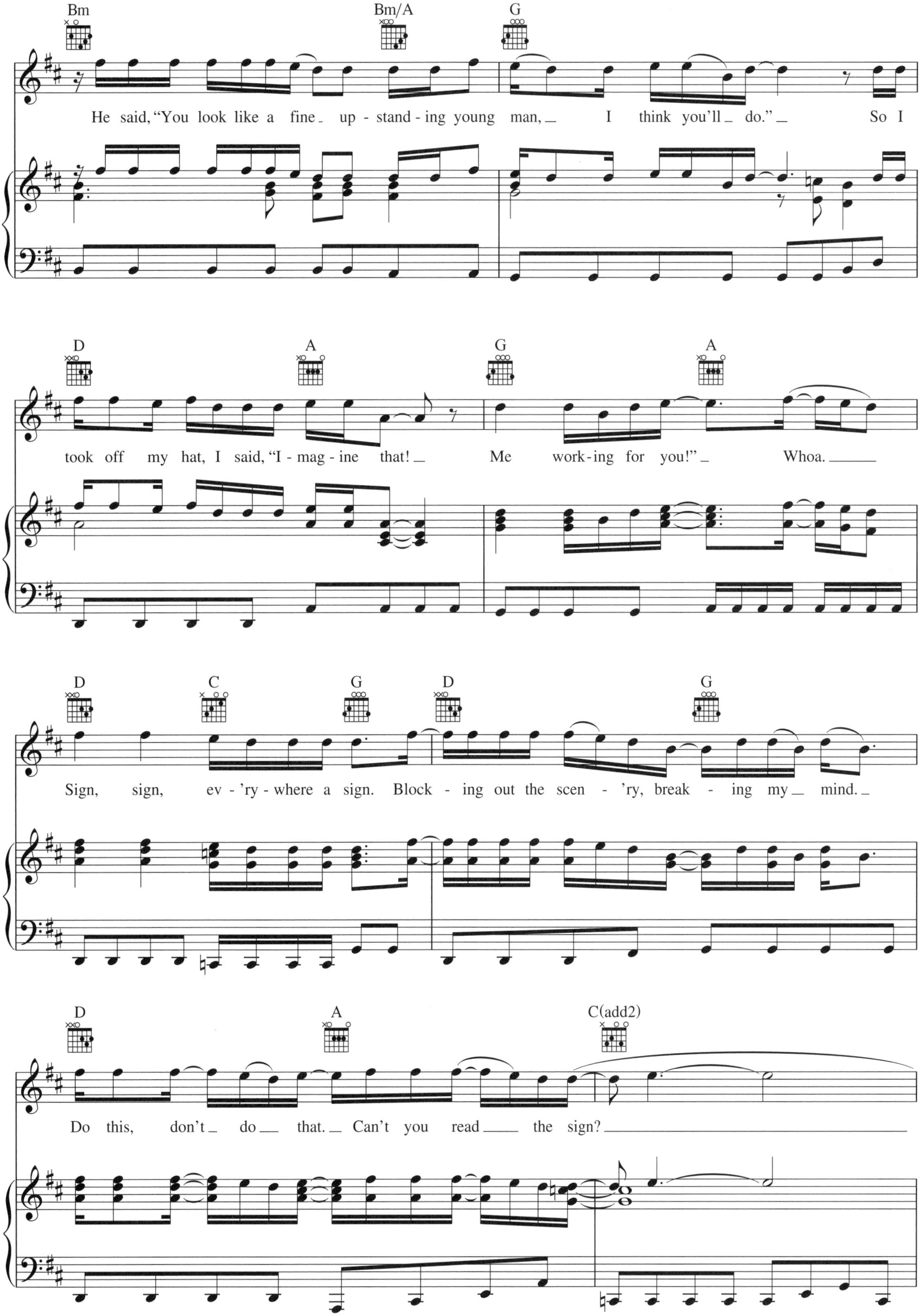

Bm
Bm/A
G
He said, "You look like a fine up - stand - ing young man, I think you'll do." So I
D
A
G
A
took off my hat, I said, "I - mag - ine that! Me work - ing for you!" Whoa.
D
C
G
D
G
Sign, sign, ev - 'ry - where a sign. Block - ing out the scen - 'ry, break - ing my mind.
D
A
C(add2)
Do this, don't do that. Can't you read the sign?

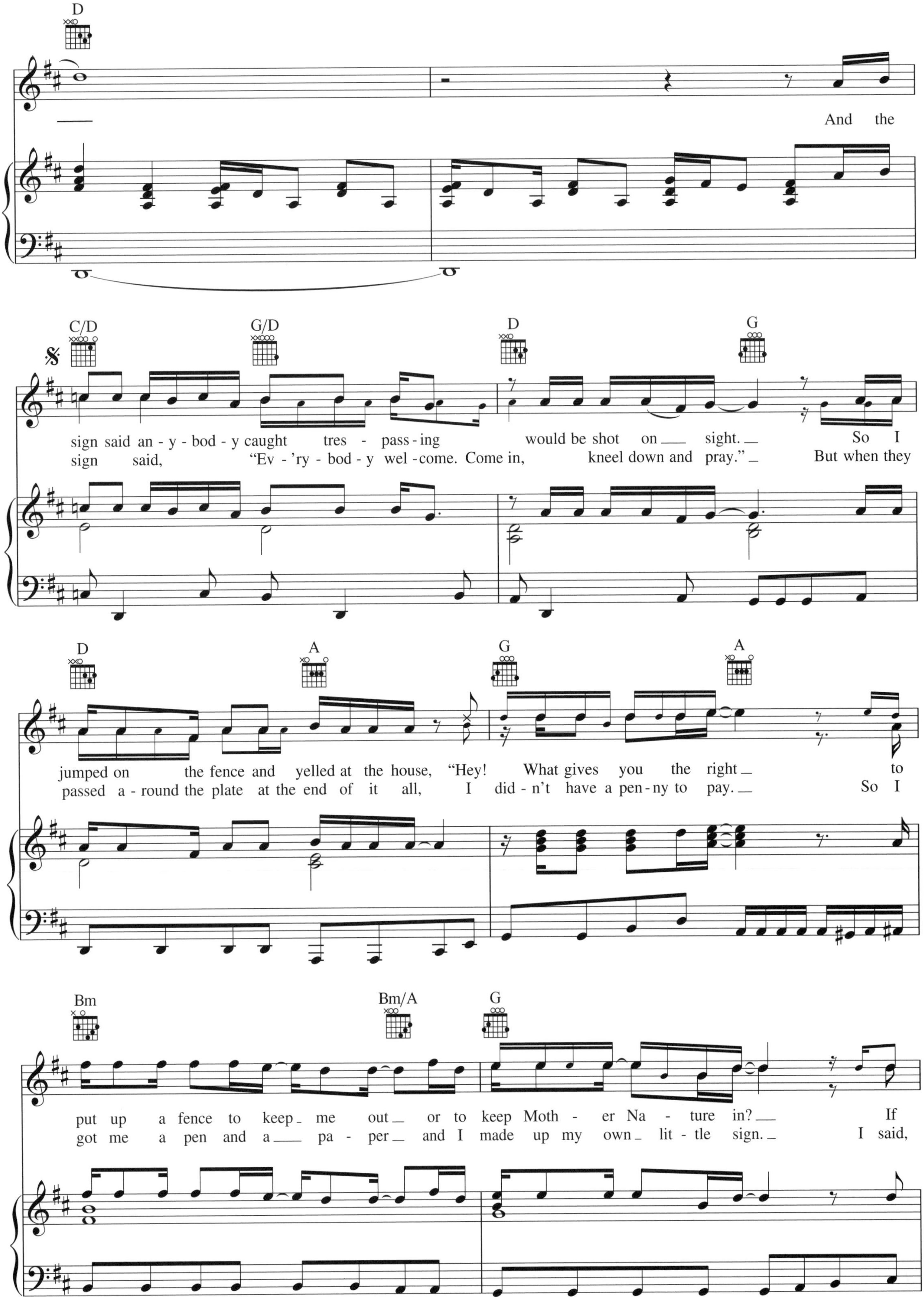
D
And the
C/D G/D D G
sign said an-y-bod-y caught tres-pass-ing would be shot on sight. So I
sign said, "Ev-'ry-bod-y wel-come. Come in, kneel down and pray." But when they
D A G A
jumped on the fence and yelled at the house, "Hey! What gives you the right to
passed a-round the plate at the end of it all, I did-n't have a pen-ny to pay. So I
Bm Bm/A G
put up a fence to keep me out or to keep Moth-er Na-ture in? If
got me a pen and a pa-per and I made up my own lit-tle sign. I said,

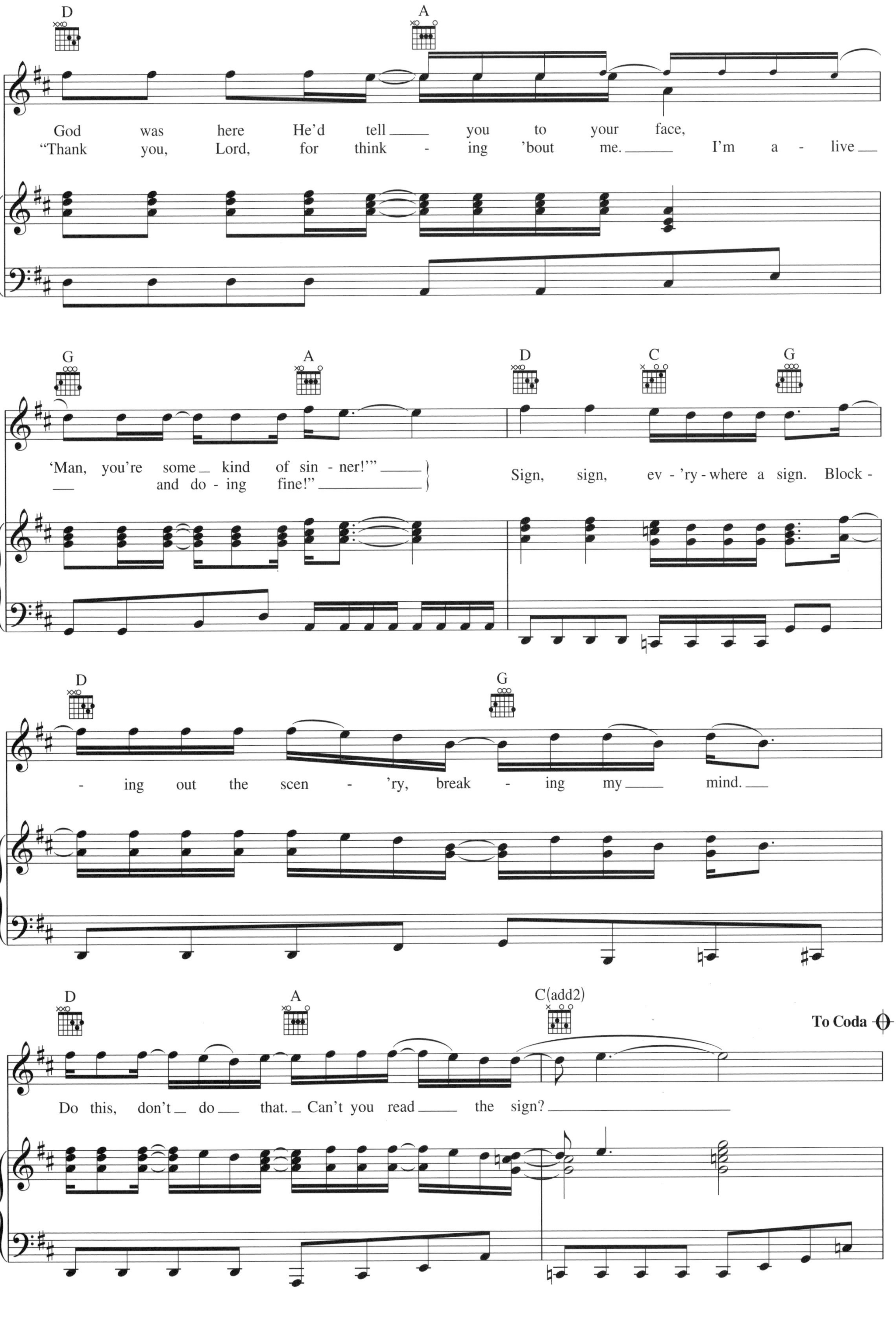
D
A
God was here He'd tell you to your face,
"Thank you, Lord, for think - ing 'bout me. I'm a - live
G
A
D
C
G
'Man, you're some kind of sin - ner!'"
and do - ing fine!"
Sign, sign, ev - 'ry - where a sign. Block -
D
G
- ing out the scen - 'ry, break - ing my mind.
D
A
C(add2)
To Coda
Do this, don't do that. Can't you read the sign?

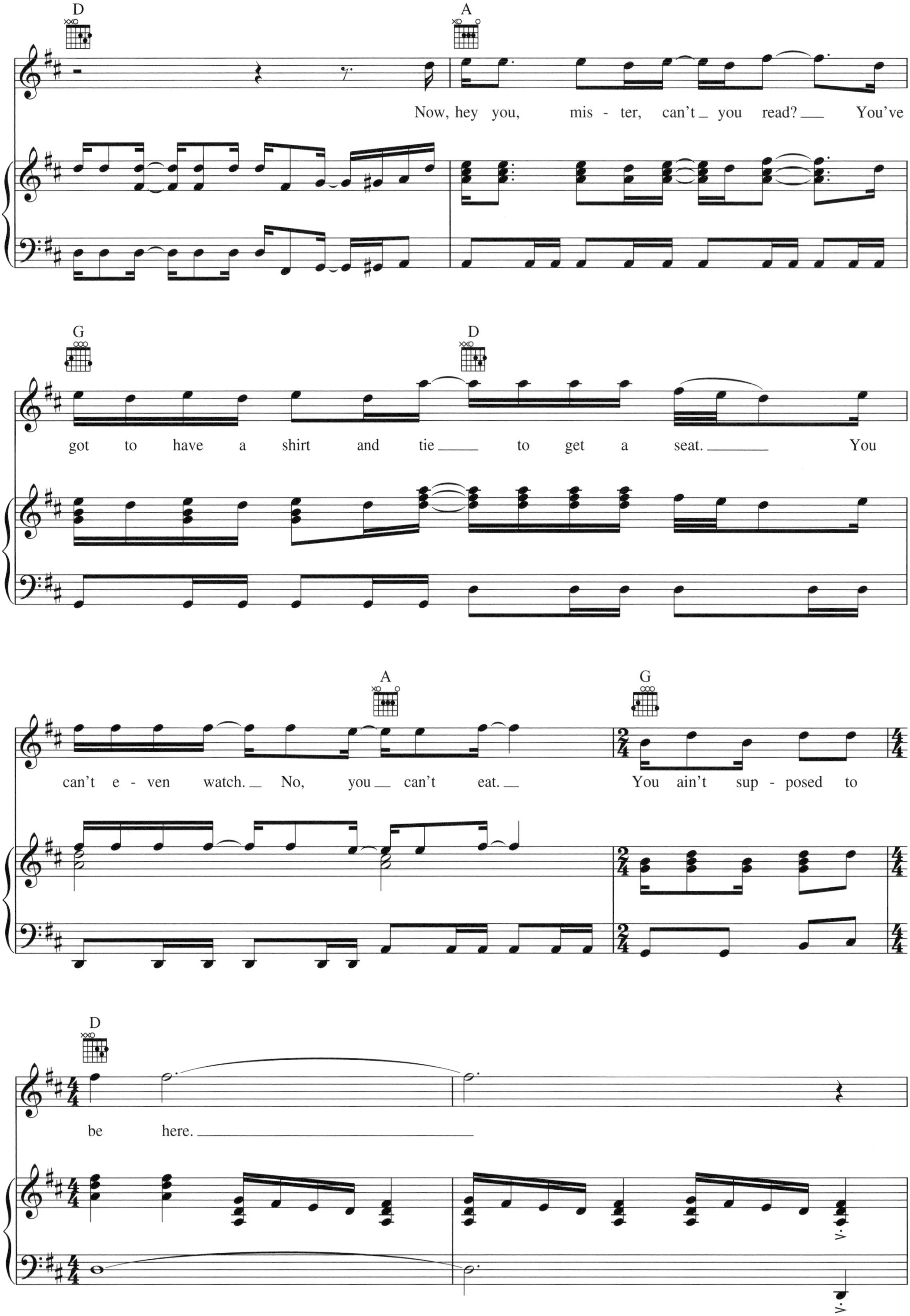
D
A
Now, hey you, mis - ter, can't _ you read? ___ You've
G
D
got to have a shirt and tie ___ to get a seat. ___ You
A
G
can't e - ven watch. _ No, you _ can't eat. _ You ain't sup - posed to
D
be here. ___

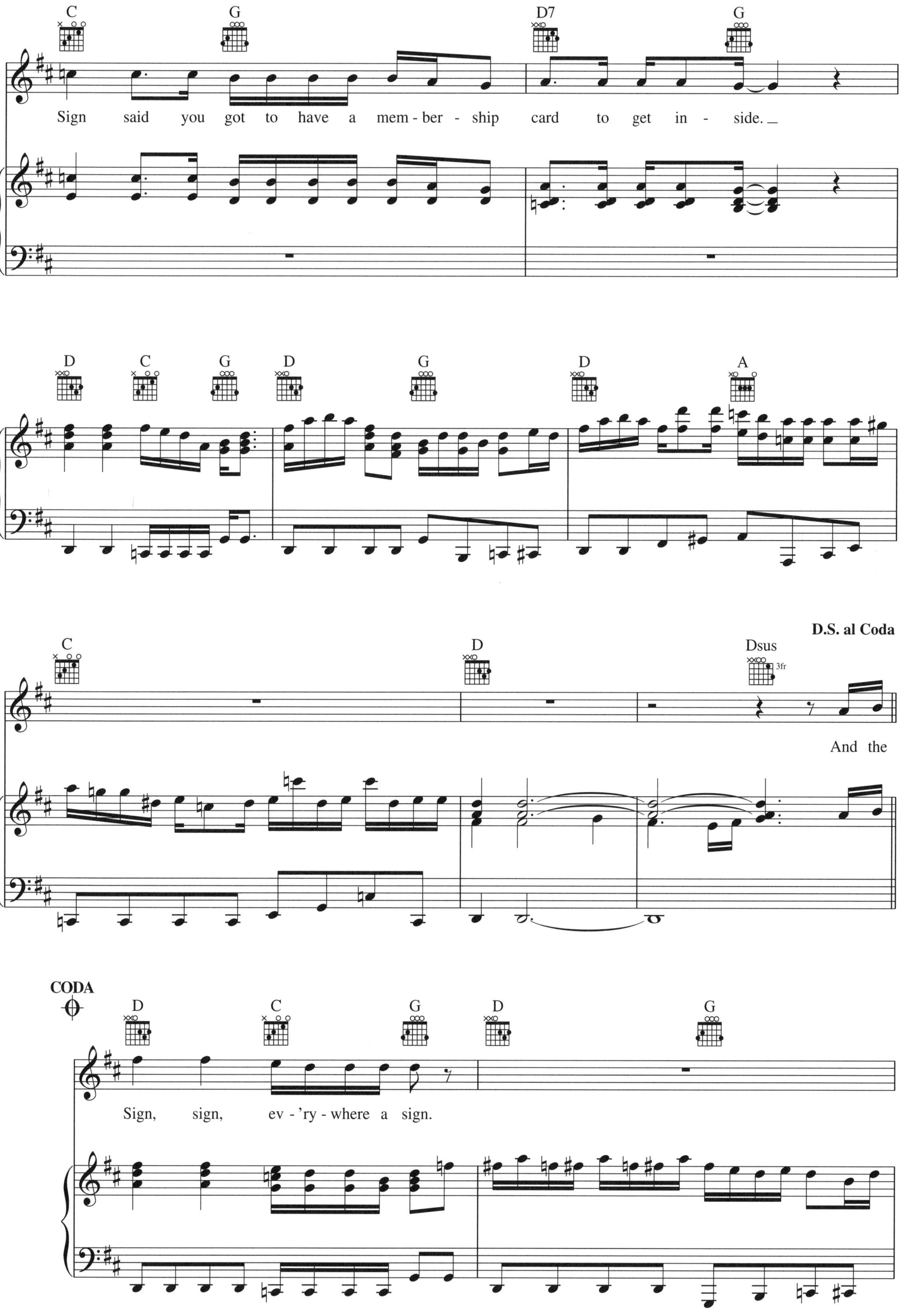
C G D7 G
Sign said you got to have a mem - ber - ship card to get in - side.
D C G D G D A
C D Dsus
3fr
D.S. al Coda
And the
CODA
D C G D G
Sign, sign, ev - 'ry - where a sign.

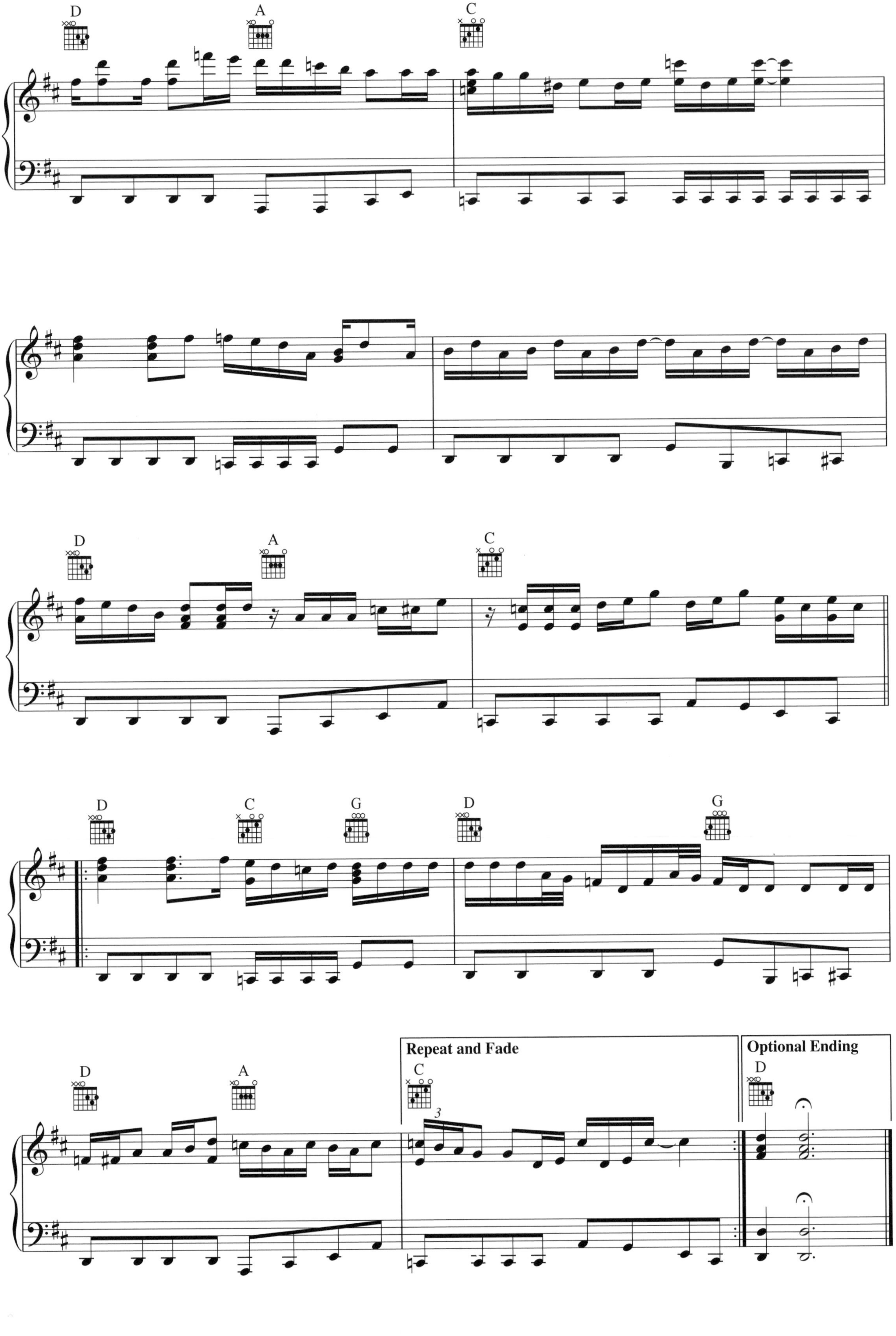
D
A
C
D
A
C
D
C
G
D
G
Repeat and Fade
Optional Ending
D
A
C
3
D

WAR

Words and Music by NORMAN WHITFIELD
and BARRETT STRONG

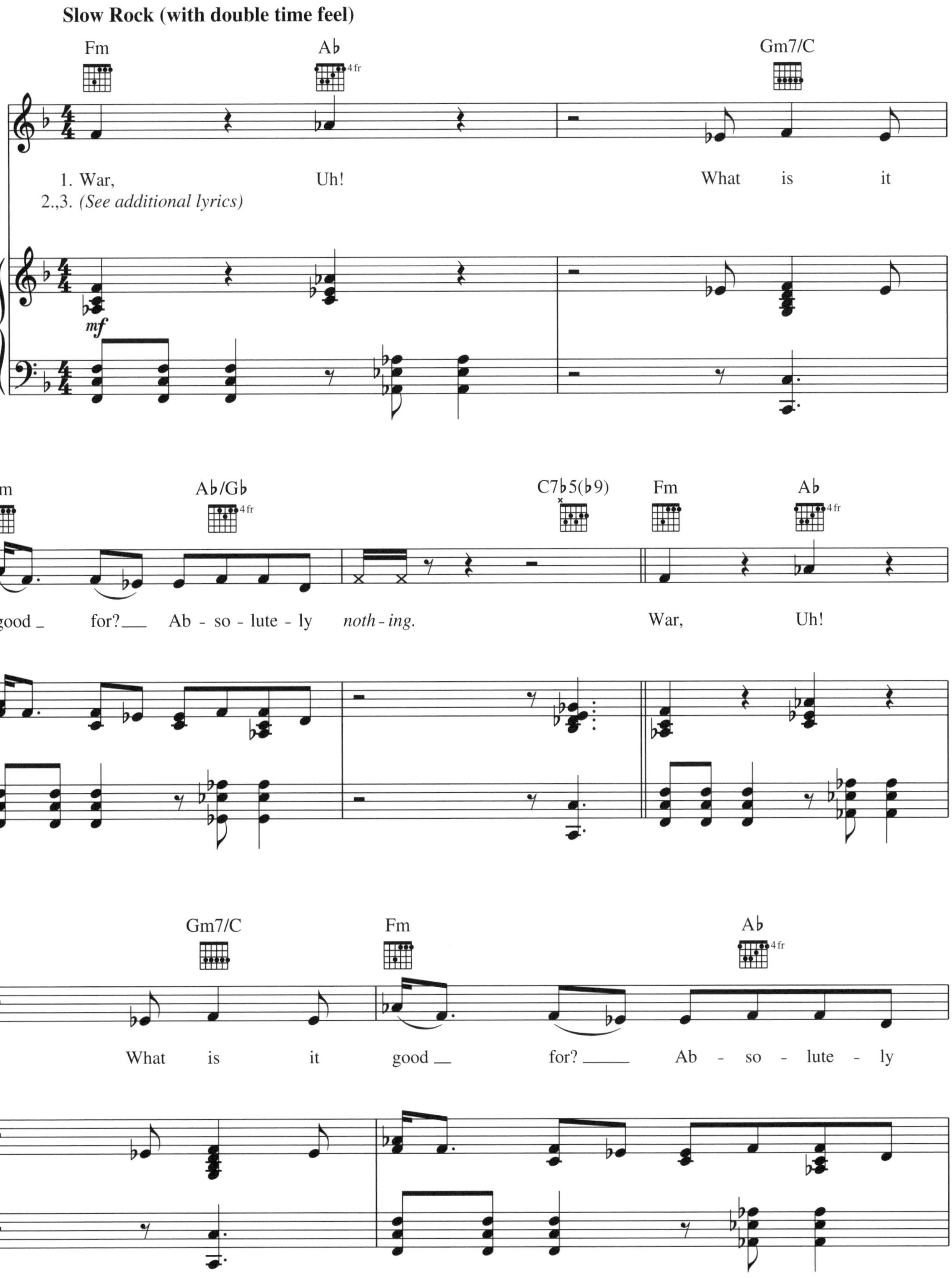

© 1970 (Renewed 1998) JOBETE MUSIC CO., INC.
All Rights Controlled and Administered by EMI BLACKWOOD MUSIC INC.
on behalf of STONE AGATE MUSIC (A Division of JOBETE MUSIC CO., INC.)
All Rights Reserved International Copyright Secured Used by Permission

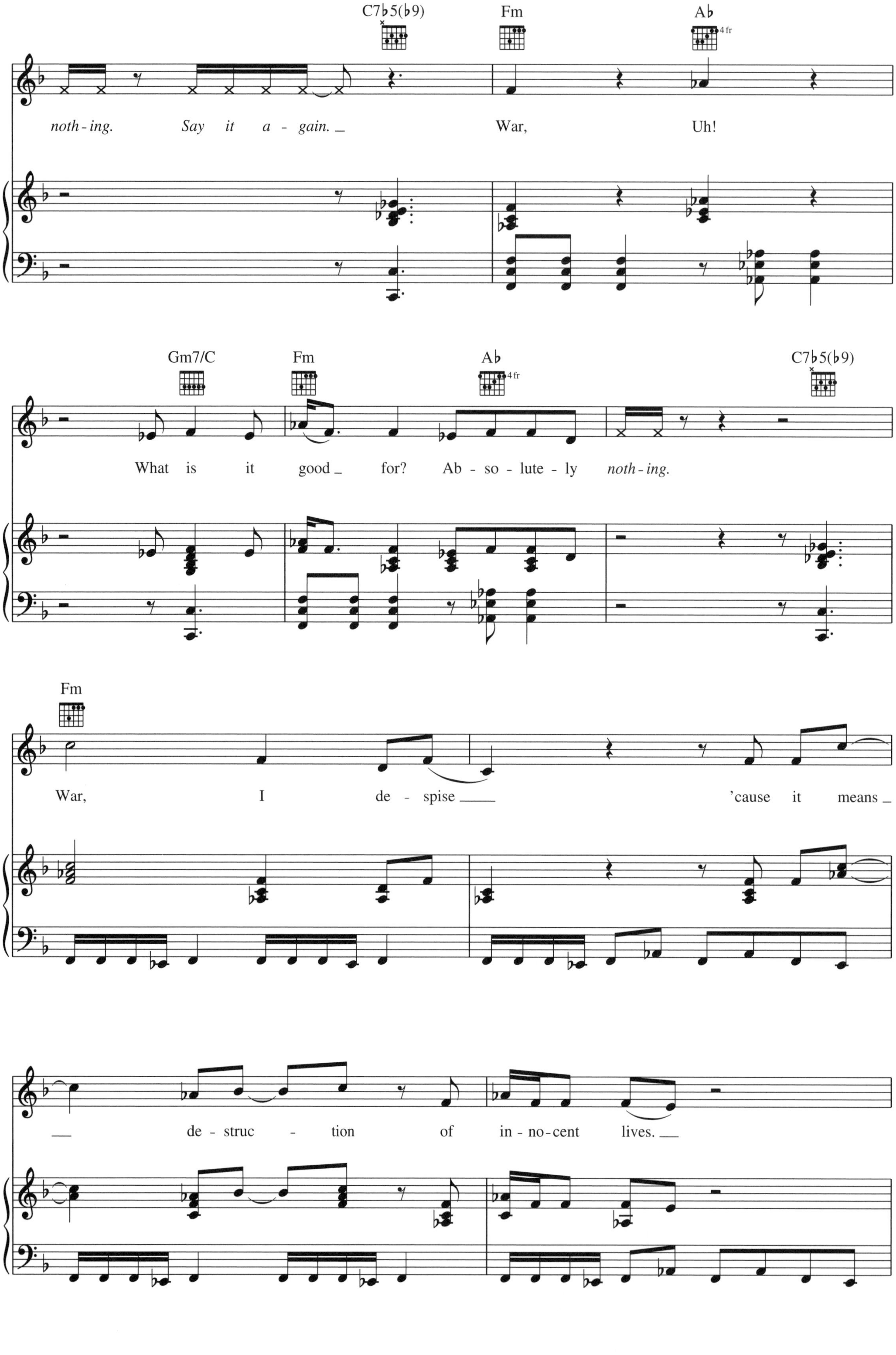
C7♭5(♭9)
Fm
A♭
4 fr
noth - ing. Say it a - gain. _ War, Uh!
Gm7/C
Fm
A♭
4 fr
C7♭5(♭9)
What is it good _ for? Ab - so - lute - ly noth - ing.
Fm
War, I de - spise ____ 'cause it means _
__ de - struc - tion of in - no - cent lives. __

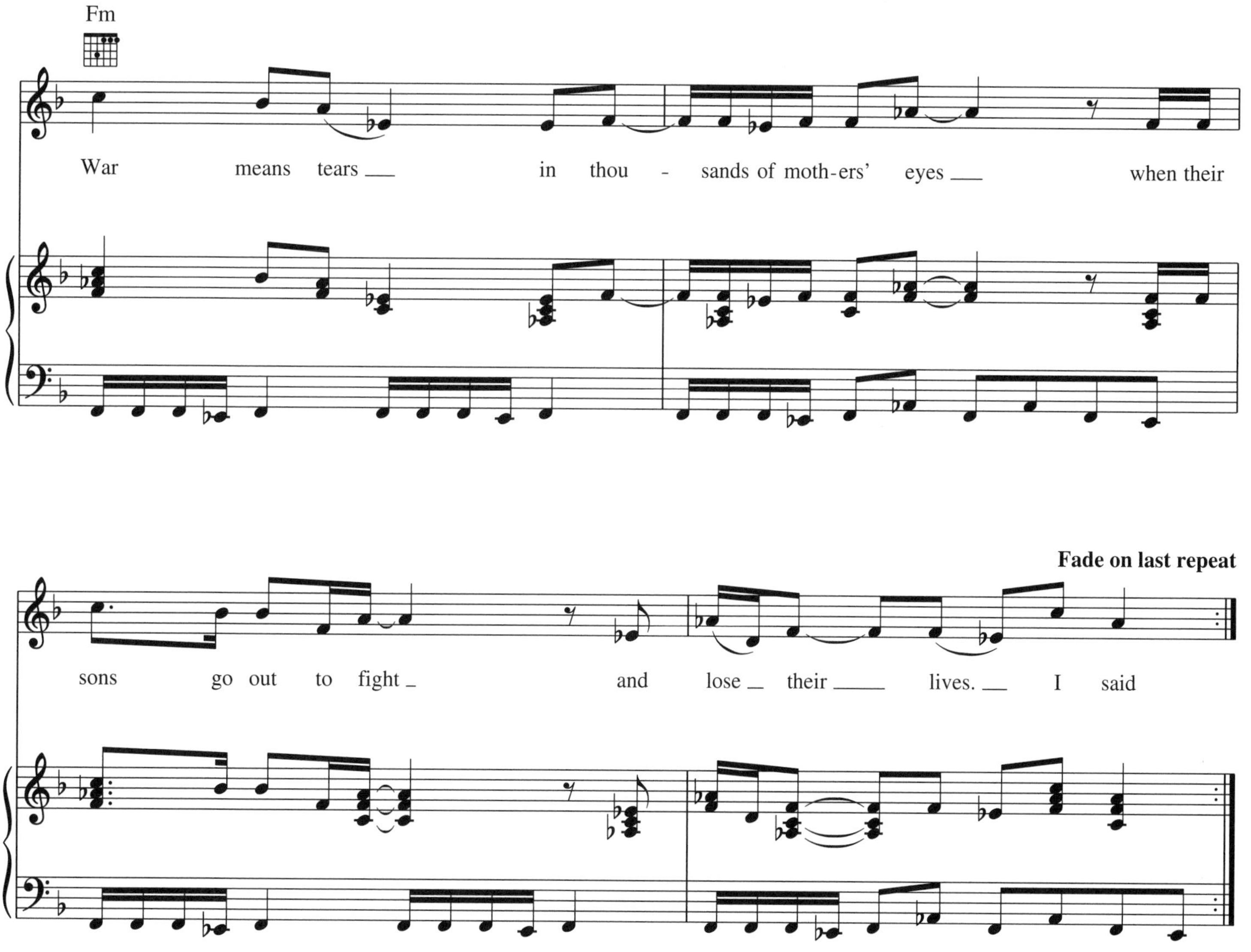

Additional Lyrics

2. War, uh! What is it good for? Absolutely nothing; say it again;
War, uh! What is it good for? Absolutely nothing.
War, it's nothing but a heartbreaker; War, friend only to the undertaker.
War is an enemy to all mankind. The thought of war blows my mind.
War has caused unrest within the younger generation;
Induction then destruction, who wants to die? Ah
War, uh um; What is it good for? You tell me nothing, um!
War, uh! What is it good for? Absolutely nothing.
Good God, war, it's nothing but a heartbreaker;
War, friend only to the undertaker;

3. Wars have shattered many a young man's dreams;
Made him disabled, bitter and mean.
Life is much too short and precious to spend fighting wars each day.
War can't give life, it can only take it away. Ah
War, Uh um! What is it good for? Absolutely nothing, um.
War, good God almighty, listen, what is it good for? Absolutely nothing, yeah.
War, it's nothing but a heartbreaker; War, friend only to the undertaker.
Peace, love and understanding, tell me is there no place for them today?
They say we must fight to keep our freedom, but Lord knows it's gotta be a better way.
I say war, uh um, yeah, yeah. What is it good for? Absolutely nothing; say it again;
War, yea, yea, yea, yea, what is it good for? Absolutely nothing; say it again;
War, nothing but a heartbreaker; What is it good for? Friend only to the undertaker.....
(Fade)

TURN! TURN! TURN!
(To Everything There Is a Season)

Words from the Book of Ecclesiastes
Adaptation and Music by PETE SEEGER

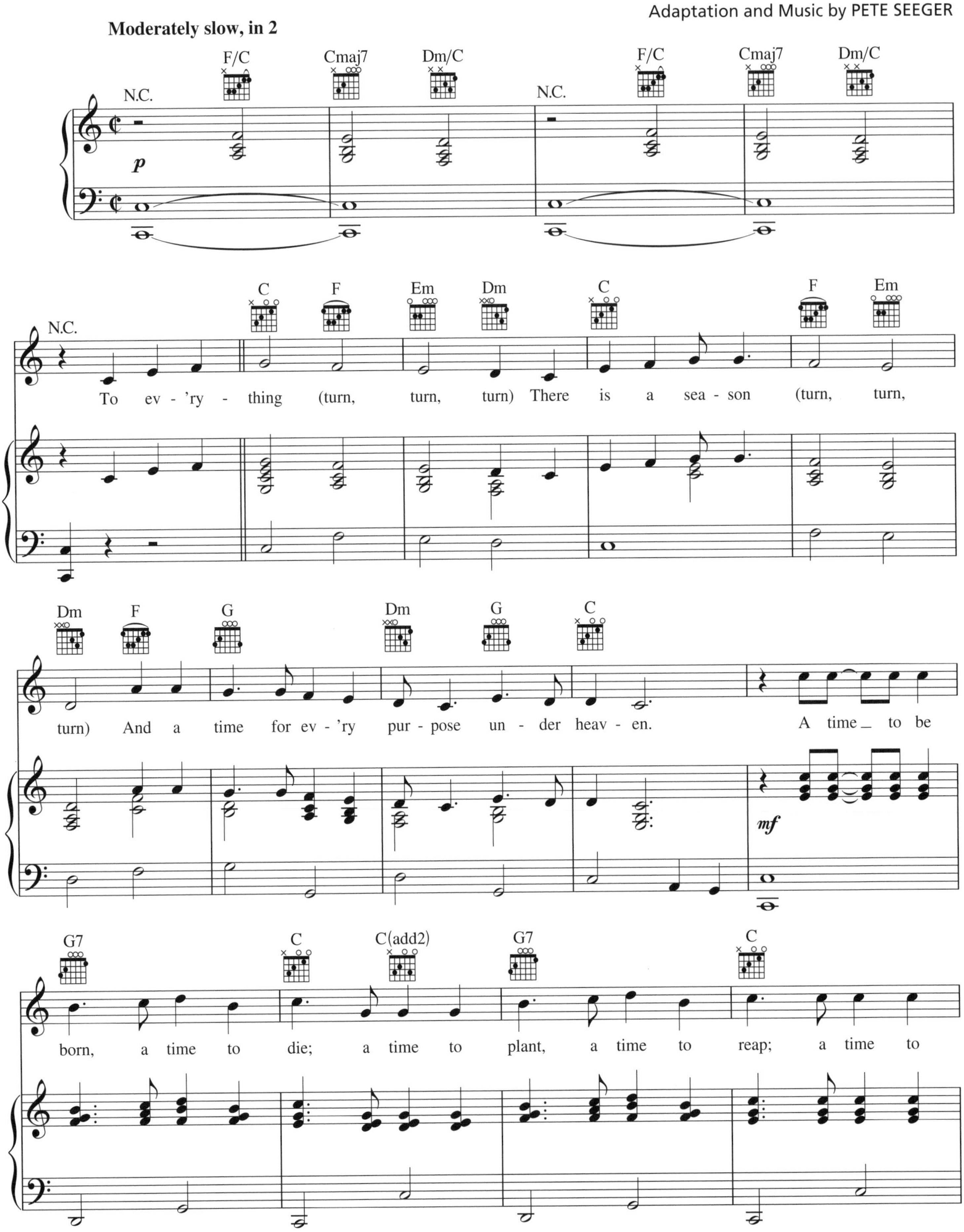

TRO - © Copyright 1962 (Renewed) Melody Trails, Inc., New York, NY
International Copyright Secured
All Rights Reserved Including Public Performance For Profit
Used by Permission

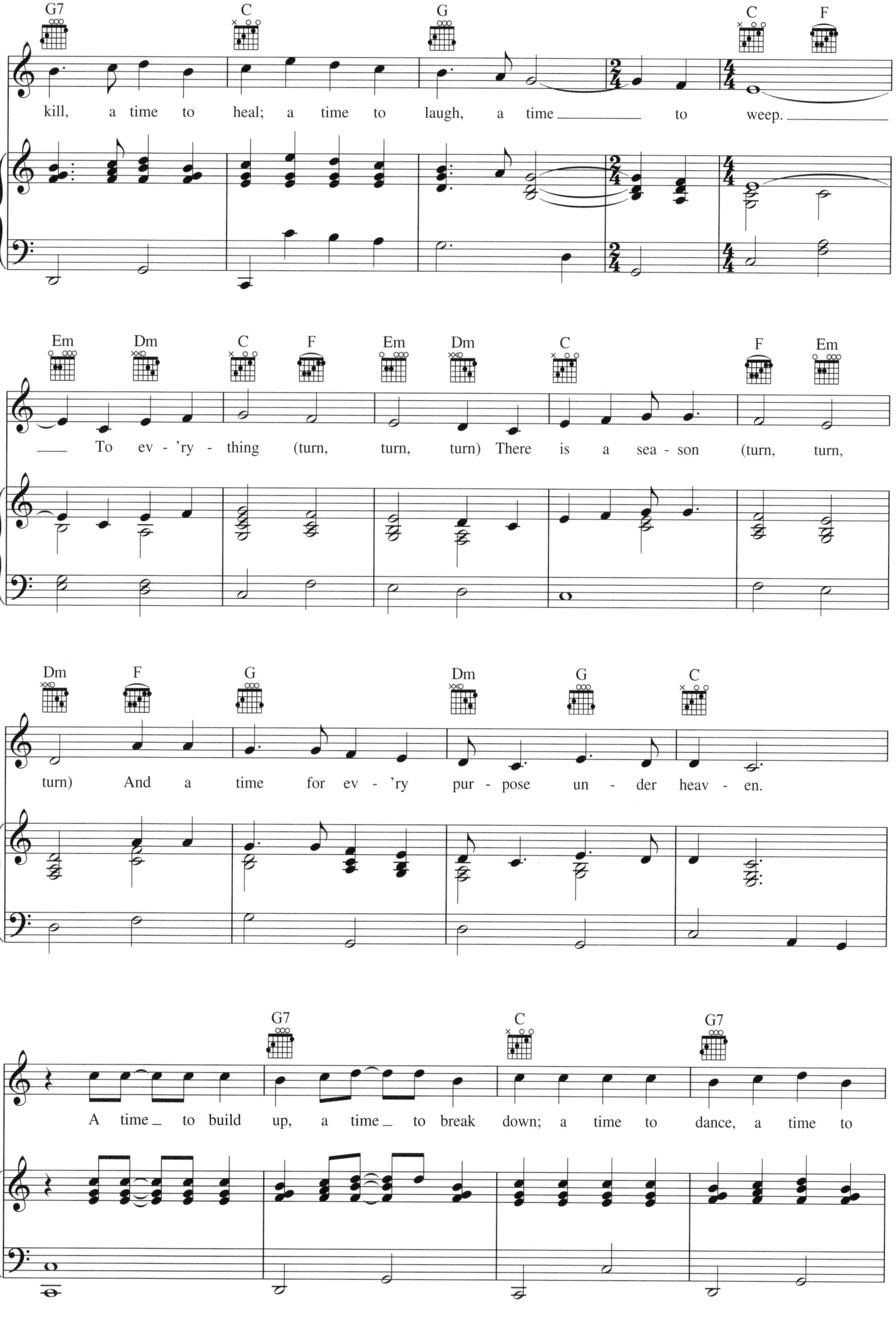
G7 C G C F
kill, a time to heal; a time to laugh, a time to weep.
Em Dm C F Em Dm C F Em
To ev - 'ry - thing (turn, turn, turn) There is a sea - son (turn, turn,
Dm F G Dm G C
turn) And a time for ev - 'ry pur - pose un - der heav - en.
G7 C G7
A time to build up, a time to break down; a time to dance, a time to

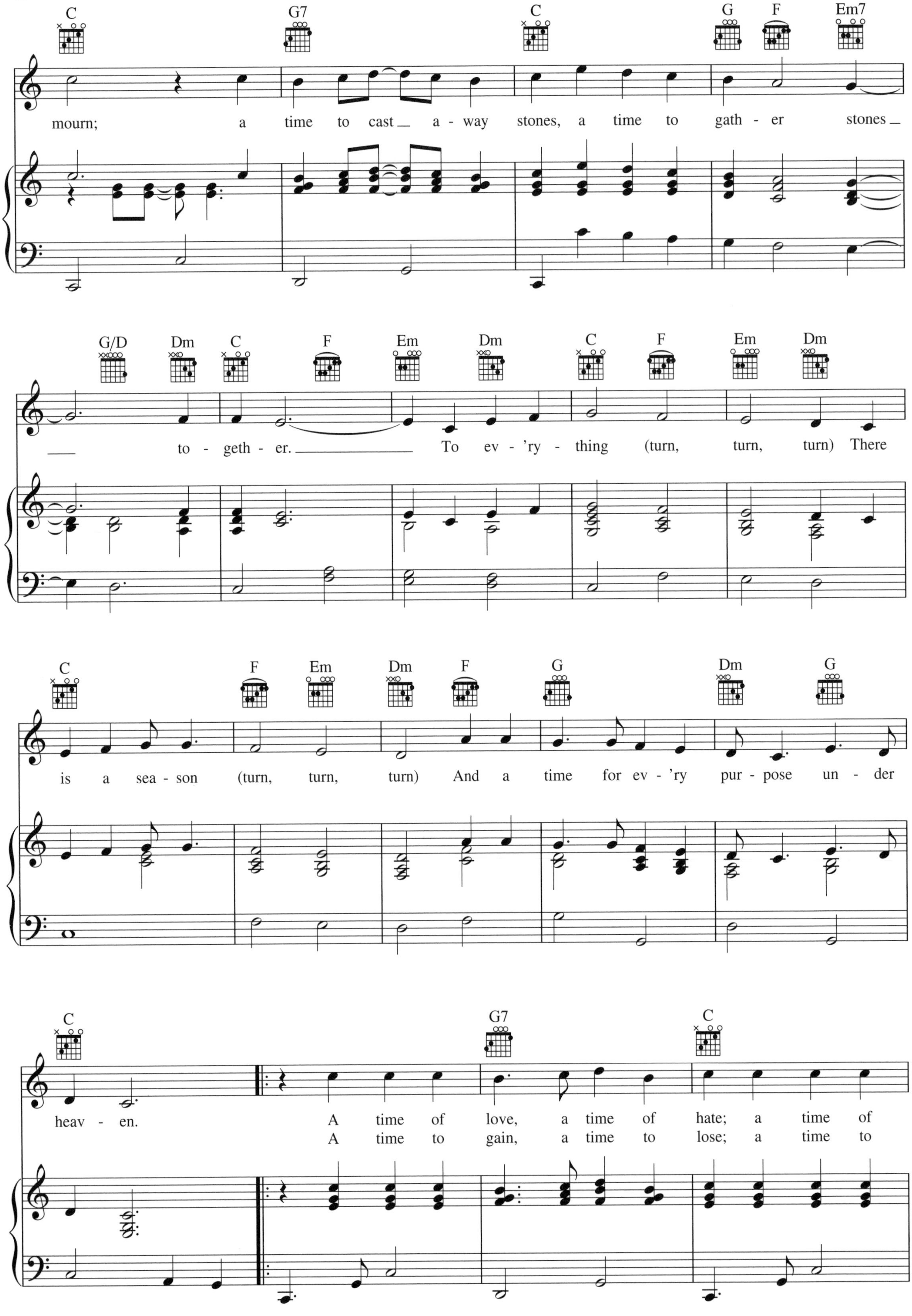
C G7 C G F Em7
mourn; a time to cast away stones, a time to gath - er stones
G/D Dm C F Em Dm C F Em Dm
to - geth - er. To ev - 'ry - thing (turn, turn, turn) There
C F Em Dm F G Dm G
is a sea - son (turn, turn, turn) And a time for ev - 'ry pur - pose un - der
C G7 C
heav - en. A time of love, a time of hate; a time of
A time to gain, a time to lose; a time to

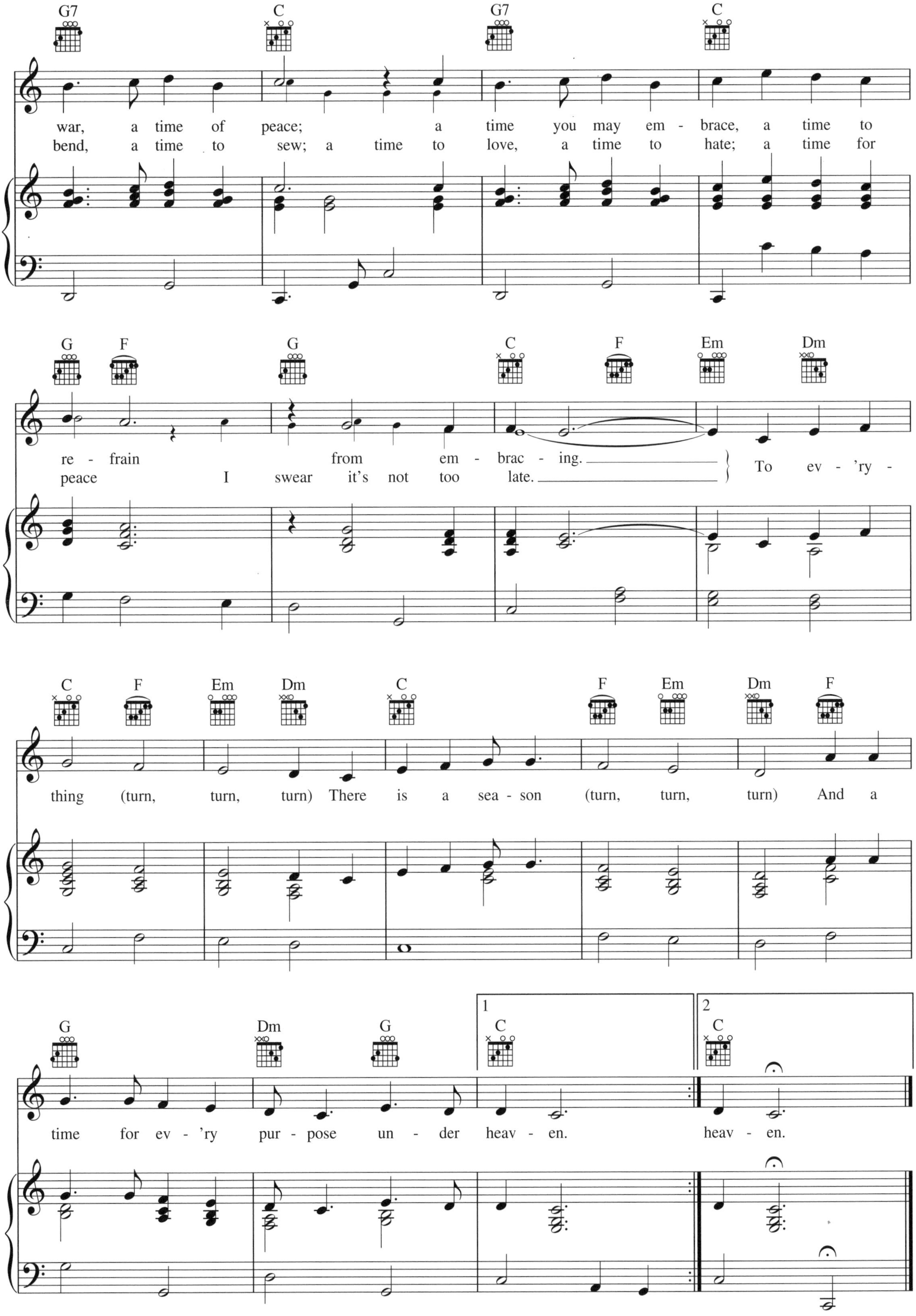
G7 C G7 C
war, a time of peace; a time you may em - brace, a time to
bend, a time to sew; a time to love, a time to hate; a time for
G F G C F Em Dm
re - frain from em - brac - ing.
peace I swear it's not too late.
To ev - 'ry -
C F Em Dm C F Em Dm F
thing (turn, turn, turn) There is a sea - son (turn, turn, turn) And a
G Dm G
1 C
2 C
time for ev - 'ry pur - pose un - der heav - en.
heav - en.

THE UNIVERSAL SOLDIER

Words and Music by
BUFFY SAINT-MARIE

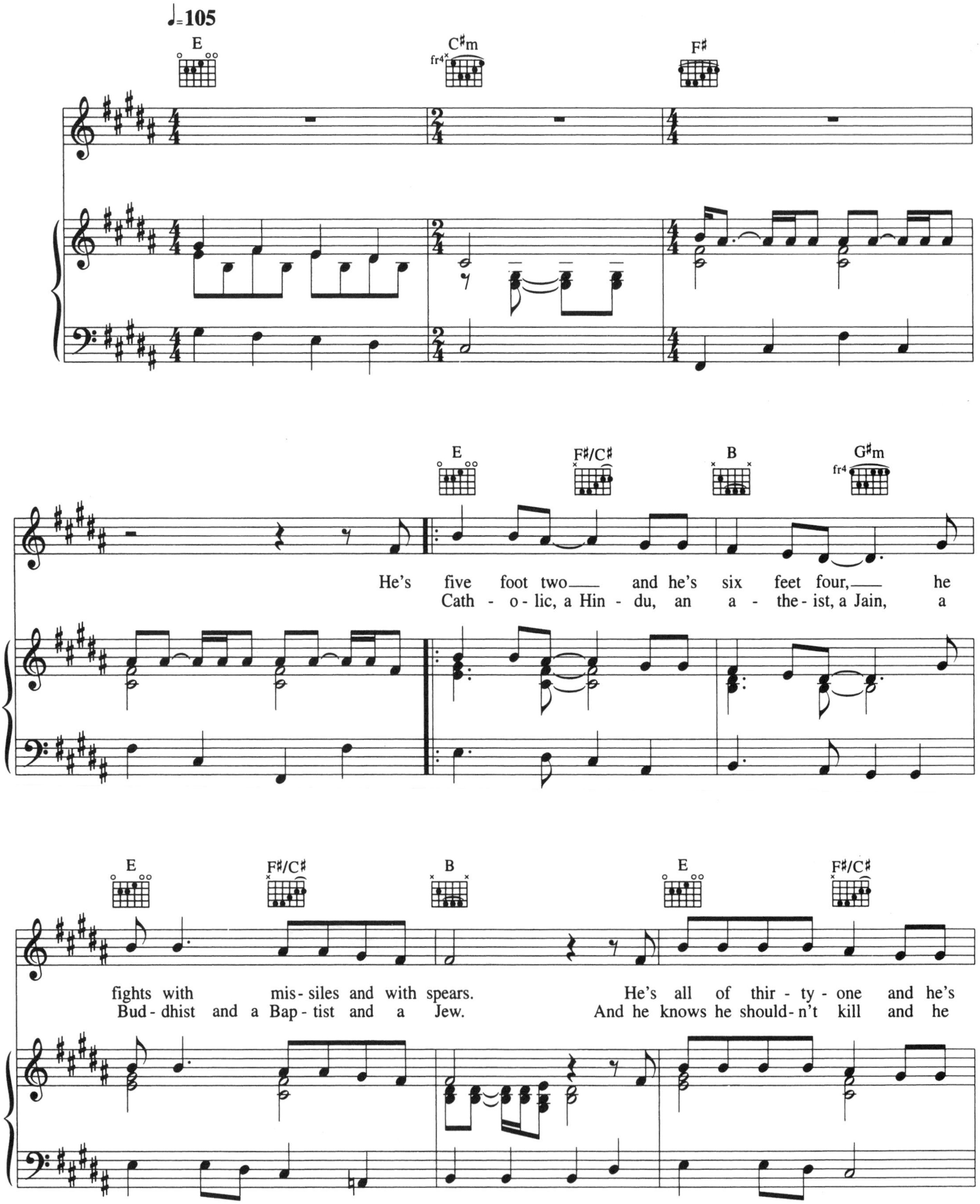
♩=105
E
C♯m
fr4
F♯
E
F♯/C♯
B
G♯m
fr4
He's five foot two and he's six feet four, he
Cath - o - lic, a Hin - du, an a - the - ist, a Jain, a
E
F♯/C♯
B
E
F♯/C♯
fights with mis - siles and with spears. He's all of thir - ty - one and he's
Bud - dhist and a Bap - tist and a Jew. And he knows he should - n't kill and he

Copyright © 1963 CALEB MUSIC
Copyright Renewed
All Rights in the U.S. and Canada Controlled and Administered by ALMO MUSIC CORP.
All Rights Reserved Used by Permission

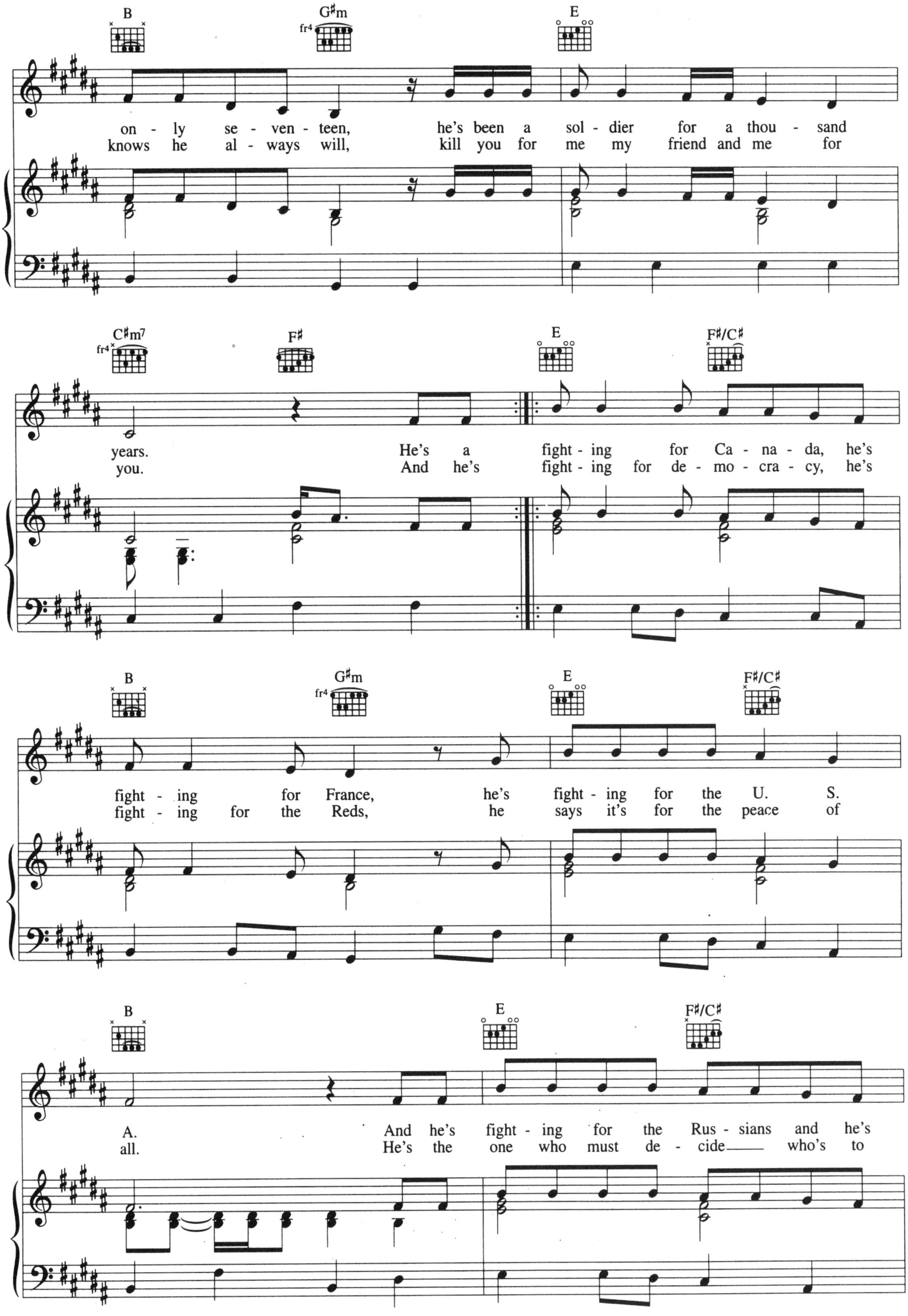
B
G♯m
fr4
E
on - ly se - ven - teen, he's been a sol - dier for a thou - sand
knows he al - ways will, kill you for me my friend and me for
C♯m7
fr4
F♯
E
F♯/C♯
years. He's a fight - ing for Ca - na - da, he's
you. And he's fight - ing for de - mo - cra - cy, he's
B
G♯m
fr4
E
F♯/C♯
fight - ing for France, he's fight - ing for the U. S.
fight - ing for the Reds, he says it's for the peace of
B
E
F♯/C♯
A. And he's fight - ing for the Rus - sians and he's
all. He's the one who must de - cide who's to

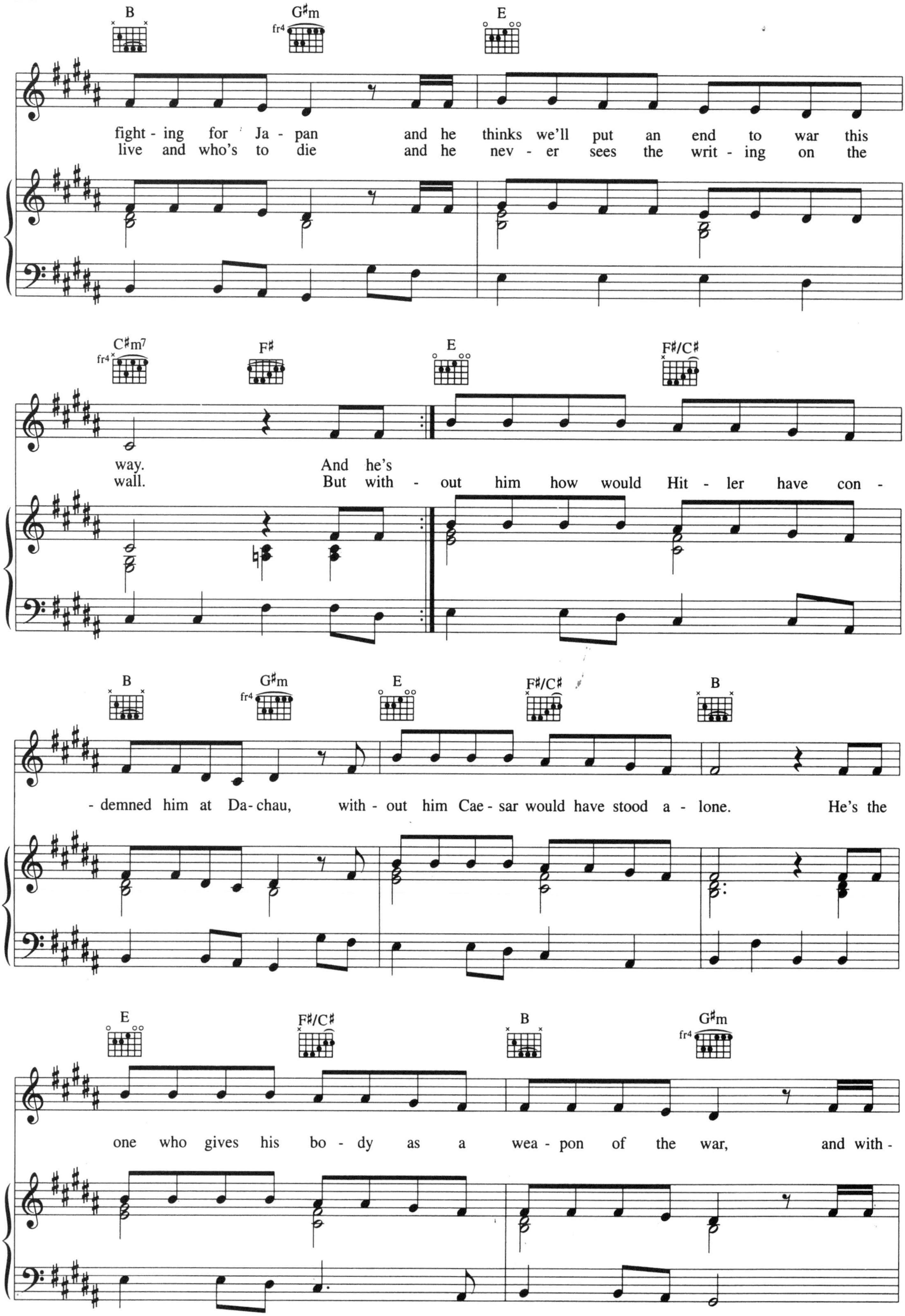
B
G♯m
E
fight - ing for Ja - pan and he thinks we'll put an end to war this
live and who's to die and he nev - er sees the writ - ing on the
C♯m7
F♯
E
F♯/C♯
way. And he's
wall. But with - out him how would Hit - ler have con -
B
G♯m
E
F♯/C♯
B
- demned him at Da - chau, with - out him Cae - sar would have stood a - lone. He's the
E
F♯/C♯
B
G♯m
one who gives his bo - dy as a wea - pon of the war, and with -
fr4

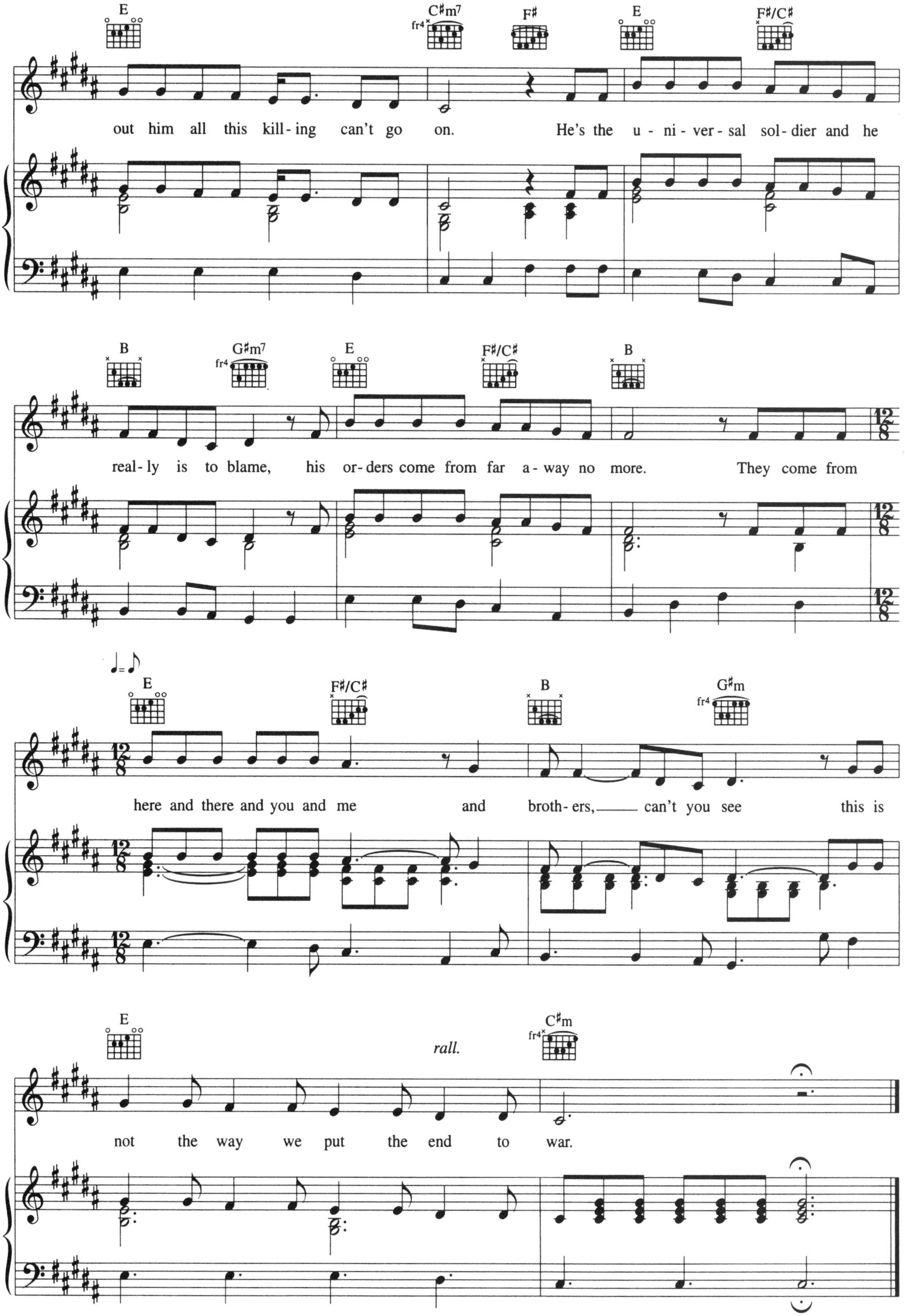
E C♯m7 F♯ E F♯/C♯
out him all this kill-ing can't go on. He's the u-ni-ver-sal sol-dier and he
B G♯m7 E F♯/C♯ B
real-ly is to blame, his or-ders come from far a-way no more. They come from
E F♯/C♯ B G♯m
here and there and you and me and broth-ers, can't you see this is
E C♯m
rall.
not the way we put the end to war.

WE ARE THE WORLD

Words and Music by LIONEL RICHIE
and MICHAEL JACKSON

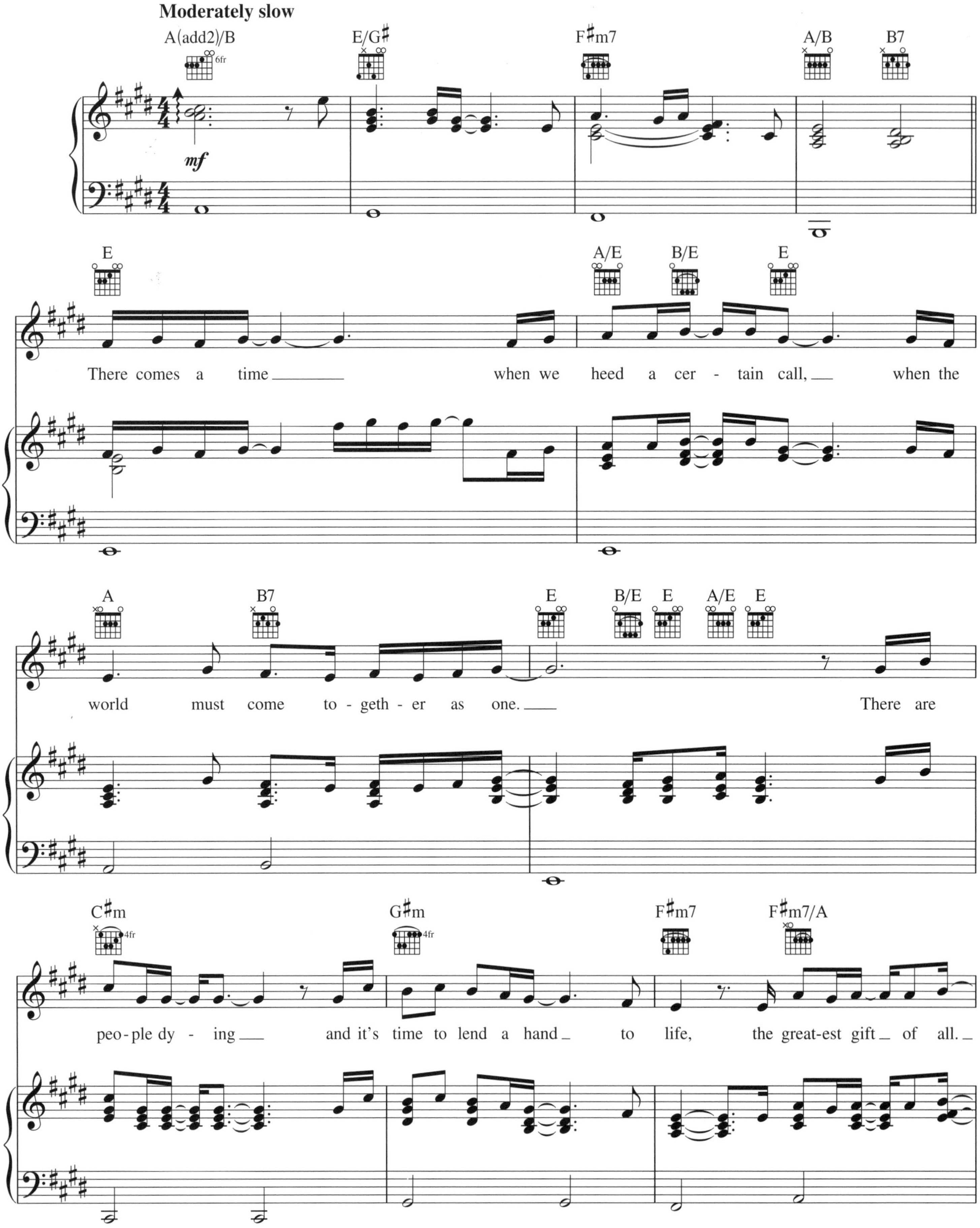

Copyright © 1985 by Brockman Music, Brenda Richie Publishing, Warner-Tamerlane Publishing Corp. and Mijac Music
All Rights Reserved Used by Permission

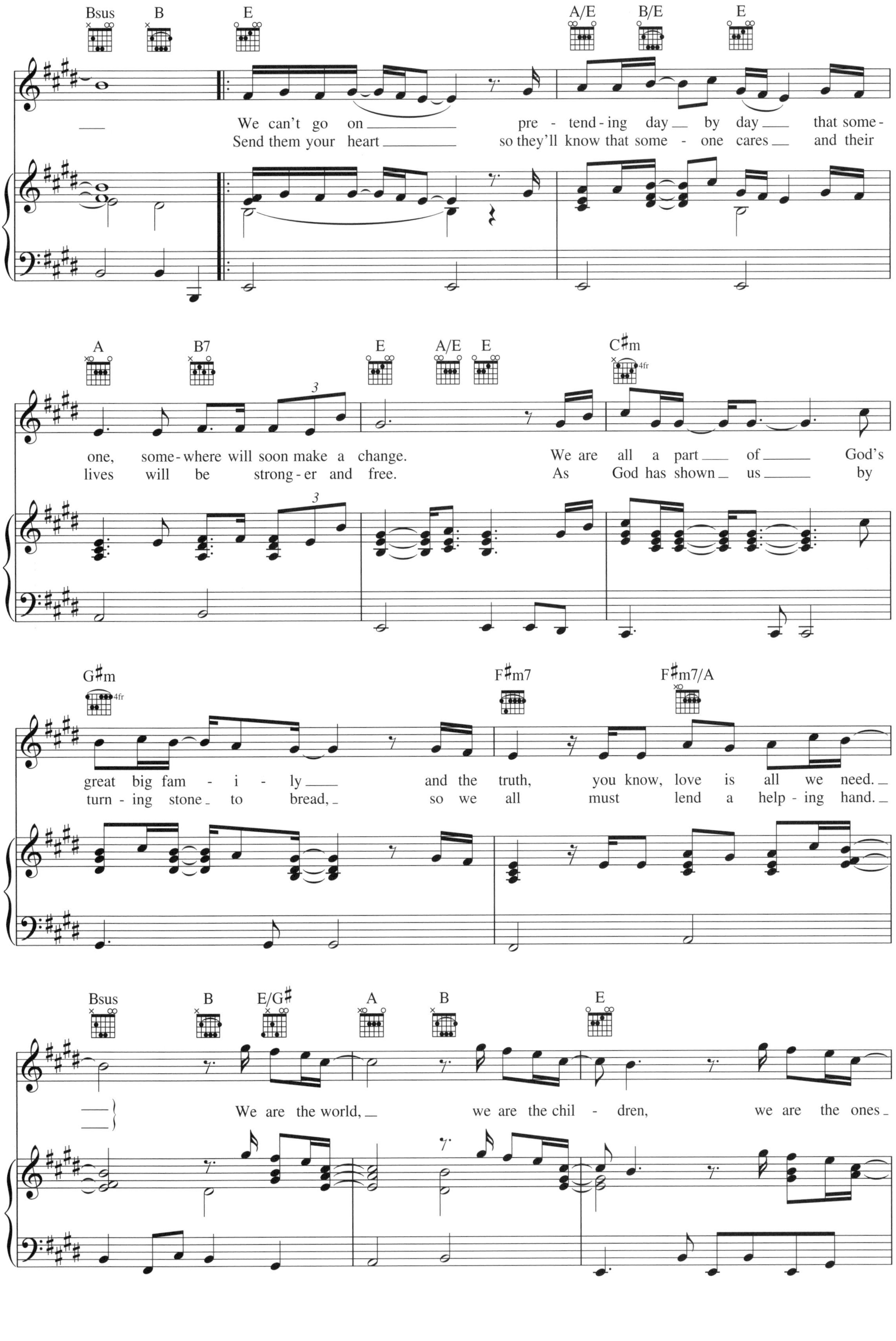
Bsus B E A/E B/E E
We can't go on pre - tend - ing day by day that some -
Send them your heart so they'll know that some - one cares and their
A B7 E A/E E C♯m
one, some - where will soon make a change. We are all a part of God's
lives will be strong - er and free. As God has shown us by
3
G♯m F♯m7 F♯m7/A
great big fam - i - ly and the truth, you know, love is all we need.
turn - ing stone to bread, so we all must lend a help - ing hand.
Bsus B E/G♯ A B E
We are the world, we are the chil - dren, we are the ones
4fr

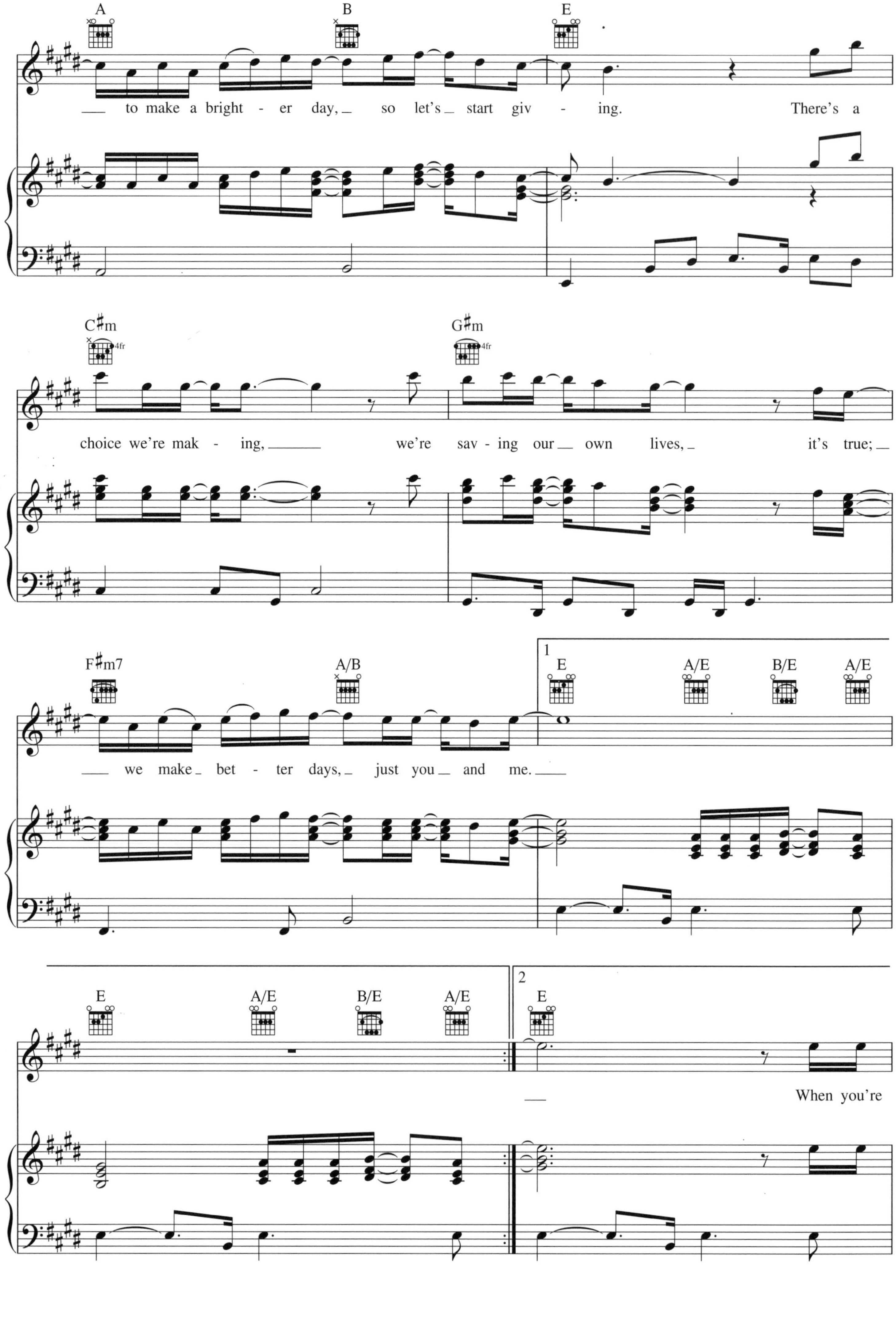
A
B
E
to make a bright - er day, so let's start giv - ing. There's a
C♯m
G♯m
4fr
choice we're mak - ing, we're sav - ing our own lives, it's true;
F♯m7
A/B
1
E
A/E
B/E
A/E
we make bet - ter days, just you and me.
E
A/E
B/E
A/E
2
E
When you're

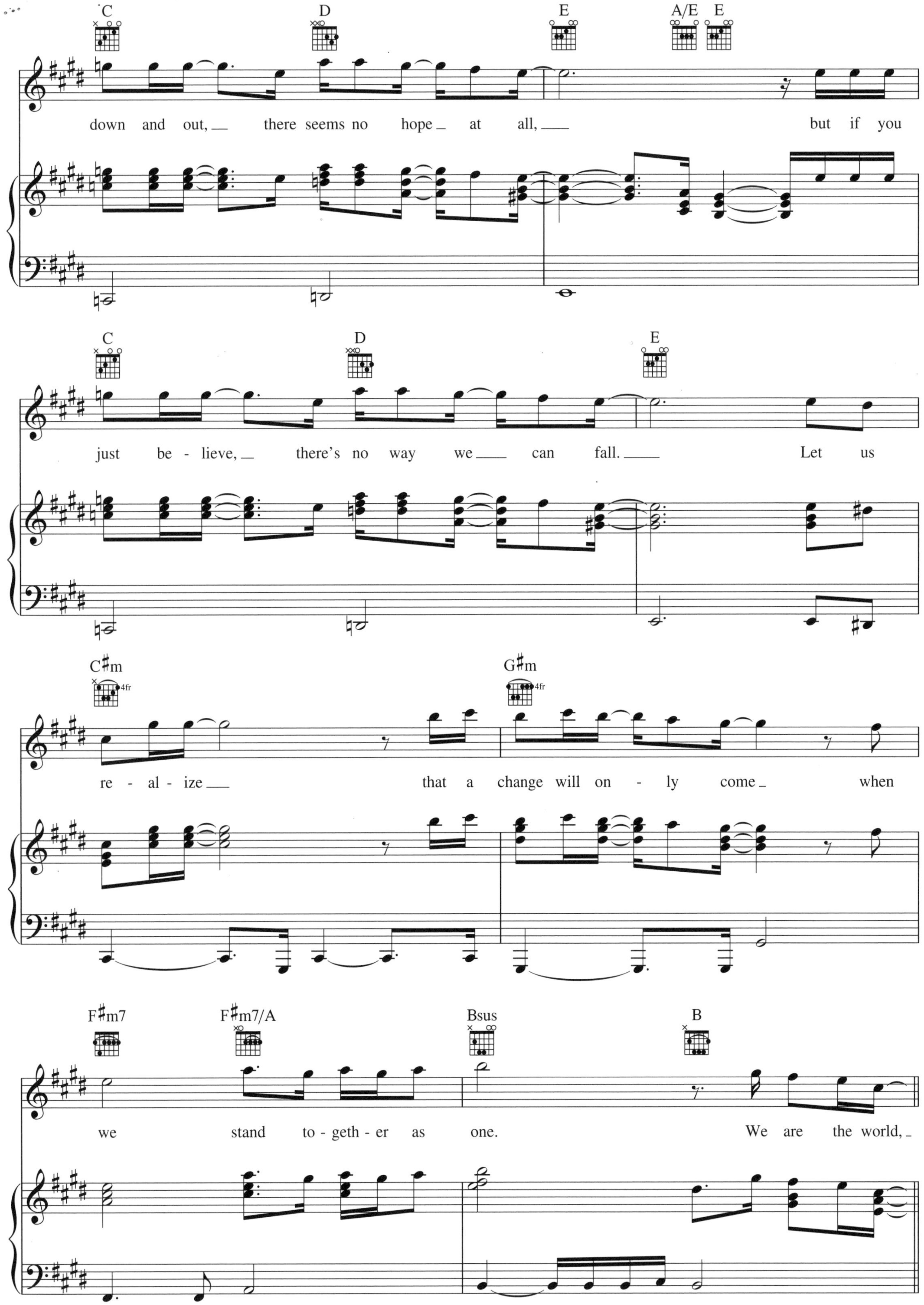
C D E A/E E
down and out, there seems no hope at all, but if you
C D E
just be - lieve, there's no way we can fall. Let us
C♯m G♯m
re - al - ize that a change will on - ly come when
F♯m7 F♯m7/A Bsus B
we stand to - geth - er as one. We are the world,

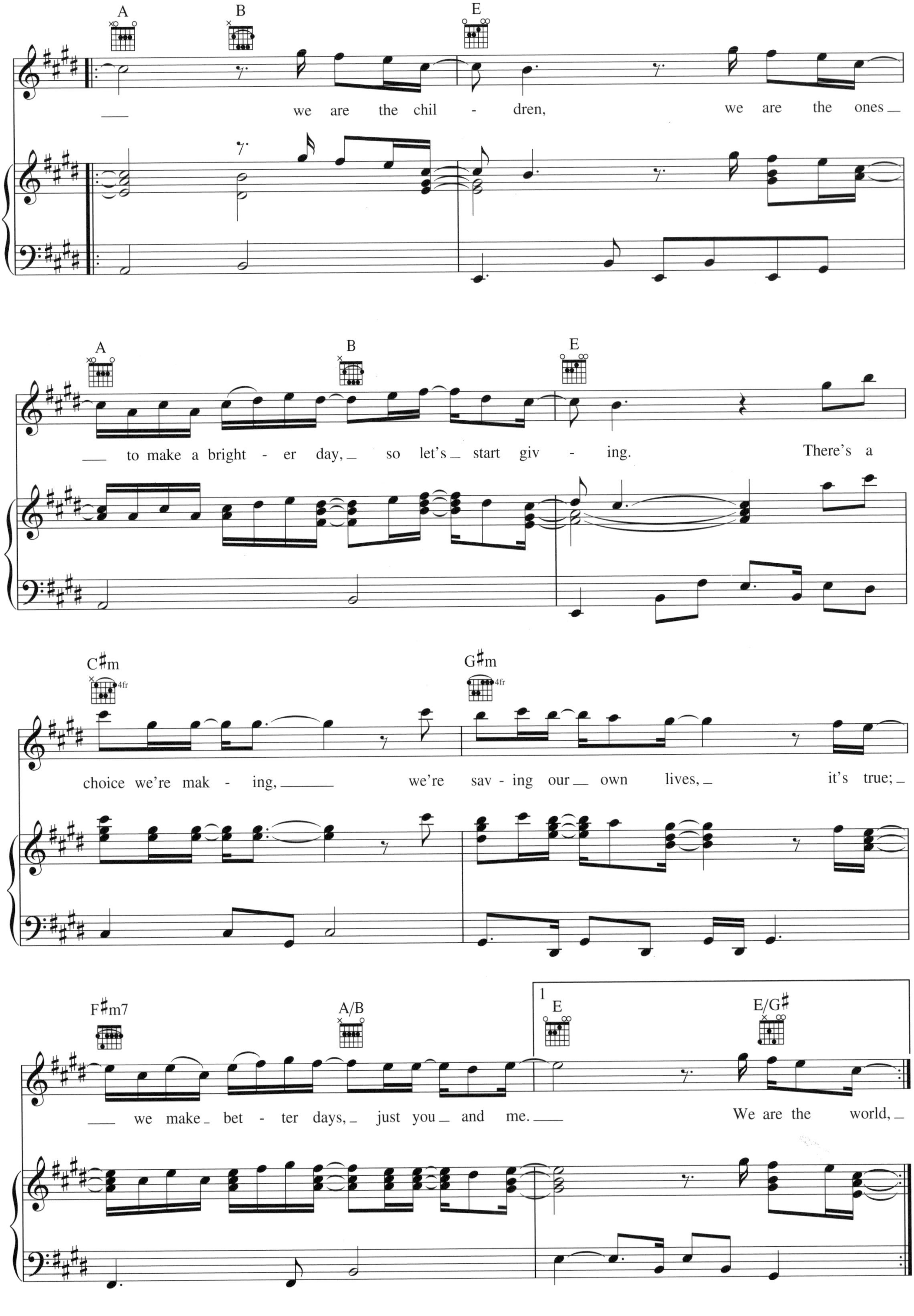
A
B
E
we are the chil - dren, we are the ones
A
B
E
to make a bright - er day, so let's start giv - ing. There's a
C♯m
4fr
G♯m
4fr
choice we're mak - ing, we're sav - ing our own lives, it's true;
F♯m7
A/B
1
E
E/G♯
we make bet - ter days, just you and me. We are the world,

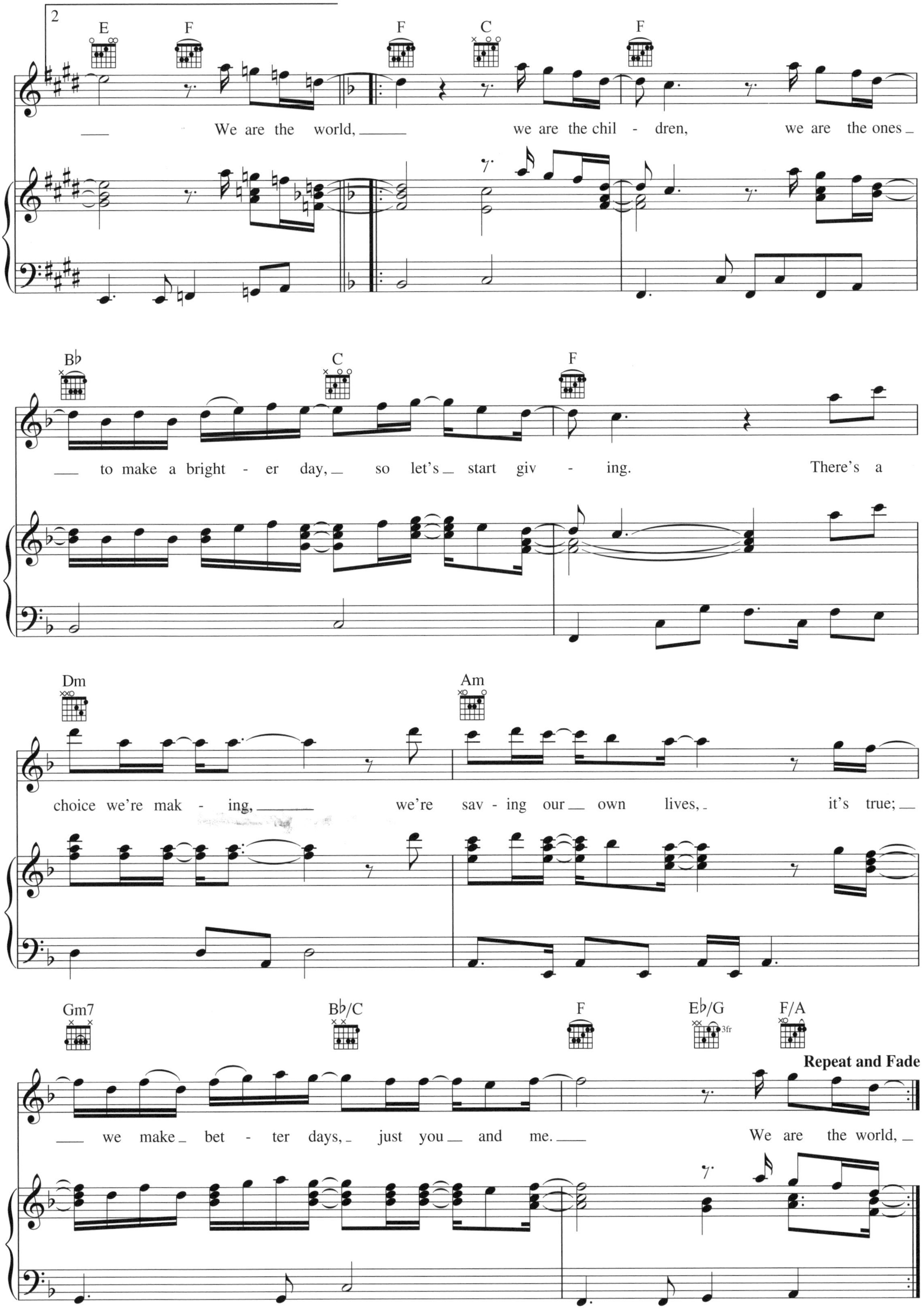
2
E F F C F
We are the world, we are the chil - dren, we are the ones
B♭ C F
to make a bright - er day, so let's start giv - ing. There's a
Dm Am
choice we're mak - ing, we're sav - ing our own lives, it's true;
Gm7 B♭/C F E♭/G F/A
3fr
Repeat and Fade
we make bet - ter days, just you and me. We are the world,

WE SHALL OVERCOME

Musical and Lyrical Adaptation by ZILPHIA HORTON,
FRANK HAMILTON, GUY CARAWAN and PETE SEEGER
Inspired by African American Gospel Singing, members of the Food and Tobacco
Workers Union, Charleston, SC, and the southern Civil Rights Movement

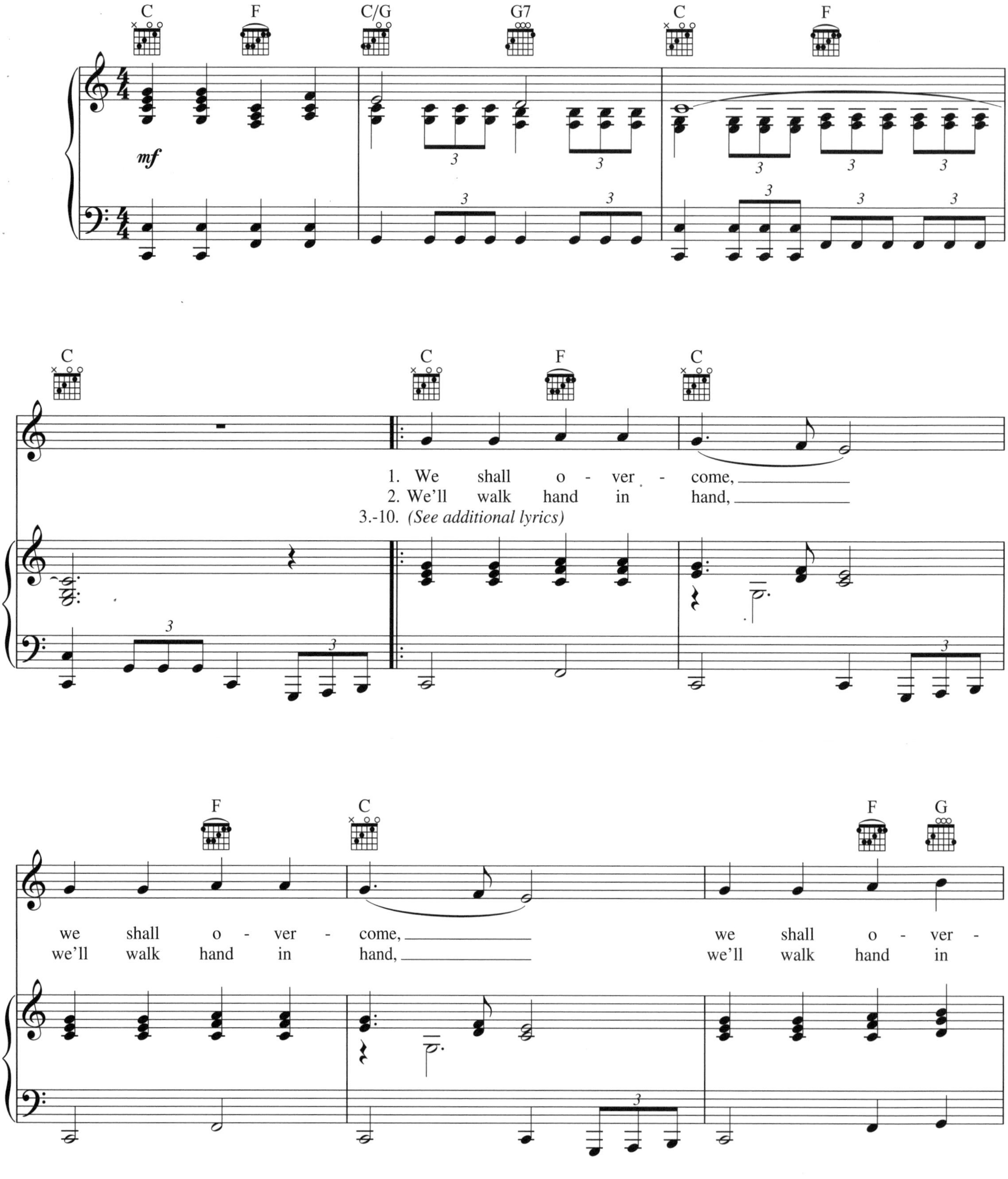
Moderately slow, with determination
C
F
C/G
G7
C
F
mf
C
C
F
C
1. We shall o - ver - come,
2. We'll walk hand in hand,
3.-10. (See additional lyrics)
F
C
F
G
we shall o - ver - come,
we'll walk hand in hand,
we shall o - ver -
we'll walk hand in

TRO - © Copyright 1960 (Renewed) and 1963 (Renewed) Ludlow Music, Inc., New York, NY
International Copyright Secured
All Rights Reserved Including Public Performance For Profit
Used by Permission
Royalties derived from this composition are being contributed to the We Shall Overcome Fund and The Freedom Movement under the Trusteeship of the writers.

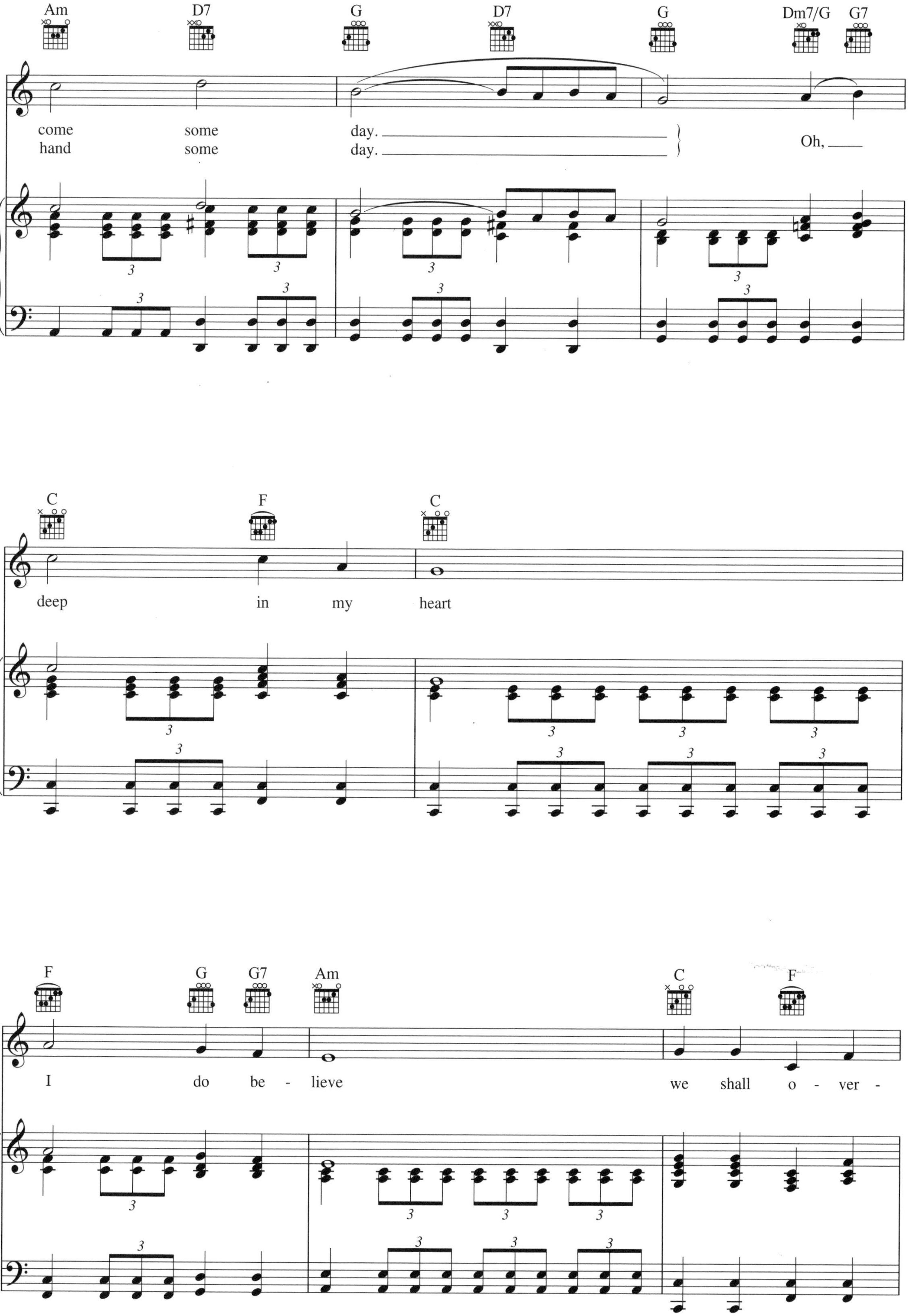
Am D7 G D7 G Dm7/G G7
come some day.
hand some day.
Oh,
C F C
deep in my heart
F G G7 Am C F
I do be - lieve we shall o - ver -
3

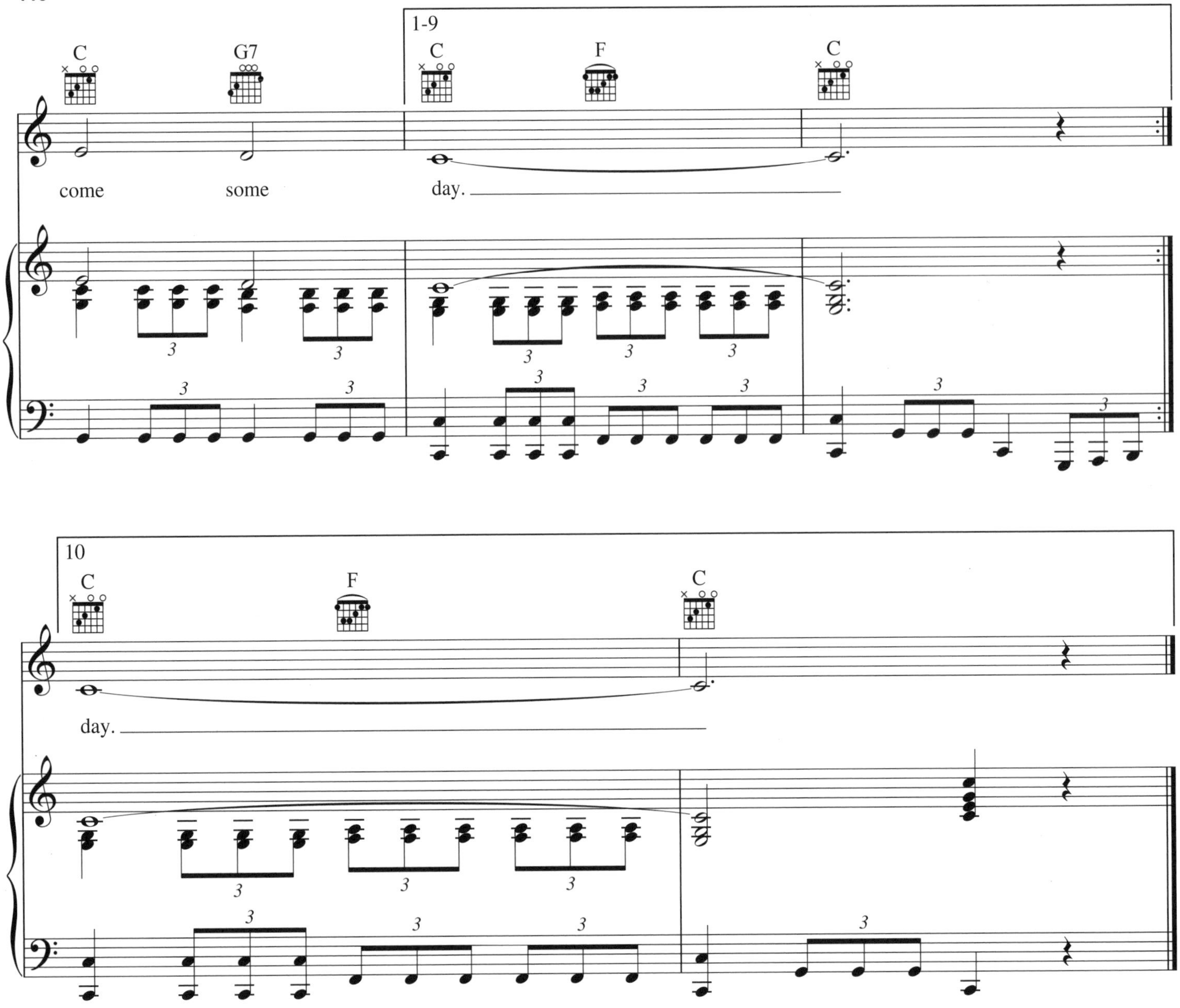

Additional Lyrics

3. We are not afraid, we are not afraid,
We are not afraid today.
Oh, deep in my heart I do believe
We shall overcome some day.

4. We shall stand together, we shall stand together,
We shall stand together now.
Oh, deep in my heart I do believe
We shall overcome some day.

5. The truth will make us free, the truth will make us free,
The truth will make us free some day.
Oh, deep in my heart I do believe
We shall overcome some day.

6. The Lord will see us through, the Lord will see us through,
The Lord will see us through some day.
Oh, deep in my heart I do believe
We shall overcome some day.

7. We shall be like Him, we shall be like Him,
We shall be like Him some day.
Oh, deep in my heart I do believe
We shall overcome some day.

8. We shall live in peace, we shall live in peace,
We shall live in peace someday.
Oh, deep in my heart I do believe
We shall overcome some day.

9. The whole wide world around, the whole wide world around,
The whole wide world around some day.
Oh, deep in my heart I do believe
We shall overcome some day.

10. We shall overcome, we shall overcome,
We shall overcome some day.
Oh, deep in my heart I do believe
We shall overcome some day.

WHAT THE WORLD NEEDS NOW IS LOVE

Lyric by HAL DAVID
Music by BURT BACHARACH

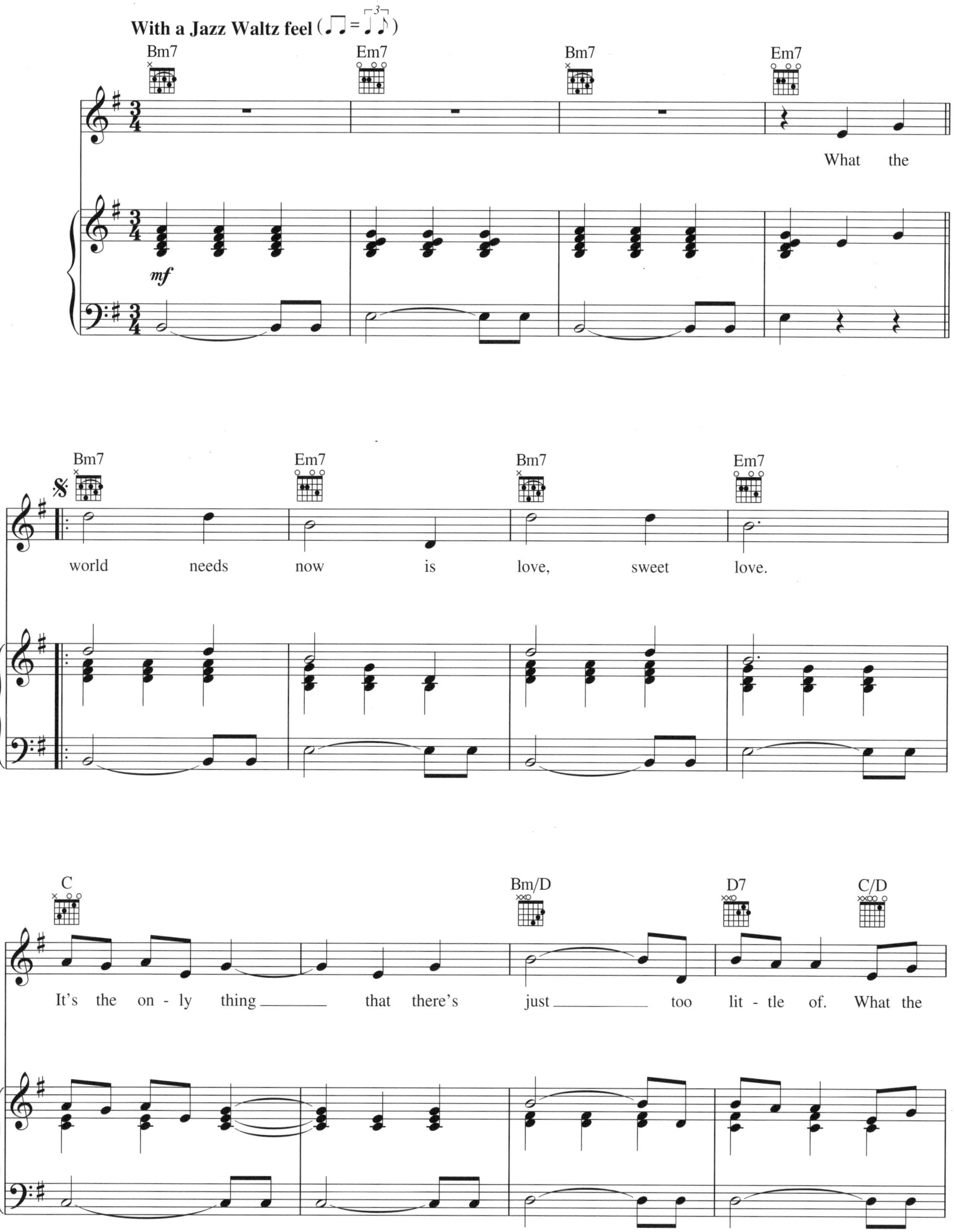

Copyright © 1965 (Renewed) Casa David and New Hidden Valley Music
International Copyright Secured All Rights Reserved

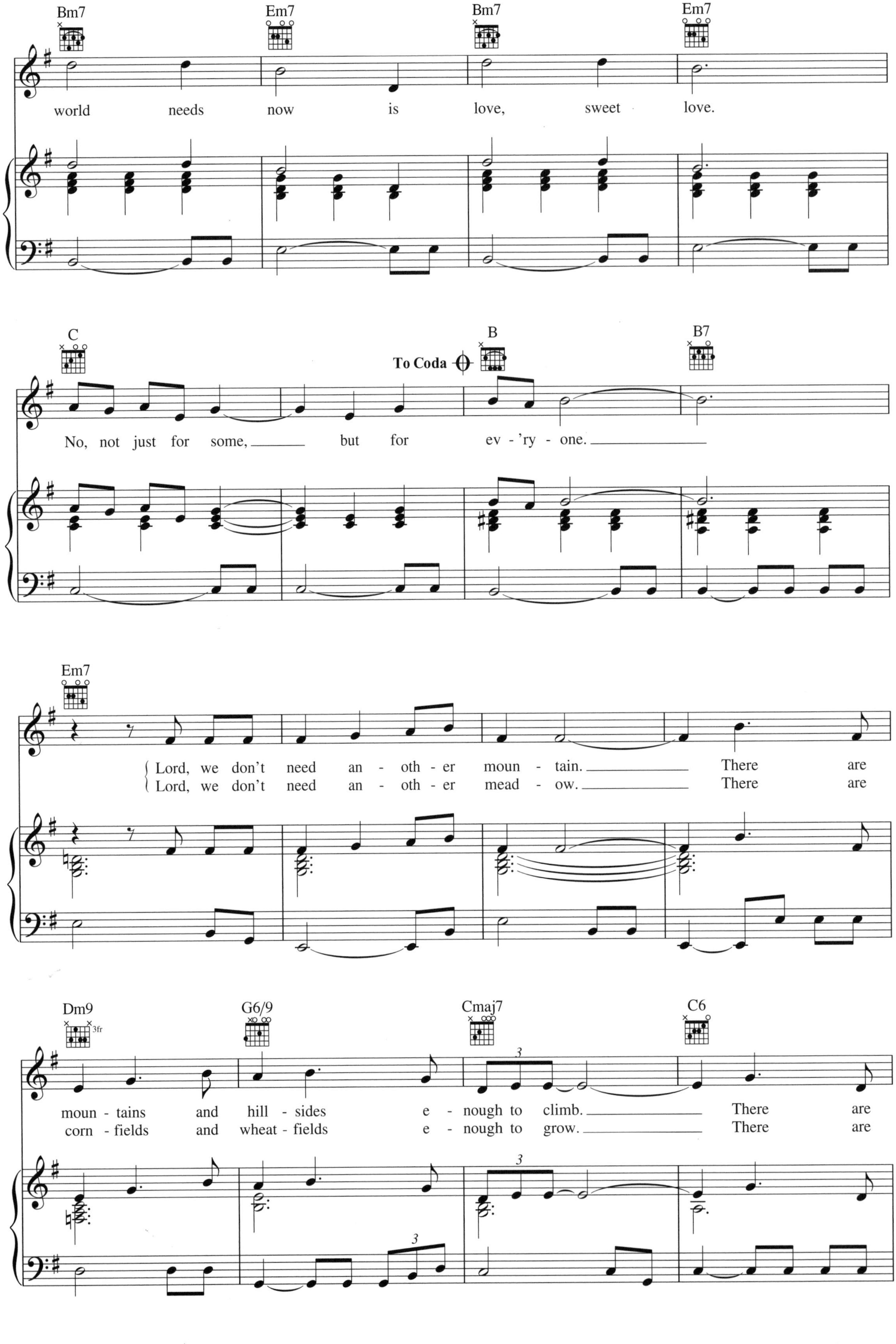
Bm7 Em7 Bm7 Em7
world needs now is love, sweet love.
C To Coda B B7
No, not just for some, but for ev - 'ry - one.
Em7
Lord, we don't need an - oth - er moun - tain. There are
Lord, we don't need an - oth - er mead - ow. There are
Dm9 3fr G6/9 Cmaj7 C6
moun - tains and hill - sides e - nough to climb. There are
corn - fields and wheat - fields e - nough to grow. There are

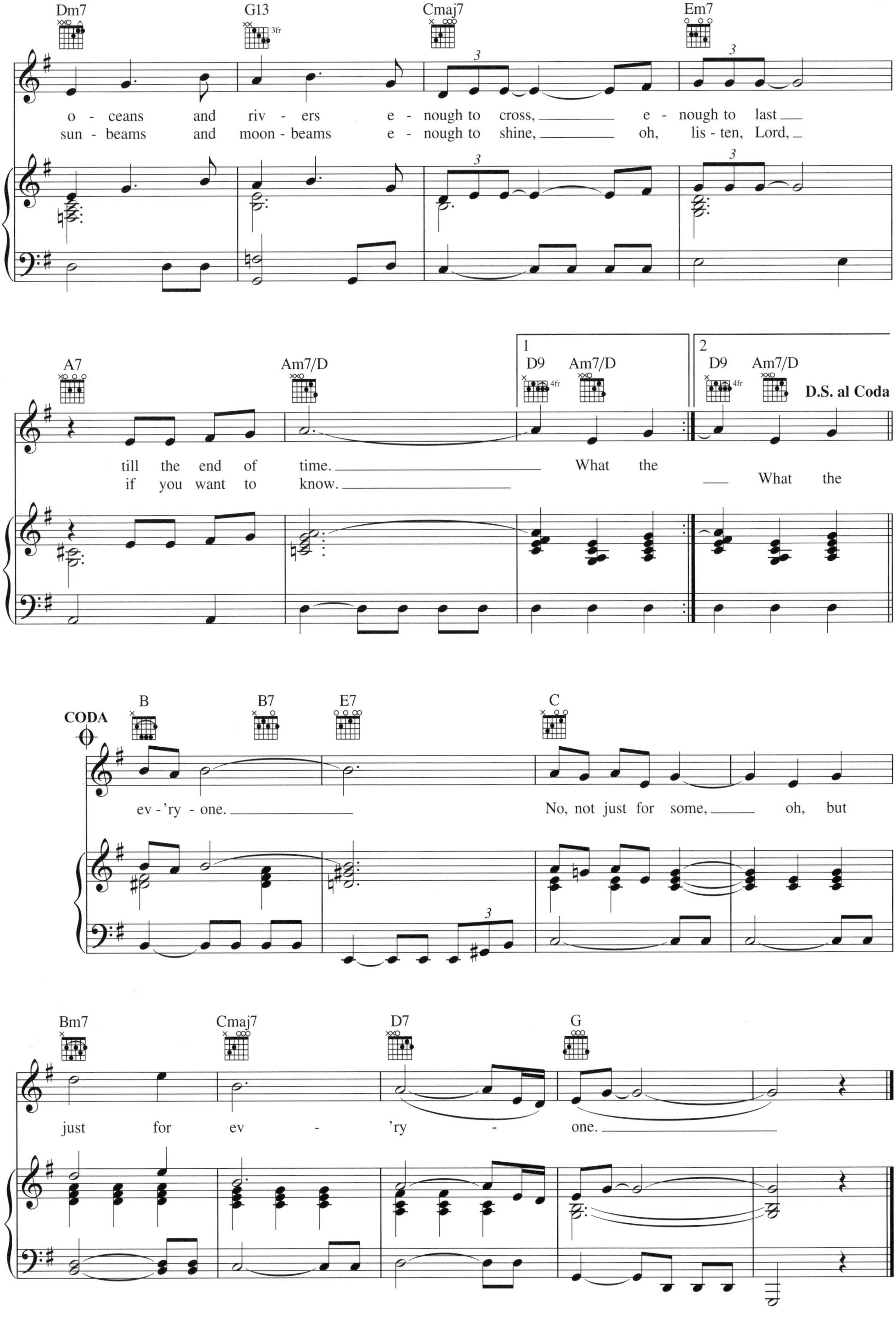
Dm7
G13
3fr
Cmaj7
Em7
o - ceans and riv - ers e - nough to cross, e - nough to last
sun - beams and moon - beams e - nough to shine, oh, lis - ten, Lord,
A7
Am7/D
1
D9
4fr
Am7/D
2
D9
4fr
Am7/D
D.S. al Coda
till the end of time. What the
if you want to know. What the
CODA
B
B7
E7
C
ev - 'ry - one. No, not just for some, oh, but
Bm7
Cmaj7
D7
G
just for ev - 'ry - one.

WHAT A WONDERFUL WORLD

Words and Music by GEORGE DAVID WEISS
and BOB THIELE

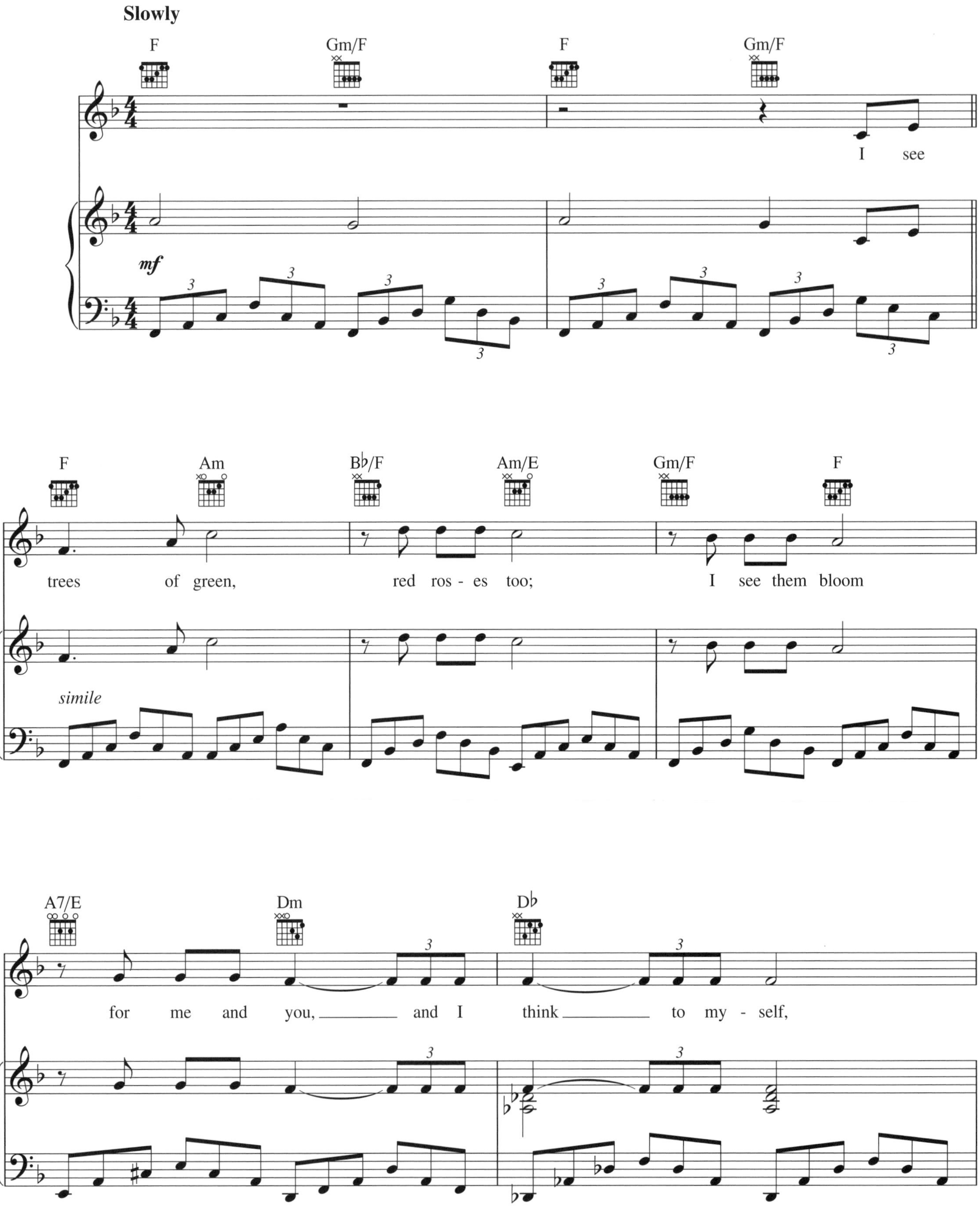

Copyright © 1967 by Range Road Music Inc., Quartet Music, Inc. and Abilene Music, Inc.
Copyright Renewed
International Copyright Secured All Rights Reserved
Used by Permission

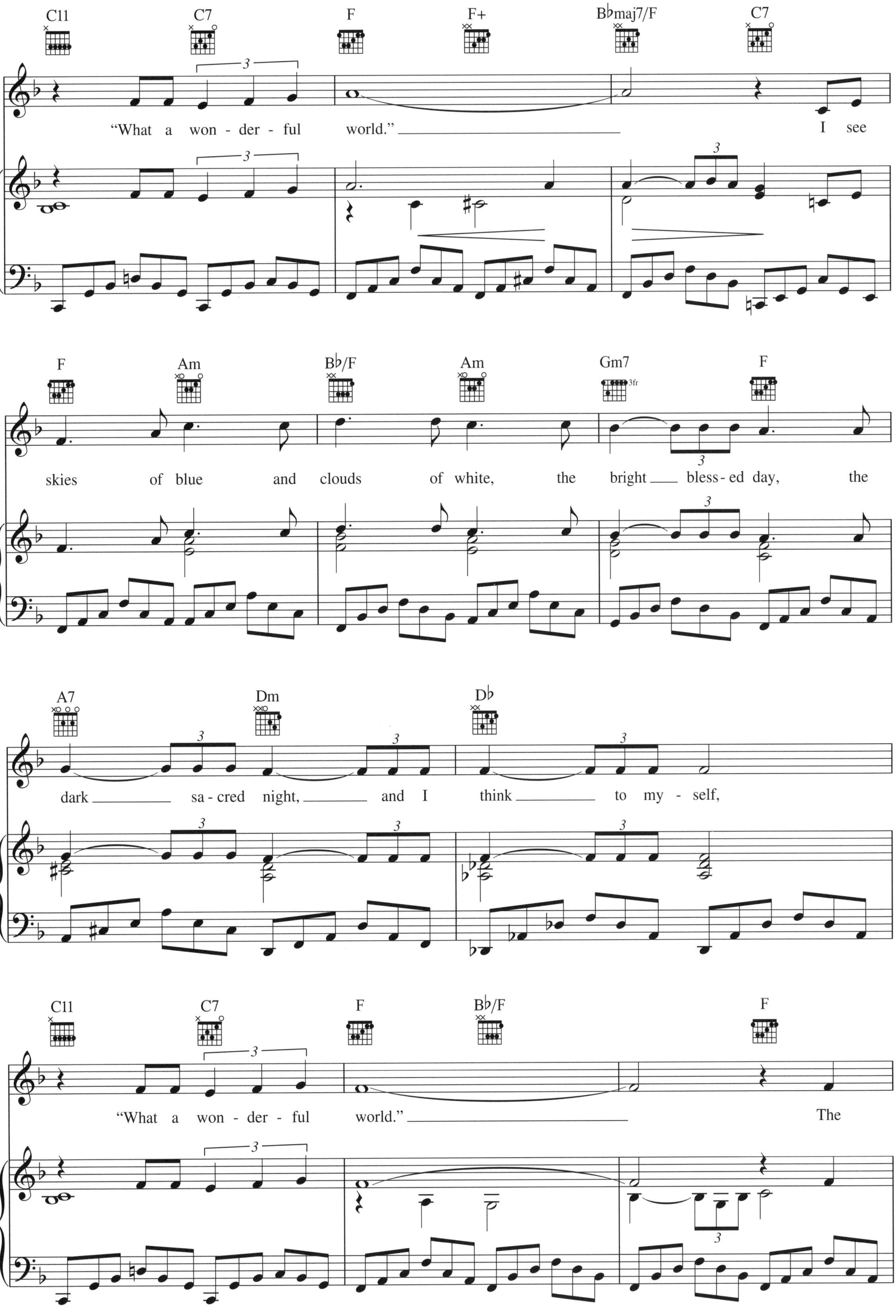
C11 C7 F F+ B♭maj7/F C7
"What a won - der - ful world." I see
F Am B♭/F Am Gm7 F
skies of blue and clouds of white, the bright blessed - ed day, the
A7 Dm D♭
dark sa - cred night, and I think to my - self,
C11 C7 F B♭/F F
"What a won - der - ful world." The

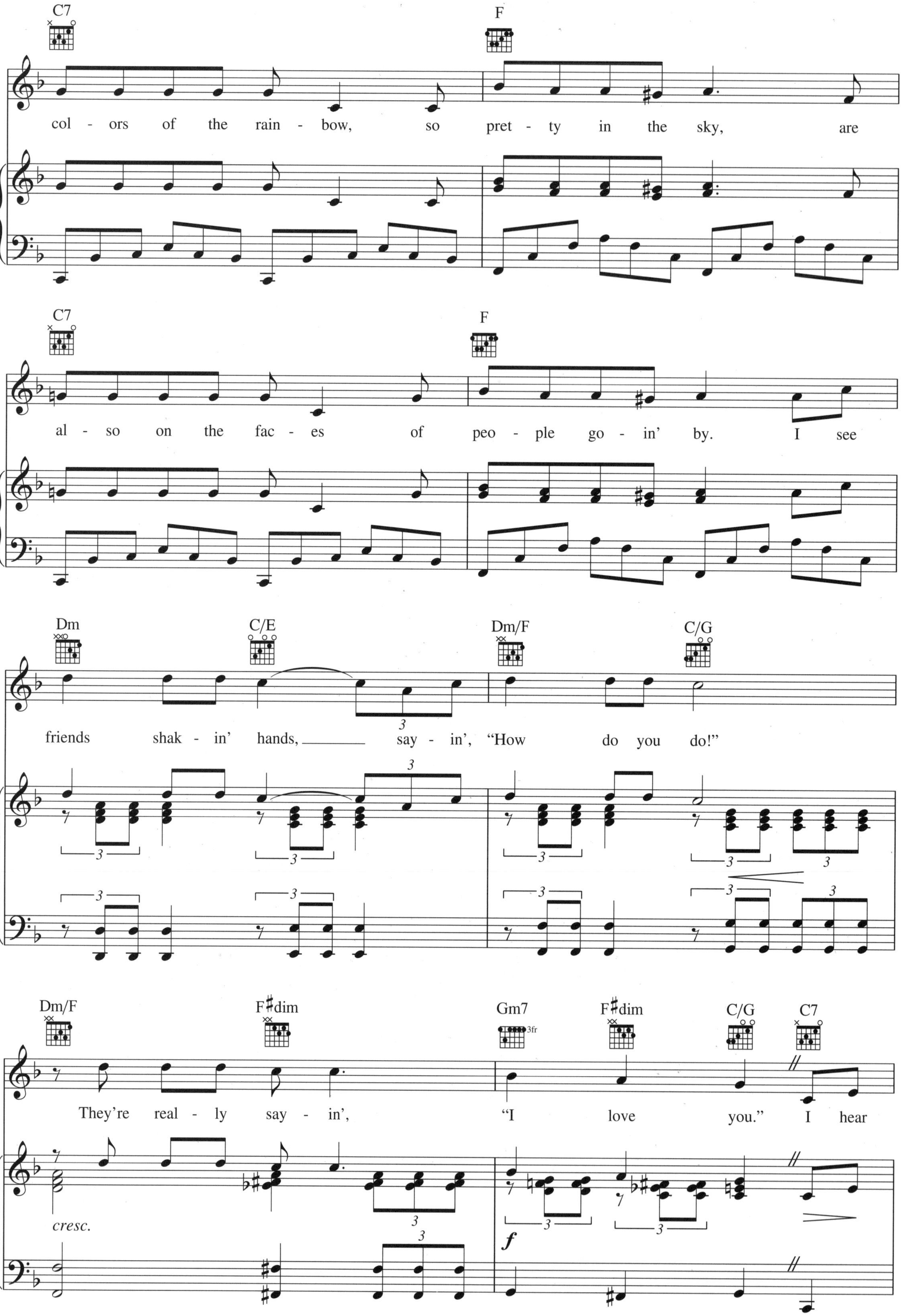
C7
F
col - ors of the rain - bow, so pret - ty in the sky, are
C7
F
al - so on the fac - es of peo - ple go - in' by. I see
Dm
C/E
Dm/F
C/G
friends shak - in' hands, say - in', "How do you do!"
Dm/F
F♯dim
Gm7
3fr
F♯dim
C/G
C7
They're real - ly say - in', "I love you." I hear
cresc.
f

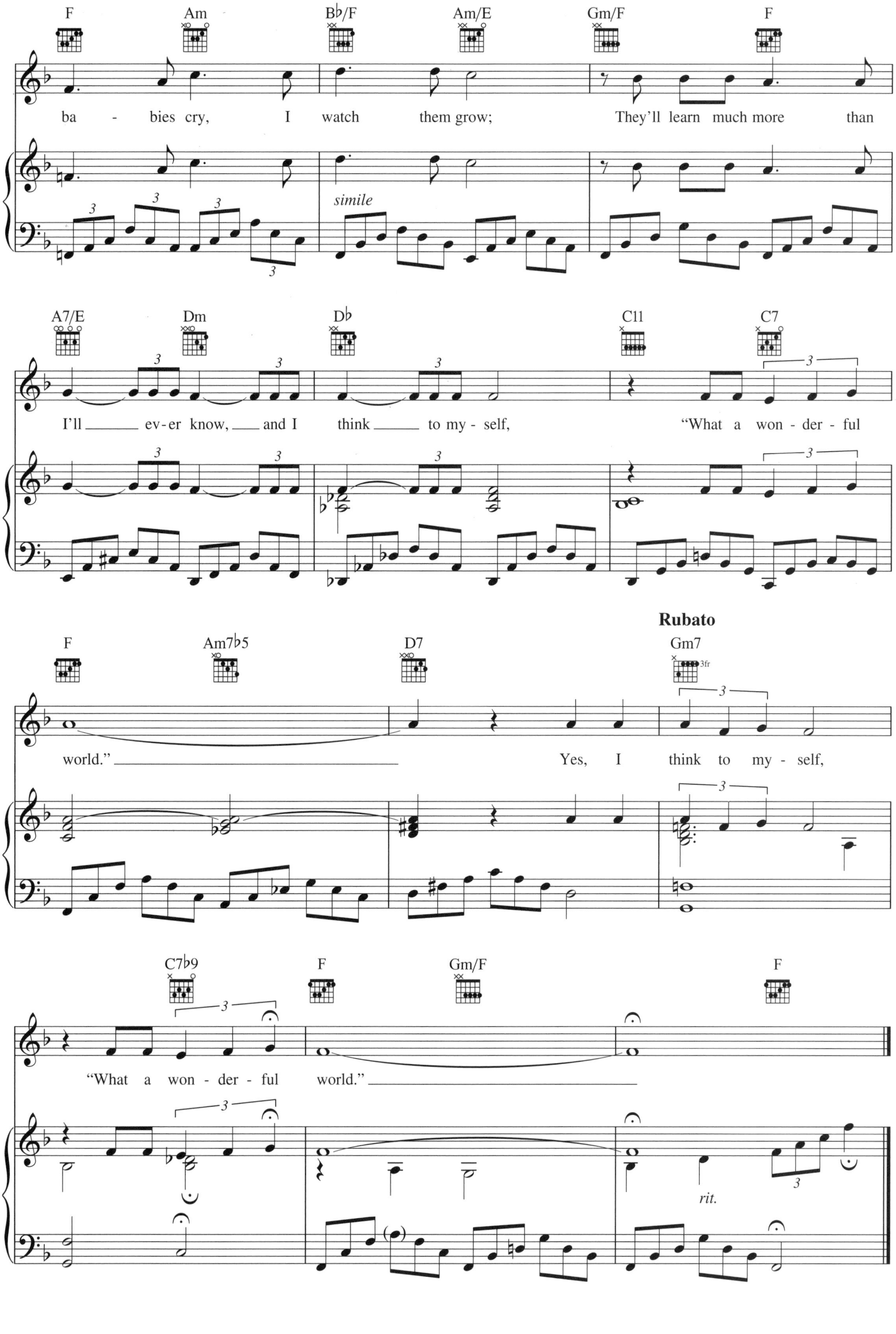
F
Am
B♭/F
Am/E
Gm/F
F
ba - bies cry, I watch them grow;
They'll learn much more than
simile
A7/E
Dm
D♭
C11
C7
I'll ev - er know, and I think to my - self,
"What a won - der - ful
Rubato
F
Am7♭5
D7
Gm7
3fr
world."
Yes, I think to my - self,
C7♭9
F
Gm/F
F
"What a won - der - ful world."
rit.

WHAT'S GOING ON

Words and Music by MARVIN GAYE,
AL CLEVELAND and RENALDO BENSON

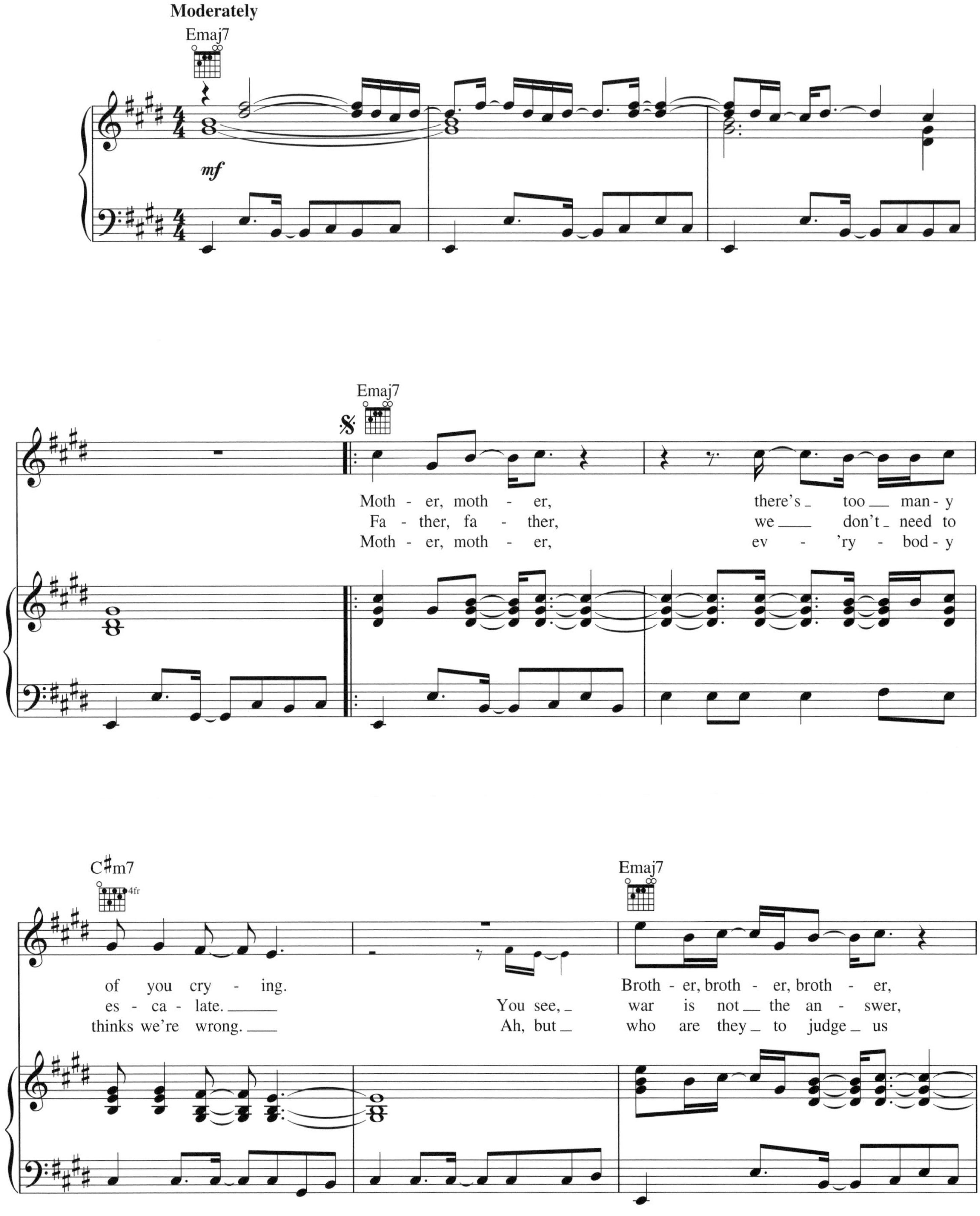
Moderately
Emaj7
mf
Emaj7
Moth - er, moth - er, there's too many
Fa - ther, fa - ther, we don't need to
Moth - er, moth - er, ev - 'ry - bod - y
C♯m7
4fr
Emaj7
of you cry - ing. Broth - er, broth - er, broth - er,
es - ca - late. You see, war is not the an - swer,
thinks we're wrong. Ah, but who are they to judge us

© 1970, 1971, 1972 (Renewed 1998, 1999, 2000) JOBETE MUSIC CO., INC.
All Rights Controlled and Administered by EMI APRIL MUSIC INC. and EMI BLACKWOOD MUSIC INC. on behalf of
JOBETE MUSIC CO., INC. and STONE AGATE MUSIC (A Division of JOBETE MUSIC CO., INC.)
All Rights Reserved International Copyright Secured Used by Permission

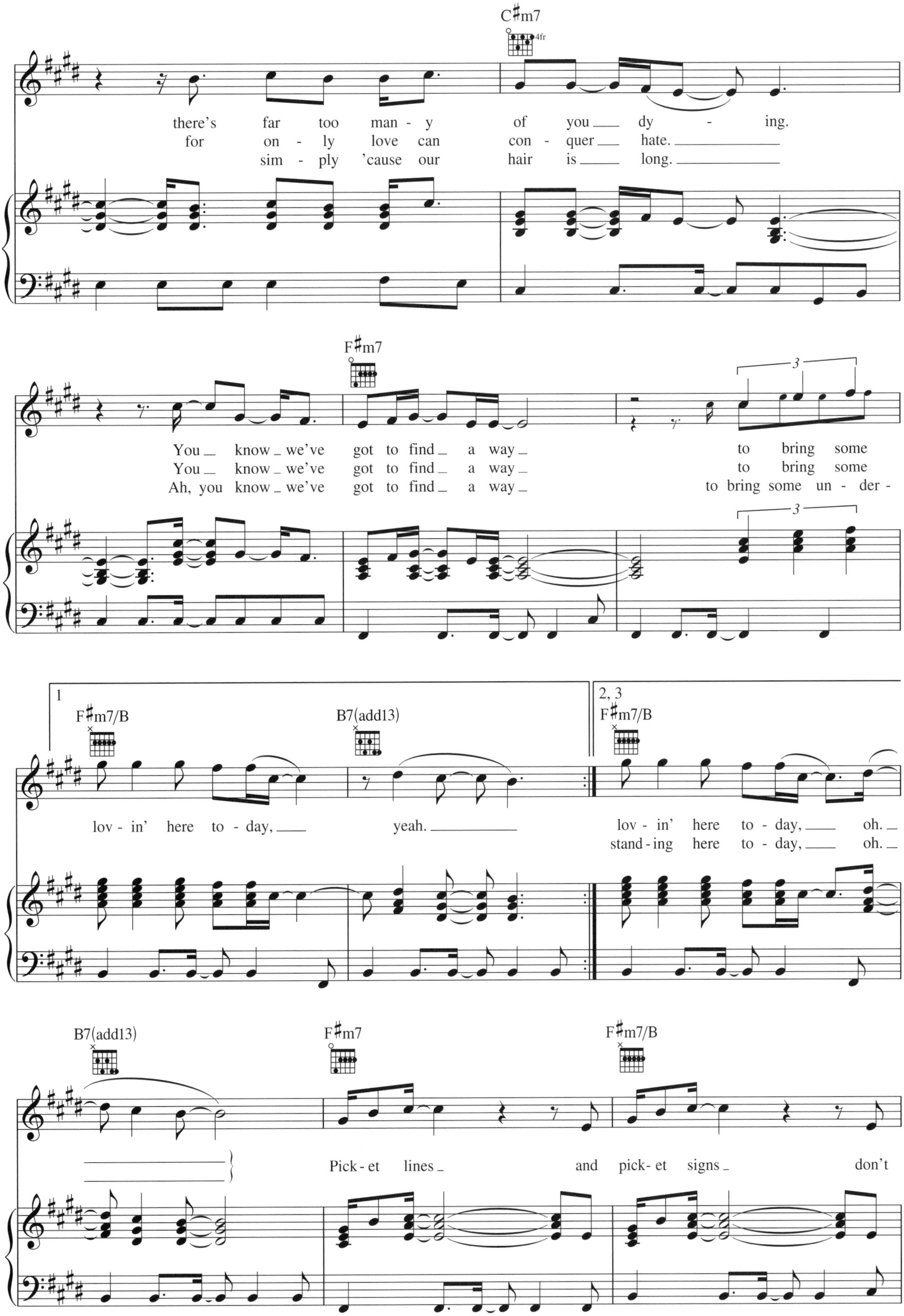
C♯m7
there's far too man - y of you dy - ing.
for on - ly love can con - quer hate.
sim - ply 'cause our hair is long.
F♯m7
You know we've got to find a way to bring some
You know we've got to find a way to bring some
Ah, you know we've got to find a way to bring some un - der -
1
F♯m7/B
B7(add13)
lov - in' here to - day, yeah.
2, 3
F♯m7/B
lov - in' here to - day, oh.
stand - ing here to - day, oh.
B7(add13)
F♯m7
F♯m7/B
Pick - et lines and pick - et signs don't

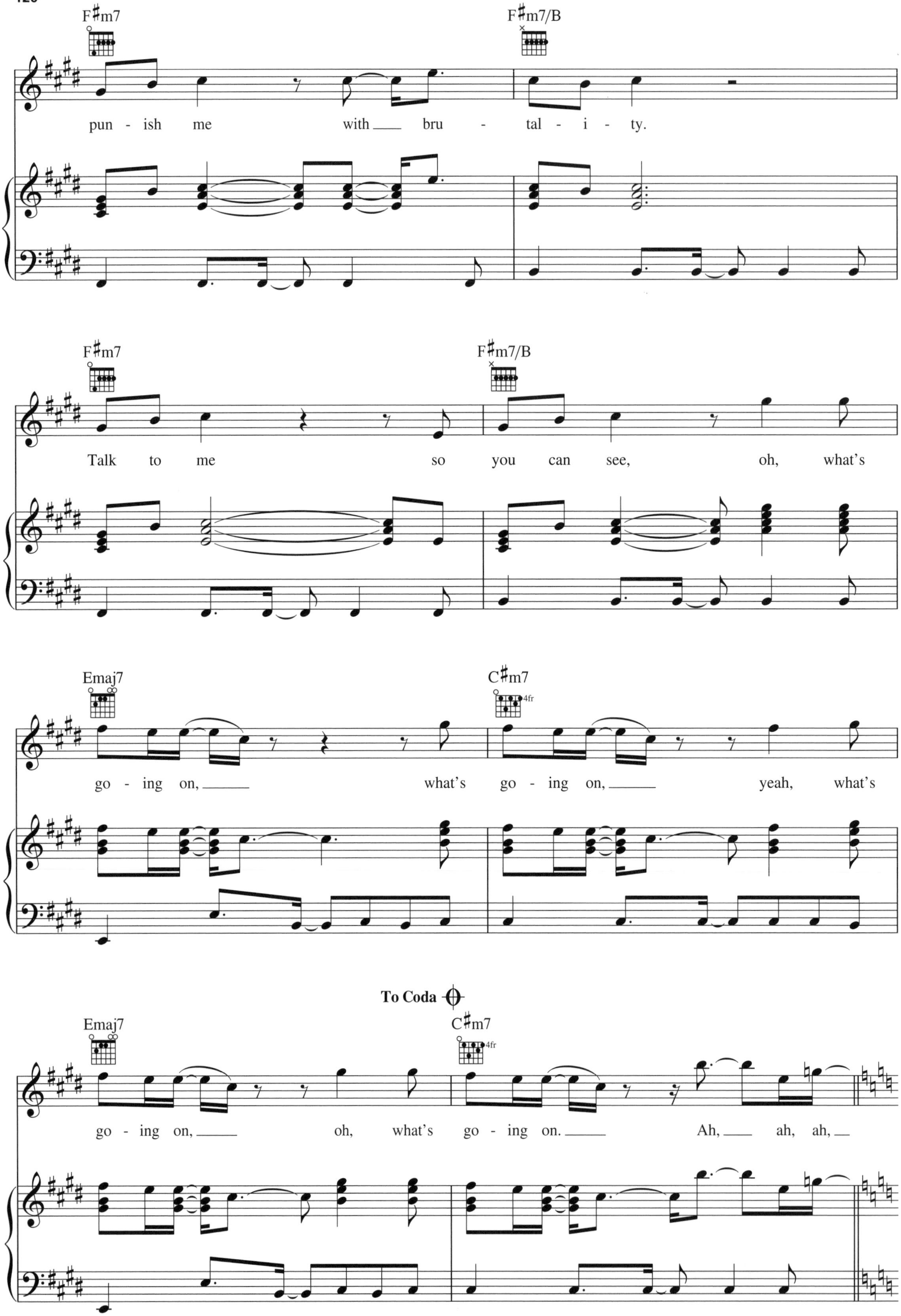
F♯m7
F♯m7/B
pun - ish me with bru - tal - i - ty.
F♯m7
F♯m7/B
Talk to me so you can see, oh, what's
Emaj7
C♯m7
4fr
go - ing on, what's go - ing on, yeah, what's
To Coda
Emaj7
C♯m7
4fr
go - ing on, oh, what's go - ing on. Ah, ah, ah,

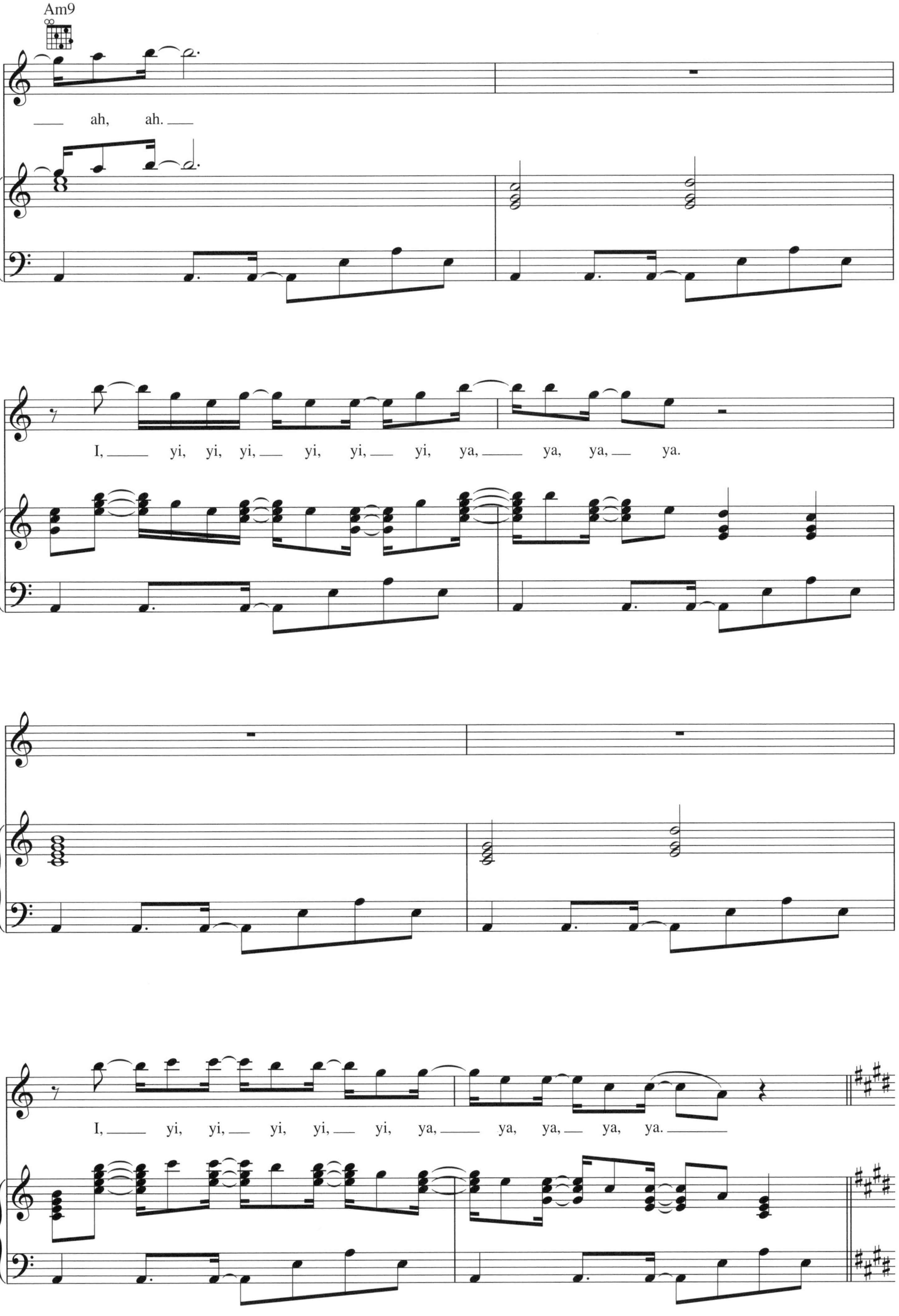
Am9
ah, ah.
I, yi, yi, yi, yi, yi, yi, ya, ya, ya, ya.
I, yi, yi, yi, yi, yi, ya, ya, ya, ya, ya.

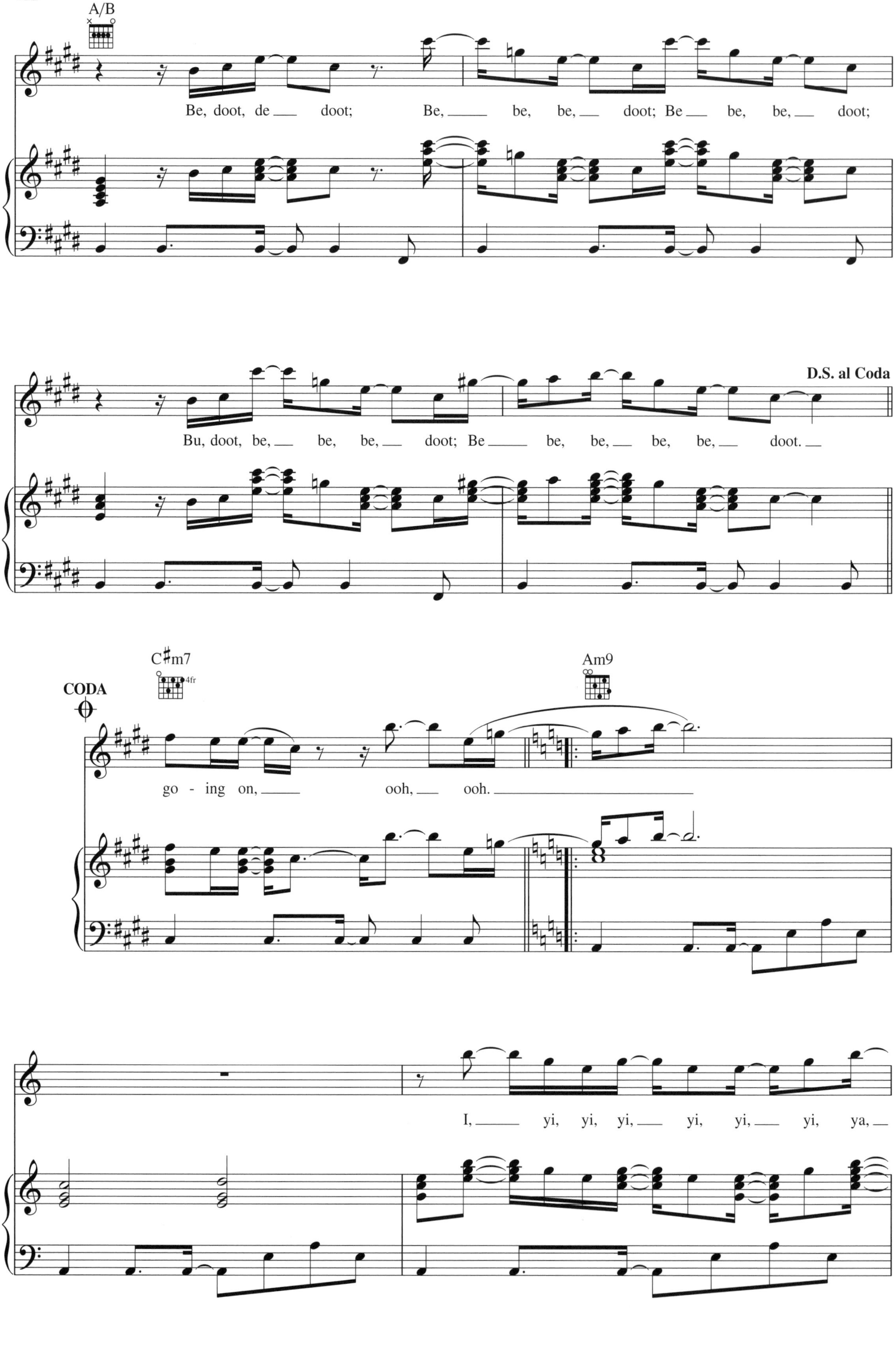
A/B
Be, doot, de doot; Be, be, be, doot; Be be, be, doot;
Bu, doot, be, be, be, doot; Be be, be, be, be, doot.
D.S. al Coda
CODA
C♯m7
4fr
Am9
go - ing on, ooh, ooh.
I, yi, yi, yi, yi, yi, yi, ya,

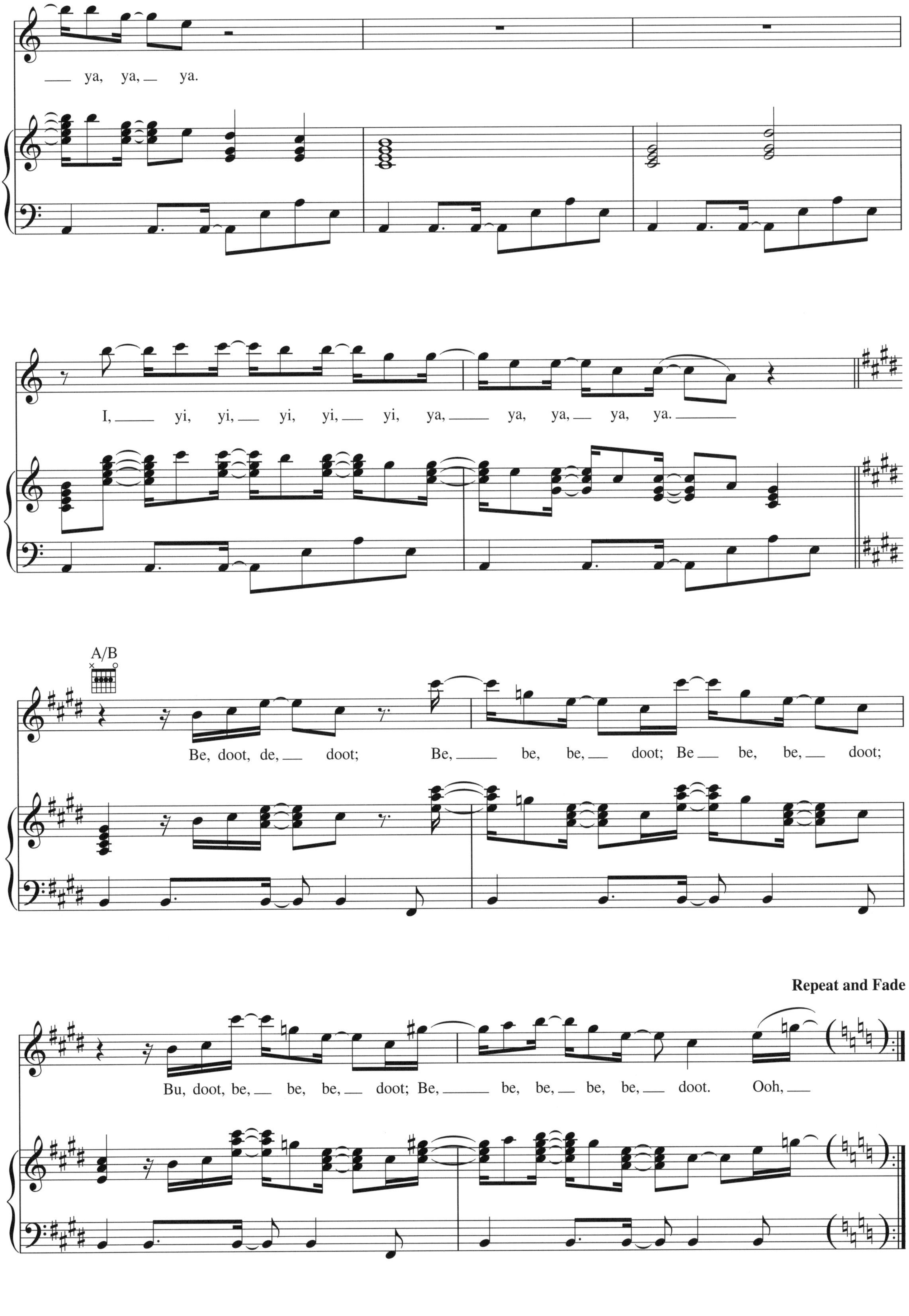
ya, ya, ya.
I, yi, yi, yi, yi, yi, ya, ya, ya, ya, ya.
A/B
Be, doot, de, doot; Be, be, be, doot; Be be, be, doot;
Repeat and Fade
Bu, doot, be, be, be, doot; Be, be, be, be, be, doot. Ooh,

WHERE HAVE ALL THE FLOWERS GONE?

Words and Music by
PETE SEEGER

Moderately slow, with simplicity

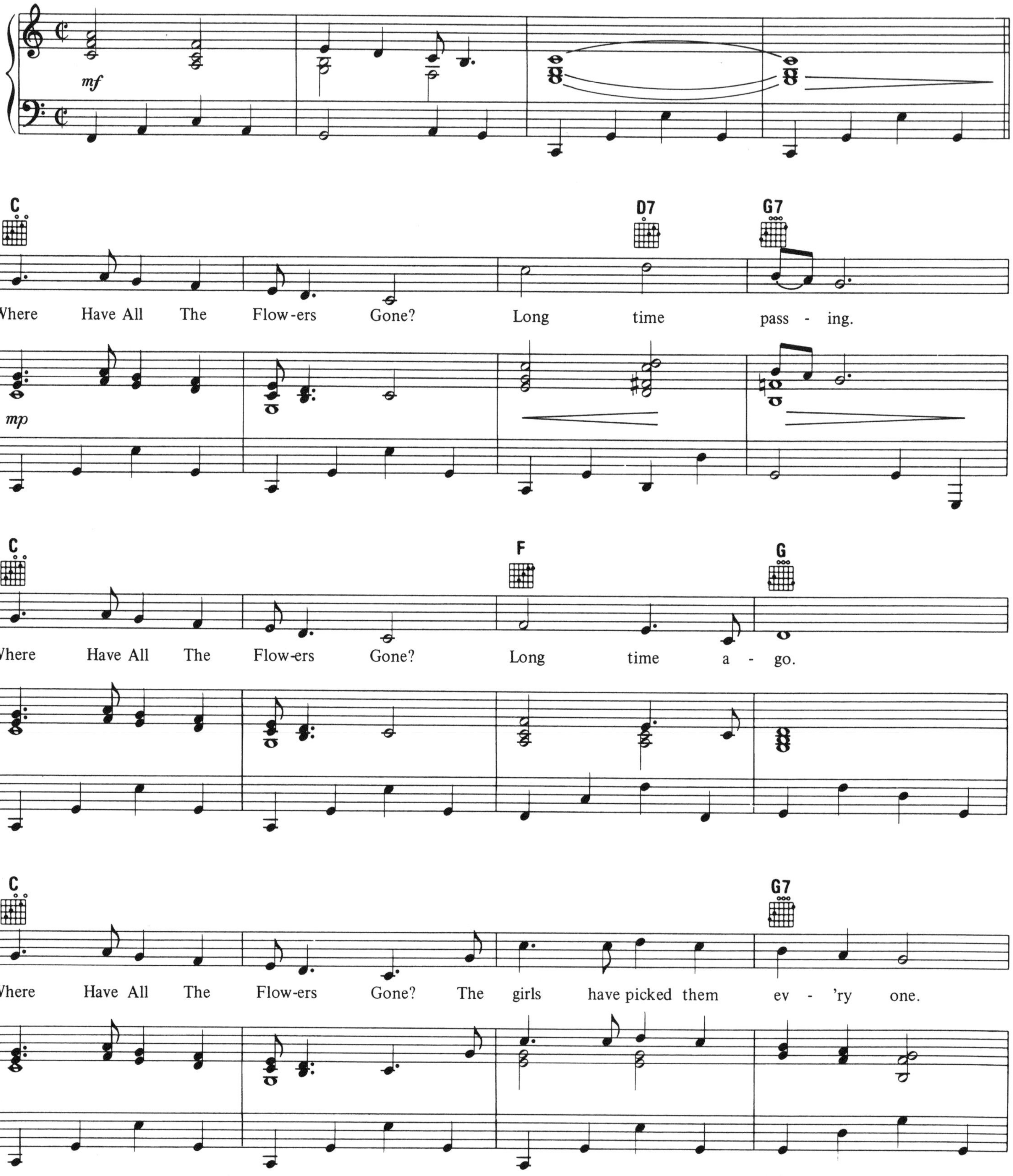
mf
mp
C
D7
G7
Where Have All The Flow-ers Gone? Long time pass - ing.
C
F
G
Where Have All The Flow-ers Gone? Long time a - go.
C
G7
Where Have All The Flow-ers Gone? The girls have picked them ev - 'ry one.

Copyright © 1961 (Renewed) by Sanga Music, Inc.
All Rights Reserved Used by Permission

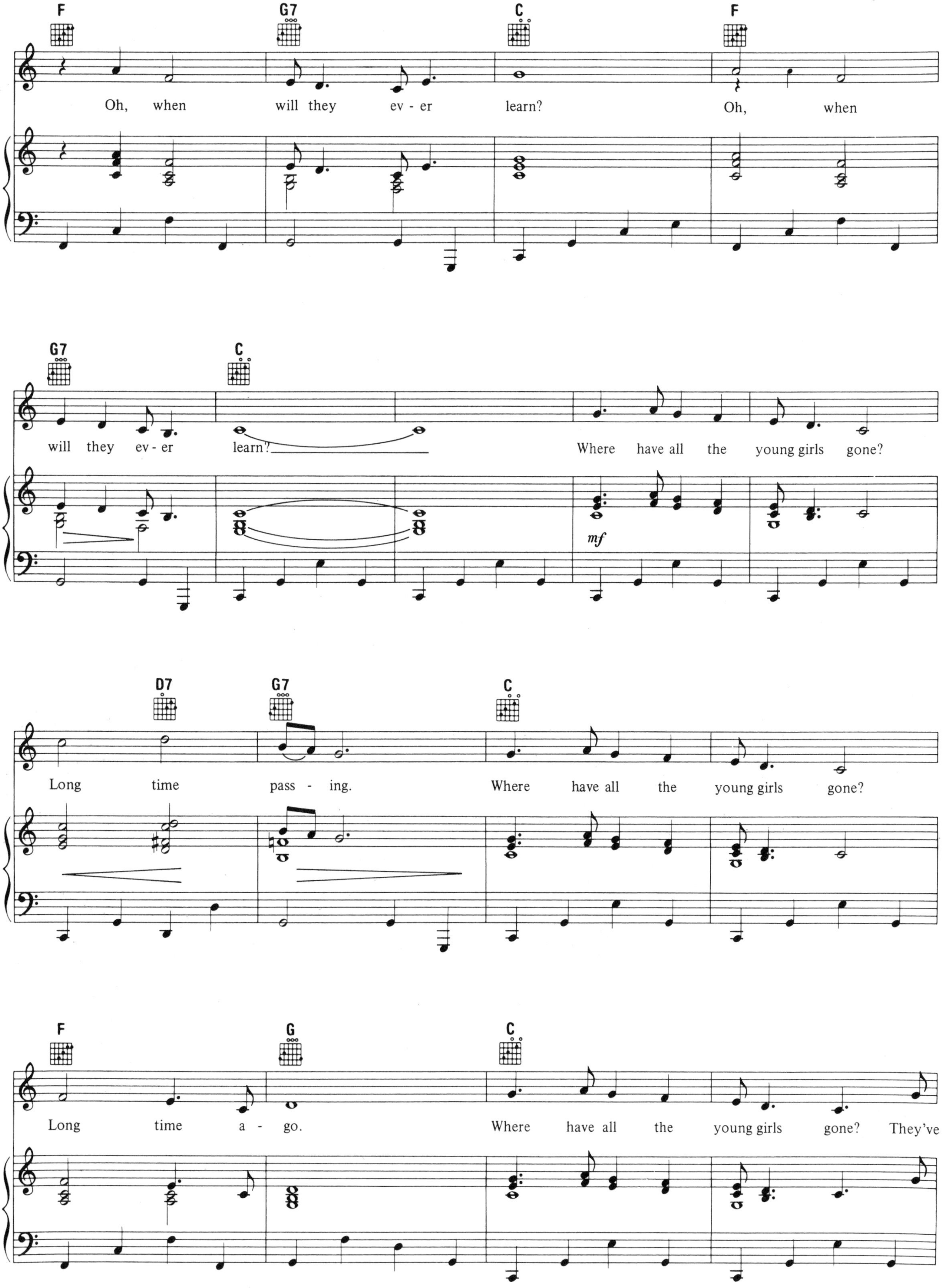
F G7 C F
Oh, when will they ev - er learn? Oh, when
G7 C
will they ev - er learn?
Where have all the young girls gone?
mf
D7 G7 C
Long time pass - ing. Where have all the young girls gone?
F G C
Long time a - go. Where have all the young girls gone? They've

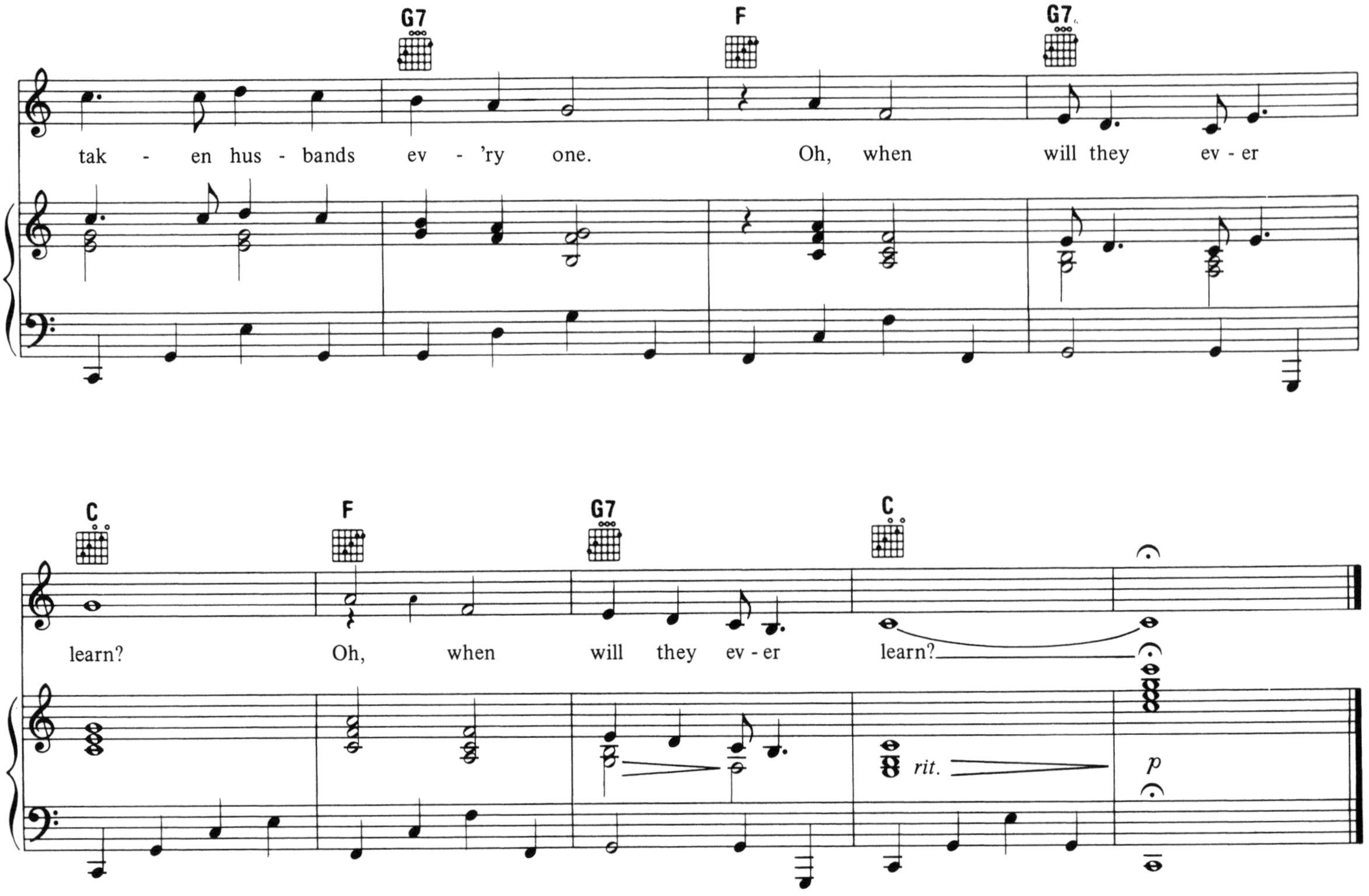

3. Where have all the young men gone? Long time passing.
   Where have all the young men gone? Long time ago.
   Where have all the young men gone?
   They're all in uniform.
   Oh, when will they ever learn?
   Oh, when will they ever learn?

4. Where have all the soldiers gone? Long time passing.
   Where have all the soldiers gone? Long time ago.
   Where have all the soldiers gone?
   They've gone to graveyards, every one.
   Oh, when will they ever learn?
   Oh, when will they ever learn?

5. Where have all the graveyards gone? Long time passing.
   Where have all the graveyards gone? Long time ago.
   Where have all the graveyards gone?
   They're covered with flowers, every one.
   Oh, when will they ever learn?
   Oh, when will they ever learn?

6. Where Have All The Flowers Gone? Long time passing.
   Where Have All The Flowers Gone? Long time ago.
   Where Have All The Flowers Gone?
   Young girls picked them, every one.
   Oh, when will they ever learn?
   Oh, when will they ever learn?

MORE INSPIRATIONAL SONGBOOKS FROM HAL LEONARD

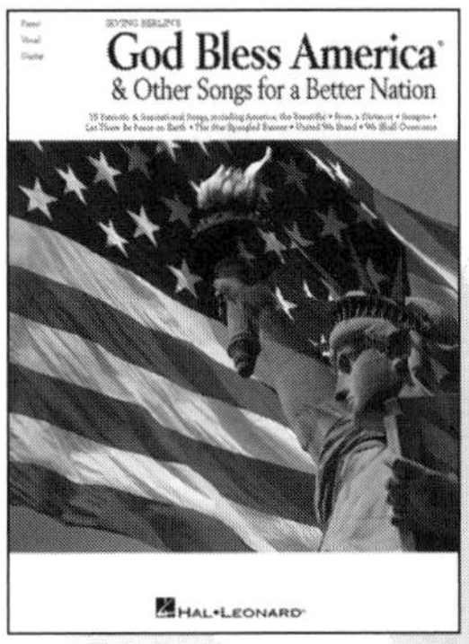

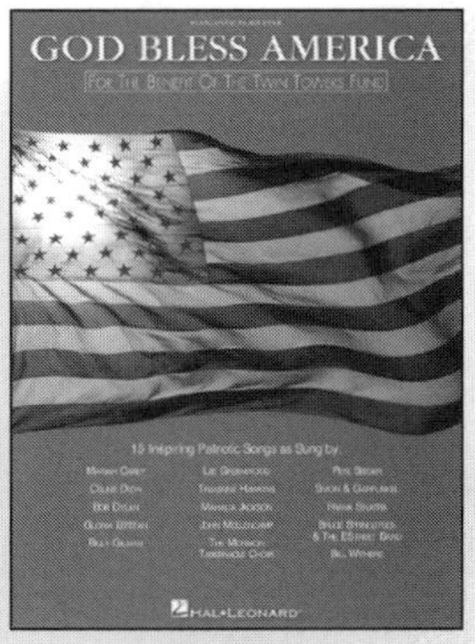

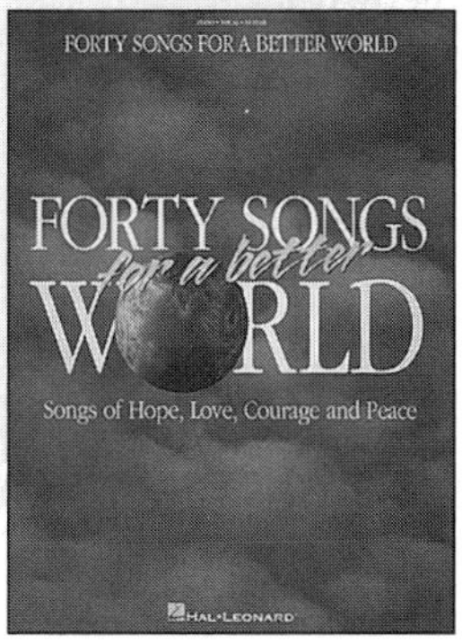

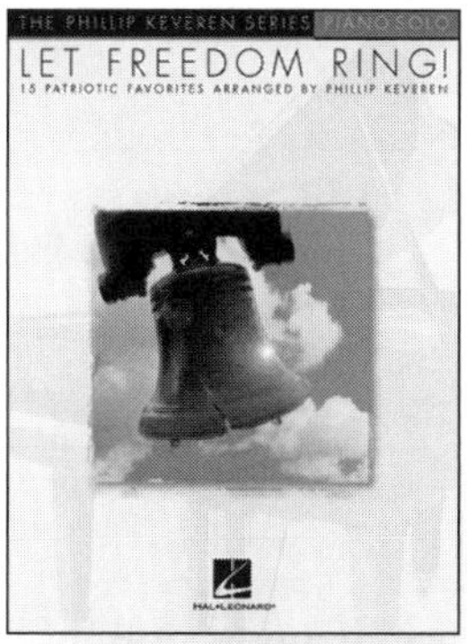

GOD BLESS AMERICA®

FOR THE BENEFIT OF THE TWIN TOWERS FUND

This special matching folio features 15 inspiring patriotic songs performed by top artists. Includes: Amazing Grace (Tramaine Hawkins) ★ America the Beautiful (Frank Sinatra) ★ Blowin' in the Wind (Bob Dylan) ★ Bridge over Troubled Water (Simon & Garfunkel) ★ Coming Out of the Dark (Gloria Estefan) ★ God Bless America® (Celine Dion) ★ God Bless the U.S.A. (Lee Greenwood) ★ Hero (Mariah Carey) ★ Land of Hope and Dreams (Bruce Springsteen and the E Street Band) ★ Lean on Me (Bill Withers) ★ Peaceful World (John Mellencamp) ★ The Star Spangled Banner (The Mormon Tabernacle Choir) ★ There's a Hero (Billy Gilman) ★ This Land Is Your Land (Peter Seeger) ★ We Shall Overcome (Mahalia Jackson).

____00313196 Piano/Vocal/Guitar............$16.95

IRVING BERLIN'S

GOD BLESS AMERICA® & OTHER SONGS FOR A BETTER NATION

This songbook features 35 songs to unite all Americans: Abraham, Martin and John ★ Amazing Grace ★ America ★ America the Beautiful ★ Battle Hymn of the Republic ★ Everything Is Beautiful ★ From a Distance ★ God Bless America® ★ God of Our Fathers ★ He Ain't Heavy...He's My Brother ★ I Believe ★ If I Had a Hammer ★ Imagine ★ Last Night I Had the Strangest Dream ★ Let Freedom Ring ★ Let There Be Peace on Earth ★ The Lord's Prayer ★ My Country 'Tis of Thee (America) ★ Pray for Our Nation ★ Precious Lord, Take My Hand ★ The Star Spangled Banner ★ Stars and Stripes Forever ★ This Is a Great Country ★ This Is My Country ★ This Land Is Your Land ★ United We Stand ★ We Shall Overcome ★ What a Wonderful World ★ What the World Needs Now Is Love ★ You'll Never Walk Alone ★ You're a Grand Old Flag ★ and more.

____00310825 Piano/Vocal/Guitar............$12.95

FORTY SONGS FOR A BETTER WORLD

40 songs with a message, including: All You Need Is Love ★ Blackbird ★ Bless the Beasts and Children ★ Candle on the Water ★ Child of Mine ★ Circle of Life ★ Colors of the Wind ★ Count Your Blessings Instead of Sheep ★ Ebony and Ivory ★ Everything Is Beautiful ★ The Flower That Shattered the Stone ★ Friends ★ From a Distance ★ God Bless the U.S.A. ★ Gonna Build a Mountain ★ He Ain't Heavy...He's My Brother ★ I Am Your Child ★ I Believe ★ If I Had a Hammer (The Hammer Song) ★ If I Ruled the World ★ If We Only Have Love (Quand on N'a Que L'amour) ★ Imagine ★ The Impossible Dream (The Quest) ★ In Harmony ★ Let's Get Together ★ Lost in the Stars ★ Love Can Build a Bridge ★ Love in Any Language ★ Make Your Own Kind of Music ★ One Song ★ Ordinary Miracles ★ The Rainbow Connection ★ Tears in Heaven ★ Turn! Turn! Turn! (To Everything There Is a Season) ★ What a Wonderful World ★ What the World Needs Now Is Love ★ With a Little Help from My Friends ★ You'll Never Walk Alone ★ You've Got a Friend ★ You've Got to Be Carefully Taught.

____00310096 Piano/Vocal/Guitar............$15.95

LET FREEDOM RING!

The Phillip Keveren Series

15 favorites celebrating the land of the free, including: America, the Beautiful ★ Anchors Aweigh ★ Battle Hymn of the Republic ★ Eternal Father, Strong to Save ★ God Bless Our Native Land ★ God of Our Fathers ★ My Country, 'Tis of Thee (America) ★ Semper Fidelis ★ The Star Spangled Banner ★ Stars and Stripes Forever ★ Washington Post March ★ Yankee Doodle ★ Yankee Doodle Boy ★ You're a Grand Old Flag.

____00310839 Piano Solo..........................$9.95

FOR MORE INFORMATION, SEE YOUR LOCAL MUSIC DEALER, OR WRITE TO:

HAL•LEONARD® CORPORATION
7777 W. BLUEMOUND RD. P.O. BOX 13819 MILWAUKEE, WI 53213

Visit Hal Leonard Online at
www.halleonard.com

Prices, contents and availability subject to change without notice.

Contemporary Classics

Your favorite songs for piano, voice and guitar.

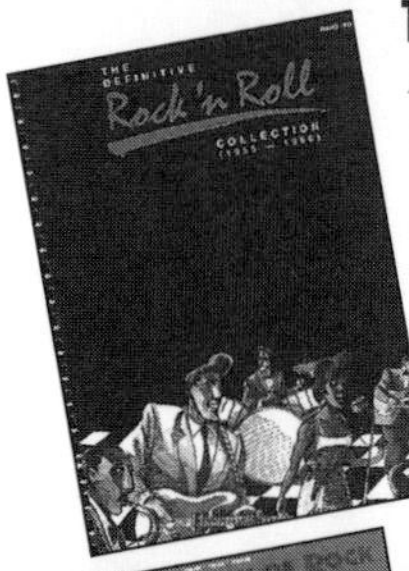

The Definitive Rock 'n' Roll Collection

A classic collection of the best songs from the early rock 'n' roll years – 1955-1966. 97 songs, including: Barbara Ann • Chantilly Lace • Dream Lover • Duke of Earl • Earth Angel • Great Balls of Fire • Louie, Louie • Rock Around the Clock • Ruby Baby • Runaway • (Seven Little Girls) Sitting in the Back Seat • Stay • Surfin' U.S.A. • Wild Thing • Woolly Bully • and more.
00490195...$29.95

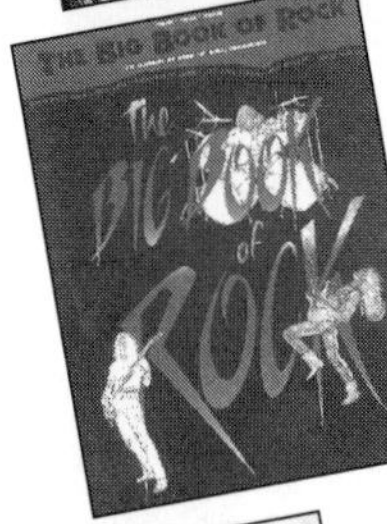

The Big Book of Rock

78 of rock's biggest hits, including: Addicted to Love • American Pie • Born to Be Wild • Cold As Ice • Dust in the Wind • Free Bird • Goodbye Yellow Brick Road • Groovin' • Hey Jude • I Love Rock 'N' Roll • Lay Down Sally • Layla • Livin' on a Prayer • Louie Louie • Maggie May • Me and Bobby McGee • Monday, Monday • Owner of a Lonely Heart • Shout • Walk This Way • We Didn't Start the Fire • You Really Got Me • and more.
00311566...$19.95

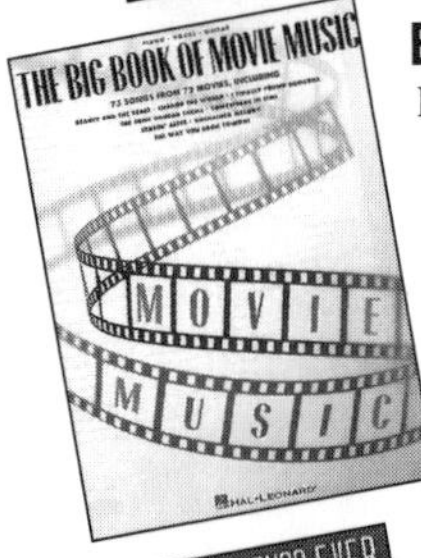

Big Book of Movie Music

Features 73 classic songs from 72 movies: Beauty and the Beast • Change the World • Eye of the Tiger • I Finally Found Someone • The John Dunbar Theme • Somewhere in Time • Stayin' Alive • Take My Breath Away • Unchained Melody • The Way You Look Tonight • You've Got a Friend in Me • Zorro's Theme • more.
00311582...$19.95

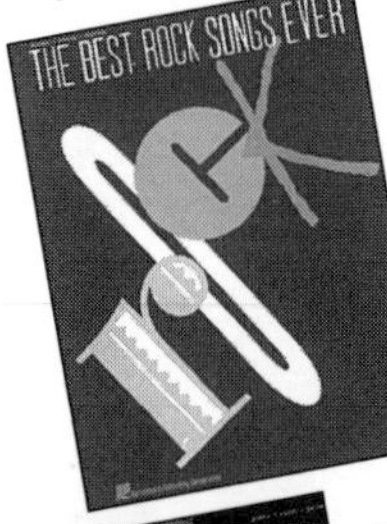

The Best Rock Songs Ever

70 of the best rock songs from yesterday and today, including: All Day and All of the Night • All Shook Up • Blue Suede Shoes • Born to Be Wild • Boys Are Back in Town • Every Breath You Take • Faith • Free Bird • Hey Jude • I Still Haven't Found What I'm Looking For • Livin' on a Prayer • Lola • Louie Louie • Maggie May • Money • (She's) Some Kind of Wonderful • Takin' Care of Business • Walk This Way • We Didn't Start the Fire • We Got the Beat • Wild Thing • more!
00490424..$18.95

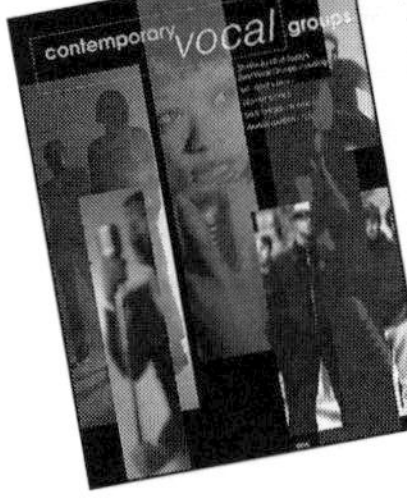

Contemporary Vocal Groups

This exciting new collection includes 35 huge hits by 18 of today's best vocal groups, including 98 Degrees, TLC, Destiny's Child, Savage Garden, Boyz II Men, Dixie Chicks, 'N Sync, and more! Songs include: Bills, Bills, Bills • Bug a Boo • Diggin' on You • The Hardest Thing • I'll Make Love to You • In the Still of the Nite (I'll Remember) • Ready to Run • Tearin' Up My Heart • Truly, Madly, Deeply • Waterfalls • Wide Open Spaces • and more.
00310605...$14.95

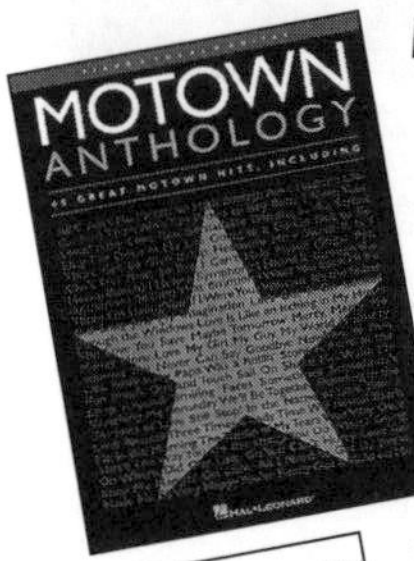

Motown Anthology

This songbook commemorates Motown's 40th Anniversary with 68 songs, background information on this famous record label, and lots of photos. Songs include: ABC • Baby Love • Ben • Dancing in the Street • Easy • For Once in My Life • My Girl • Shop Around • The Tracks of My Tears • War • What's Going On • You Can't Hurry Love • and many more.
00310367..$19.95

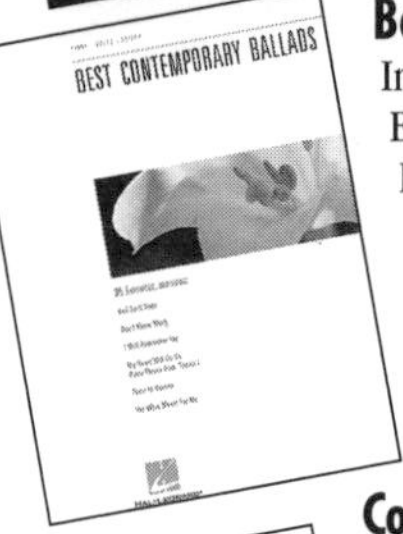

Best Contemporary Ballads

Includes 35 favorites: And So It Goes • Angel • Beautiful in My Eyes • Don't Know Much • Fields of Gold • Hero • I Will Remember You • Iris • My Heart Will Go On • Tears in Heaven • Valentine • You Were Meant for Me • You'll Be in My Heart • and more.
00310583...$16.95

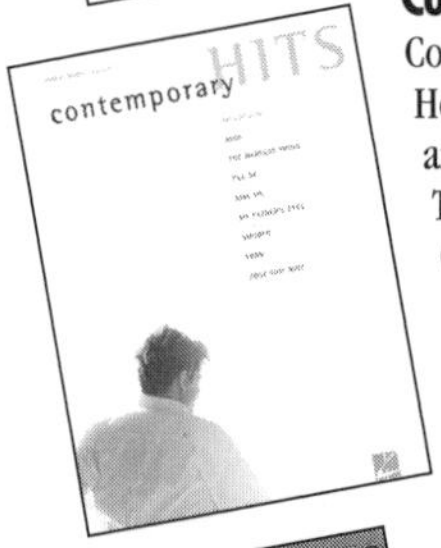

Contemporary Hits

Contains 35 favorites by artists such as Sarah McLachlan, Whitney Houston, 'N Sync, Mariah Carey, Christina Aguilera, Celine Dion, and other top stars. Songs include: Adia • Building a Mystery • The Hardest Thing • I Believe in You and Me • I Drive Myself Crazy • I'll Be • Kiss Me • My Father's Eyes • Reflection • Smooth • Torn • and more!
00310589...$16.95

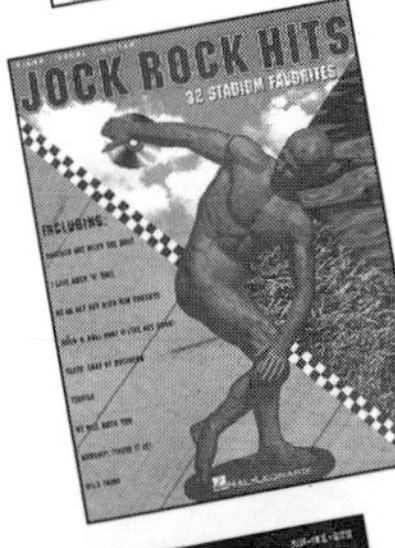

Jock Rock Hits

32 stadium-shaking favorites, including: Another One Bites the Dust • The Boys Are Back in Town • Freeze-Frame • Gonna Make You Sweat (Everybody Dance Now) • I Got You (I Feel Good) • Na Na Hey Hey Kiss Him Goodbye • Rock & Roll – Part II (The Hey Song) • Shout • Tequila • We Are the Champions • We Will Rock You • Whoomp! (There It Is) • Wild Thing • and more.
00310105...$14.95

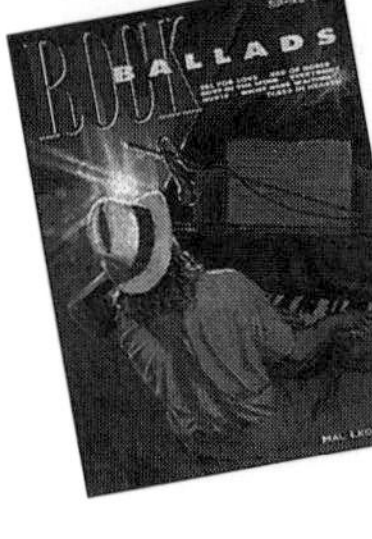

Rock Ballads

31 sentimental favorites, including: All for Love • Bed of Roses • Dust in the Wind • Everybody Hurts • Right Here Waiting • Tears in Heaven • and more.
00311673...$14.95

FOR MORE INFORMATION, SEE YOUR LOCAL MUSIC DEALER, OR WRITE TO:

HAL•LEONARD®
CORPORATION

7777 W. BLUEMOUND RD. P.O. BOX 13819 MILWAUKEE, WI 53213

Visit Hal Leonard Online at www.halleonard.com

Prices, contents & availability subject to change without notice.

0402